THE MEANING OF
THE LOCAL

This book examines the meaning of locality in urban India through studies of social, spatial and historical associations between peoples and places. By focusing on specific localities, it unpacks the meaning of the local in a variety of urban contexts. Moving beyond the assertion that space is socially constructed, it explores the ways in which social and political relations are spatially and historically contingent. Through a focus on metropolitan areas as well as small towns, detailed ethnographies highlight the vitality of place-making in the lives of city dwellers and the centrality of a 'politics of the local' in the production of power, difference and inequality. The book demonstrates how urban space is increasingly interconnected while local boundaries and group-based identities are reconstructed, and often consolidated, through the use of 'traditional' idioms and localised practices.

Geert De Neve is Senior Lecturer in Anthropology at the University of Sussex.

Henrike Donner is Lecturer in Anthropology at the London School of Economics and Political Sciences.

THE MEANING OF THE LOCAL

Politics of Place in Urban India

Edited by Geert De Neve and Henrike Donner

Routledge
Taylor & Francis Group
LONDON AND NEW YORK

First published 2006 by
by Routledge
2 Park Square, Milton Park, Abingdon, Oxon, OX14 4RN

Simultaneously published in the USA and Canada
by Routledge
270 Madison Ave, New York NY 10016

Routledge is an imprint of the Taylor & Francis Group, an informa business

Transferred to Digital Printing 2010

Typeset in Times by
Taylor & Francis Books

British Library Cataloguing in Publication Data
A catalogue record for this book is available from the British Library

Library of Congress Cataloguing in Publication Data
The meaning of the local : politics of place in urban India / edited by Geert De
Neve and Henrike Donner.
    p. cm.
Includes bibliographical references and index.
ISBN 1-84472-114-0 (hardback : alk. paper) 1. Human geography--India. 2.
India--Social conditions. I. Neve, Geert de. II. Donner, Henrike.
    GF661.M43 2006
    307.760954--dc22
    2006018603

ISBN10: 1-844-72114-0 (hbk)
ISBN10: 0-415-59623-8 (pbk)

ISBN13: 978-1-84472-114-6 (hbk)
ISBN13: 978-0-415-59623-7 (pbk)

CONTENTS

List of illustrations   vii
Notes on contributors   viii
Acknowledgements   xi

1   Space, place and globalisation: revisiting the urban
    neighbourhood in India   1
    HENRIKE DONNER AND GEERT DE NEVE

2   Economic liberalisation, class restructuring and social
    space in provincial south India   21
    GEERT DE NEVE

3   'Establishing territory': the spatial bases and practices of
    the DPI   44
    HUGO GORRINGE

4   Local governance: politics and neighbourhood activism
    in Calcutta   68
    INDRANIL CHAKRABARTI

5   Temples and charity: the neighbourhood styles of the
    Komati and Beeri Chettiar merchants of Madras City   89
    MATTISON MINES

6   Parhai ka mahaul? An educational environment in Bijnor,
    Uttar Pradesh   116
    ROGER JEFFERY, PATRICIA JEFFERY AND CRAIG JEFFREY

CONTENTS

7 The politics of gender, class and community in a central
Calcutta neighbourhood   141
HENRIKE DONNER

8 Anonymous encounters: class categorisation and social
distancing in public places   159
KATHINKA FRØYSTAD

9 Conformity and contestation: social heterogeneity in
south Indian settlements   182
PENNY VERA-SANSO

10 The rituals of rehabilitation: rebuilding an urban
neighbourhood after the Gujarat earthquake of 2001   206
EDWARD SIMPSON

Index   232

LIST OF ILLUSTRATIONS

Tables

4.1	Percentage distribution of households by place of origin	71
6.1	Sizes and characteristics of towns in Uttar Pradesh as defined by the Census 2001 compared with Bijnor	118
6.2	Educational institutions on the Main NW Road run by the Charitable Trust	121

Figures

7.1	Mixed housing in Taltala, central Calcutta	145
7.2	New development in Rajarhat, at the outskirts of the city	146
10.1	Soniwad cleared of rubble after the earthquake	207
10.2	Kili Pujan	214

Maps

2.1	The town of Bhavani and the neighbourhood of Sengadu Thottam	25
5.1	Madras in 1733 (based on Subrahmanya Aiyar's 1902	92
5.2	Madras in 1755 (based on *A Plan of Fort St. George and The Bounds of Madraspatnam* by F.L. Conradi)	94
5.3	George Town and Fort St. George, Madras City, *c.* 2000	95
5.4	Chetpet in Egmore, *c.* 1950	107
6.1	Bijnor town, showing secondary schools and neighbourhoods, 2002	119

NOTES ON
CONTRIBUTORS

Indranil Chakrabarti completed his PhD on local governance in Calcutta at the Development Studies Institute (DESTIN), London School of Economics, in 2001. Since then, he has joined the Financial Services Authority (FSA) in London, and is currently working for the Department for International Development (DFID) in Dhaka, Bangladesh, as a social development adviser. He continues to nurture an interest in social movements and civil society as important elements of an effective and well-functioning state that serves the interests of poor people.

Geert De Neve is Senior Lecturer in Social Anthropology at the University of Sussex, UK. He has a specific interest in the study of labour and industrialisation in India, as well as a more general interest in processes of migration, modernity and social transformation. He is the author of *The Everyday Politics of Labour: Working Lives in India's Informal Economy* (Social Science Press, 2005) and co-editor of *Critical Journeys: The Making of Anthropologists* (Ashgate, 2006).

Henrike Donner is Research Fellow in the Department of Anthropology at the London School of Economics, UK. She has worked extensively in Calcutta, India, and has published on gender, kinship and reproductive change among Indian middle-class families. She is the author of a forthcoming monograph, entitled *Domestic Godesses: Maternity, Globalisation and Middle-Class Identity in Contemporary India* (Ashgate, 2007).

Kathinka Frøystad is a Postdoctoral Research Fellow at the Department of Social Anthropology, University of Oslo, Norway. She has done fieldwork in Kanpur, Haridwar and New Delhi, and her publications include *Blended Boundaries: Caste, Class and Shifting Faces of 'Hinduness' in a North Indian City*, (Oxford University Press, 2005). She is currently involved in a research project on new forms of Hinduism in India and abroad.

Hugo Gorringe is Lecturer in Sociology at the University of Edinburgh with research interests in social movements and politics. His earlier work focused on Dalit movements in Tamil Nadu – their organisation, objectives, participants and outcomes, on which he published a monograph entitled *Untouchable Citizens: The Dalit Panthers and Democratisation in Tamilnadu* (Sage, 2005). He is currently working on the localisation of 'global protest' with specific reference to the 2005 G8 summit.

Patricia Jeffery is Professor of Sociology at Edinburgh University. Her research focuses on gender and communal politics among Hindus and Muslims in South Asia. Recent publications include *Don't Marry me to a Plowman! Women's Everyday Lives in Rural North India* (with Roger Jeffery, Westview Press, Boulder, CO, and Vistaar Publications, New Delhi, 1996), *Resisting the Sacred and the Secular: Women's Activism and Politicized Religion in South Asia* (edited with Amrita Basu, Kali for Women, 1999), *Educational Regimes in Contemporary India* (edited with Radhika Chopra, Sage Publications, 2005) and *Confronting Saffron Demography: Religion, Fertility and Women's Status in India* (with Roger Jeffery, Three Essays Collective, 2006).

Roger Jeffery is Professor of Sociology of South Asia at Edinburgh University. His interests include social demography, agrarian change and education in post-liberalisation India. Recent publications include *Population, Gender and Politics: Demographic Change in Rural North India* (with Patricia Jeffery, Cambridge University Press, 1997), *Social and Political Change in Uttar Pradesh: European Perspectives* (edited with Jens Lerche, Manohar, 2003) and 'Patterns and discourses of the privatisation of secondary schooling in Bijnor, UP' (with Patricia Jeffery and Craig Jeffrey, in *The Politics of Education in South Asia* (Joachim Österheld and Krishna Kumar (eds), Orient Longman, forthcoming).

Craig Jeffrey is Assistant Professor at the Department of Geography and Henry M. Jackson School of International Studies at the University of Washington. His research focuses on youth, education, agrarian change and state / society relations with primary reference to north India. Craig undertook his doctoral research in the mid-1990s on the political networks of rural elites in western Uttar Pradesh. More recently, he has conducted a collaborative project on the relationship between educational expansion and the reproduction of social inequalities, and a project on the cultures of student politics in Meerut city.

Mattison Mines is Professor Emeritus of Anthropology at the University of California, Santa Barbara, and Visiting Professor of Humanities and Social Sciences, Indian Institute of Technology, Madras. He has done field research in Tamil Nadu among the Tamil-speaking Muslims, the

Kaikkoolar weavers, and, in Chennai, among the Beeri Chetti and Komati Chetti merchants. His most recent book is *Public Faces, Private Voices Community and Individuality in South India* (University of California Press, 1994).

Edward Simpson is Lecturer in Social Anthropology at Goldsmiths College, London. He has published a monograph *Muslim Society and the western Indian Ocean: The Seafarers of Kachchh* (London: RoutledgeCurzon, 2006) and a number of articles on politics and learning in Gujarat. More recently, his research has focused on the political and moral economies of reconstruction following large-scale natural disasters in South Asia.

Penny Vera-Sanso teaches development studies at Birkbeck College, University of London. She has undertaken field research in urban and rural Tamil Nadu since 1989. She has published widely on how gender and family relations shape and are shaped by the local economy and globalisation, and how they produce Tamil identities. Her current research is a study of intergenerational relations among castes living in Chennai's squatter and municipal tenements, and landless Scheduled Caste labourers in rural Tamil Nadu.

ACKNOWLEDGEMENTS

This volume has emerged from papers delivered in the course of two work-shops on urban space that were held at the London School of Economics in 2001 and at the University of Sussex in 2002. We would like to thank the Department of Anthropology, London School of Economics, and the then School of African and Asian Studies, University of Sussex, for financial support. This volume has benefited a great deal from the discussions in these workshops, and we thank both the discussants and the participants for their many critical comments. We are particularly grateful to Akhil Gupta, Thomas Blom Hansen and the late Rajnarayan Chandavarkar for their suggestions and illuminating discussions of the papers. Barbara Harriss-White, Sunil Kumar and Jonathan Parry also made valuable contributions that are not included in this volume. Furthermore, we would like to thank the anonymous reviewers, and Dorothea Schäfter and Marianne Bulman of Routledge for their support in producing this volume.

1

SPACE, PLACE AND GLOBALISATION
Revisiting the urban neighbourhood in India

Henrike Donner and Geert De Neve

This volume is concerned with urban localities and the way they relate to processes of globalisation. By zooming in on specific localities like neighbourhoods in different cities and towns across the Indian subcontinent, we investigate how these are made into meaningful places, what such localities reveal about urban space and urban life more generally, and how global processes are articulated here. All chapters in this volume contribute to a critical analysis of urban space by focusing on processes of place-making and by documenting the differences and similarities in the making of localities under processes of socio-economic change. In particular, the contributions reveal the complexities of place-based politics as well as the ways in which these processes shape the making, contesting and reconstruction of places. By way of introduction, we first situate our argument within a rapidly growing body of scholarship on space and place. We therefore briefly present some literature on urban life and urbanism more generally, followed by a short overview of the study of cities and urban places in India. Finally, we introduce our specific focus on the urban locale and indicate how the contributors to this volume employ such a perspective to study politics, culture and change in contemporary urban India.

Space, place and globalisation

Recently, much literature on place and locality has emerged as part of discussions on 'globalisation' – some see their work as a reaction to sweeping generalisations that depict cultures and societies as 'de-territorialised', 'dislocated' and increasingly 'disembedded'; others attempt to understand new forms of place-making and relatedness. In spite of the many definitions of globalisation, one point that scholars from a wide range of disciplines agree on is the fact that, with globalisation and economic restructuring, new spatial relationships have emerged that shape contemporary cultural forms and the experience of social relations in

1

unprecedented ways (Appadurai 1990; Featherstone 1990; Giddens 1990; Escobar 2001).

These new structures have been described in terms of global flows that transform local cultures. But critics of the globalisation literature have pointed out that much of the writing on globalisation suffers from a striking asymmetry, whereby the local increasingly 'derives its meaning from its juxtaposition to the global', while the latter is privileged in the writings about globalisation (Dirlik 2001: 17). The local has received much less attention, partly because its implicit attributes seem to make it a thing of the past, less exciting to study than the 'new' worldwide links and global flows of people, goods and ideas. Or, as Dirlik puts it, 'space' is often associated with capital, history and activity, while the 'local' or 'place-based' is associated with labour, stasis and immobility (ibid. 17).

In spite of the new emphasis on the spatial aspects of society, debates on globalisation tend to treat the local as a less central concern in contemporary social analysis, and Escobar aptly argues that place has increasingly been marginalised, if not altogether erased, in current debates on globalisation. Even among geographers, who have been at the forefront of the study of spatial relations, research on global flows and spatial movements (reflected, for example, in the burgeoning field of migration studies) continues to supersede the study of the place-based (Harvey 1990; Escobar 2001). In Escobar's view, it is time to redress the balance 'by focusing anew . . . on the continued vitality of place and place-making for culture, nature and economy' (2001: 141). While the analysis of 'global flows', such as the national and global imagery (Hansen and Stepputat 2001), global economic networks (Castells 1996) or new media spaces (Sassen 1996), has shaped much current debate on culture and society against a background of massive transformations, the renewed demand for a study of the 'local' or of 'place-making' testifies to the continued importance of spatial relations that appear more localised or rooted. This demand is often phrased in terms of a need to study 'everyday lives' and 'local forms of globalisation', but there is more to it than a mere return to the certainties and fixities of place. While social scientists have for long engaged with particular localities and localised social relations – often at the risk of losing sight of the wider picture – they too have to face the new challenge of how to conceptualise the 'local' in a radically changing global world. The global transformations of the last decades have not only brought about new forms of relatedness between regions, communities and individuals, and new dependencies in the economic sphere, but they have also transformed the political contexts in which these are embedded. The 'local' and 'locality' have themselves acquired radically new meanings and contents, often counteracting the homogenising tendencies of cultural globalisation.

But why should we study place as constituted in urban contexts to understand wider processes such as globalisation? Discussing the role that information technologies play in the globalisation of cities and urban culture, Sassen argues that a focus on metropolitan cities 'allows us to recover the concrete, localized processes through which globalization exists' (1996: 206). We would like to emphasise, however, that smaller towns are equally important sites for the study of globalisation and its related processes, and that South Asia has seen much urbanisation and global integration taking place in non-metropolitan urban contexts. More specifically, the contributions of this volume relate the social relations that produce localities in older metropolitan cities, such as Kolkata, Mumbai and Chennai, to the newly booming and often more provincial Indian towns that have been transformed under the influence of recent economic liberalisation policies.

In this volume, we focus on a specific instance of place-making, the role that the locality plays in the construction of social relations against the background of changed global-local connections. The chapters contained in this volume address social transformations through a focus on urban localities and urban lifestyles, alongside global transformations. They do this through detailed ethnographies of urban neighbourhoods across India. While the contributors approach 'the meaning of the local' from different disciplinary angles, all of them employ an ethnographic methodology to explore everyday spatial practices and representations.

Studying urban place and spatial imagination

In an early article on urban anthropology, Richard Fox argued that the study of cities called for a holistic approach because, to the ethnographer, 'the city becomes only one of many institutions such as kinship, value systems, and subsistence activity which he has always treated as part of a socio-cultural whole' (Fox 1980: 106). Urban space should thus be seen as a realm that plays an active role in the organisation of society at large, since the city 'is both product and producer of particular political alignments, economic sectors and social structures' (ibid. 106). The contributions to this volume similarly consider urban localities as constitutive of social relationships, which they reflect, challenge or reproduce. Through their focus on localities, and more specifically urban neighbourhoods, they attempt to move beyond the basic and oft repeated assertion that place is socially constructed, and examine the varied ways in which places themselves are highly political and fluid – that is, gender, caste and community identities are constantly produced, negotiated and challenged through spatial practices and shifting spatial concepts.

By relating spatial concepts to the reproduction of social relationships in urban India, we continue a recent line of critical inquiries into the role that place plays in the relationship between culture and power. Geographers like Massey (1994) have pointed the way for an analysis of spatial relations in terms of power, and this perspective is today fruitfully employed by other disciplines, which have begun to critique what the anthropologists Gupta and Ferguson have called the 'assumed isomorphism of space, place, and culture' (Gupta and Ferguson 1997: 34), so often presupposed in the social sciences. The contributions to this volume underline the latter authors' assertion 'that all associations of place, people and culture are social and historical creations to be explained, not given natural facts' (ibid. 4). A common interest in the contributions to this volume lies in the ethnographic exploration of social and political space in urban India, and the production of differences – cultural, social and economic – that occur locally over time. New theoretical approaches in geography and urban studies have led the way for a rethinking of space as a constructed and political force that contributes to the constitution of localities. The ethnography of various localities can show us the micropolitics employed in the creation of such relations of power. In this context, the local-global dichotomy is gradually being discarded in favour of a notion of space as always 'hierarchically interconnected, instead of naturally disconnected' (ibid. 35).

This hierarchical interconnection of places, we argue, reflects hierarchies of power and struggles over power. Power is always distributed at different levels, and people everywhere have differential access to its sources; the same is the case for places. Foucault, for example, has emphasised that space is central to any form of communal life and fundamental in any exercise of power (1975). In this vein, we subscribe to Low and Lawrence-Zúñiga's suggestion to look at the 'concept of space as a strategy and / or technique of power and social control' (2003: 30), and we focus on the politics of place-making (or spatial strategies) in order to provide a dynamic perspective on localities and to avoid replicating the older concept of place as static and unchanging. We also suggest that an ethnographic analysis of spatial strategies can shed new light on the lives of urbanites in India, as elsewhere, in the age of globalisation.

Of particular interest to our approach is the work of those who have questioned what we mean by 'places' in the age of globalisation and have asked how people relate to places in the face of current processes of disjunction and interconnectedness. Starting with the question 'can we rethink a sense of place that is adequate to this era of time-space compression' (Massey 1994: 147), Massey proposes alternative interpretations of place, in which place is no longer associated with essential identities, with community or with the past and tradition. She suggests instead that 'what gives place its specificity is not some long internalised history but the fact that it is constructed out of a particular constellation of social relations, meeting and weaving together at a particular locus' (ibid. 154). Such a view recognises that a sense of place comes about not only through essentialised histories, but also through ongoing struggles about access to resources, the politics of difference and contested social relations played out through specific spatial practices. Here, place constitutes a *product* of socio-political relations as well as the *material* with which such relations are created. In such an approach, the structuring power of place (Giddens 1990), or the spatial imagination, is taken as seriously as the historical imagination (Soja 1989: 15).

Since concepts, ideas and practices generate social relations of difference and sameness, a dynamic approach to space explores the 'politics of mobility and access' (Massey 1994: 150). The emphasis in this volume, therefore, is on the ways in which places emerge through movements: of people, goods and resources at different times and in different urban contexts. The contributions stem from different disciplines, but share a preoccupation with the *political* nature of space – that is, the ways in which places reflect, disguise or reinforce relations of power and the politics of difference. They endorse the notion of 'places as projects', as advocated by Dirlik (2001: 36), and highlight varied ways in which places are imagined, created and contested. Similar to the languages of stateness, discussed by Hansen and Stepputat (2001: 5–10), we will look into languages of place-making to explore how people talk about places, how boundaries are negotiated and how places feed into projects of identity and difference.

Urban environments in India

In order to explore these issues in a specific context, we have chosen to focus on urban localities and, more specifically, on urban neighbourhoods in India. Although localities have been central to research on cities, notably in African and American contexts, since at least the 1920s, they have rarely been the object of research in the sociology and anthropology of South Asia. Who, then, has studied cities and urban places in India? For long, research on urban issues in India was left to policy makers, economists, geographers and urban planners, who favoured quantitative approaches over qualitative research in order to explore processes of urbanisation (for instance, Ramachandran 1989; Sharma and Sita 2001; Sandhu 2003). Although some attempts to diversify this approach towards an exploration of urbanity and urbane lifestyles have been made (see, for instance, the volumes edited by Bose 1968; Siddique 1982; Patel and Thorner 1996; Dupont *et al.* 2000), most ethnographers ignored the centrality of urban places in the lives of ordinary Indians across the subcontinent. If anything, urban settings figured as background to the study of planning problems and localised cultures, whereas urban cultures and institutions were rarely critically addressed in themselves.

Despite the rather thin ethnographic record, urban social relations have attracted the attention of many historians. First, there are those historians who focused on urbanism (Ballhatchet and Harrison 1980; Banga 1991), on the imperial Moghul city (Frykenberg 1986) and on the ways in which trade and agrarian relations shaped processes of early urbanisation and urban politics (Subrahmanyam 1990). Other historians – alongside a few influential anthropologists – explored the ways in which the colonial project transformed political, social and religious relationships in and around major urban centres. This approach is reflected, for instance, in a number of studies of changing temple administration and (royal) power relations in the larger towns of south India (Appadurai 1981; Dirks 1987). However, much of this work also emphasised the continuities of pre-colonial and colonial urban forms, and demonstrated how the urbanism of the modern city is still marked by earlier forms of urban life, which were transformed but not erased during the colonial period. Urban centres predating colonial rule remained prominent as centres of religious, political and economic power and as models of urban politics during the colonial period. This is particularly obvious in the imperial city of Delhi, which predates the colonial period (Dupont *et al.* 2000), or in the case of port cities such as Surat (Haynes 1991). Mines, in this volume, similarly discusses how social relations from at least the seventeenth century fashioned the spatial layout of Madras and continue to shape Chennai up to this day, while Simpson (also in this volume) illustrates the ways in which longstanding social and religious divisions mould post-earthquake reconstruction in Gujarat.

Finally, those historians interested in the nature of urban industrial transformation studied the effects of capitalist modes of production on urban forms and relationships. They focused on localities, often urban neighbourhoods that were the sites of struggles about labour relations, public culture, social identity and state control (Subrahmanyam 1990; Haynes 1991; Chandavarkar 1994; Subramanian 1996; Gooptu 2001).

Following independence, cities, as modernising and industrialising spaces, gained a new centrality, first in popular and political imagination and later in the social sciences. After independence, they began to preoccupy an ambivalent place in the imagination of the Indian nation after independence. While the Gandhian version of nationalism employed the imagery of 'village India', which became the 'true' site of Indian tradition, the contemporary Nehruvian vision highlighted cities as places of progress and modernity, to be achieved through planned urbanisation and industrialisation (Prakash 2002). The most famous materialisation of this imagery is Chandigar, the city designed by Le Corbusier. Less well-known, yet equally significant, are the industrial towns built in rural areas such as Bhilai, Durgapur and Jamshedpur, all of which pay tribute to this vision of progress and the role of the developmentalist state.

It was especially following the second phase of extensive urbanisation in the 1960s and 1970s that cities attracted the attention of social sciences in a major way. In order to come to terms with rapid urban growth, urban poverty and changing relationships in the city, social scientists began to investigate the nature of social change in urban localities and neighbourhoods using qualitative research methods. Whereas urban planners and geographers continued to study towns and cities to address questions of governance, infrastructure and livelihoods, other social sciences became interested in metropolitan areas and growing provincial towns to gain insight into changing patterns of (in)equality, segregation, mobility and morality (see below).

Much of this qualitative research in urban places focused on the transformation of 'traditional' patterns of organisation – specifically, those of caste and family, and the effects of migration on social status and mobility (Bose 1968; Vatuk 1971; Sinha 1972; Siddique 1982; Rao 1986). Sociologists and anthropologists studying urban localities in India during the 1970s emphasised the resilience of specific South Asian forms of social organisation, as reflected in the volume edited by Siddique (1982). Long-term fieldwork, mostly undertaken by anthropologists, explored the dynamics and representations of new group-based identities among different strata of urban society, ranging from industrialists in Madras (Singer and Cohn 1968; Singer 1972) to untouchables in Agra (Lynch 1969).

In many of these studies, however, the assumed congruence between social relations and territory continued to be reflected in the uncritical use of 'community', 'locality' and 'neighbourhood' as interchangeable terms. The neighbourhood became the site within which changing relationships of caste, gender and family could be researched and contained, and they continued to be conceived of as something akin to villages, as local and fixed. The sociological literature on urban India barely explored the form and meaning of neighbourhoods as socially constructed places (see, for instance, Vatuk 1971; Searle-Chatterjee 1981; Ramachandran 1989). Consequently, most accounts of urban life tend to provide a brief introduction to the neighbourhood through a description of its main physical and social characteristics before moving on to the 'real' concerns of the study (that is, caste, community, family, household structure and patterns of migration). Terms like *mohalla, para* or *nagar*, used to describe neighbourhoods, are often only loosely defined and then relegated to a glossary. By taking the neighbourhood itself as a point of departure, however, the present volume unpacks the ways in which neighbourhoods are made into meaningful places and are fundamental to an understanding of urban life more generally.

In their early approaches to the city and city life in India, scholars also replicated to a considerable degree a view of the urban that had become influential in much anthropological and sociological writing on the West at the time. Following the publication of Wirth's seminal paper, 'Urbanism as a Way of Life' (1938), the city as a whole was represented as a distinctly social form, associated with heterogeneity, anonymity and impersonal relationships, with social relations marked by breakdown, decay and deterioration. Town and village emerged as contrasting spheres of social life and organisation, with an almost exclusive focus on the urban poor and urban slums. Many studies 'depicted the city as a pathological milieu, difficult for residents and scholars alike, especially anthropologists who stressed the normative rather than the deviant' (Press and Smith 1980: 4). In line with American urban anthropology and British studies of African towns, scholars studying South

7

Asia reproduced this negative perspective on urban contexts through stereo-types of danger, immorality and misery. Moreover, this imagery fitted with both the colonial view of cities as sites of criminal activities where law and order (and thus colonial rule) were under constant threat (Chandavarkar 1994; Ferguson 1999; Nair 1999) and with prevalent folk models of towns, imagined as seats of changing values (Nandy 2001; Parry 2003).

Nevertheless, this largely negative image of the city has also been revisited in more recent writings. In-depth studies of inner city areas began to demonstrate that social relations in urban contexts are often as homogeneous, stable and familiar as those in the village. Thus, Herbert Gans coined the term 'urban village' to refer to urban pockets in which people are closely related, interact on a regular basis and share similar socio-economic circumstances (1962: 3–4). Along the same line, recent ethnographic accounts of urban India have drawn attention to people's much more ambivalent attitudes to towns and cities. In fact, today, the urban is seen as a source of employment, a site of emancipation and increasingly as the very location of modernity itself, desired for its available goods, assumed freedoms and accessible opportunities (Pinney 1999). Parry, for one, has argued that the long-distance migrants to the steel town of Bhilai in Central India have 'internalised a vision of modernity which antithetically constructs the village as an area of darkness – a "waiting room" from which one hopes to escape' (Parry 2003: 217). And it is not only in Bhilai that representations of the rural and the urban are being inversed. Even the period after independence saw a certain romanticisation of rural India, although the contemporary city-dweller rarely subscribes to such a view of village life. She or he is more likely to subscribe to the moral denouncement of the rural as the seat of backwardness, illiteracy and tradition. The village is increasingly contrasted with representations of cities as seats of new and clean industries, as in the case of information technology (IT) hubs, and sites of desired consumption practices and indeed modernity (Parry 1999, 2003; Fernandes 2000).

From the 1970s, urbanisation began to take new forms with the rise of satellite towns around bigger cities, which were often planned either as sites for middle-class residences or as sites for the relocation of industries. Throughout the 1970s and 1980s, planners and development theorists analysed state-controlled developments of such satellite towns as well as their potential to remedy urban housing crises and infrastructure problems (Sharma and Sita 2001; Mitra 2002). Attempts to capture 'cultural aspects' of metropolitan areas were made (Patel and Thorner 1996), yet they did not combine cultural with spatial perspectives on urbanism, leaving discussions of concrete localities disconnected from notions of culture defined in more general terms. By and large, the spatial interests of planners and geographers in cities and urban areas remained far removed from the socio-cultural debates of purity and pollution, caste and rituals that preoccupied the leading sociologists of India during the 1970s and 1980s, who again showed little interest in the field of cultural studies and urban lifestyles emerging else-where. For the former, it was ultimately their interest in the transformation of values and social institutions that led them to take the study of urban space and urban life more seriously (see, for instance, Béteille 1992), as reflected, for example, in the recent volume edited by Sandhu (2003). Moreover, what had looked to planners as philosophical discussions of little practical value, such as the study of pollution, hierarchy and social status, became more politically relevant once they were fused with wider studies of social change, reservation policies, migration, and social and political move-ments (see D'Souza 1975; Berreman 1979; Searle-Chatterjee 1981; Karlekar 1982; Khare 1985; Béteille 1992).

Unfortunately, while urban places provided the material for much of the research on social change and politics in India, such places remained the *sites* rather than the *objects* of inquiry. The papers in this volume, on the other hand, take urban places *per se* as the objects of research, and carefully scru-tinize these places in an attempt not only to reveal cultural and historical dimensions of change but also to uncover the spatial dimensions of social change in contemporary India. It is with this particular fusion of cultural, historical and spatial aspects of urban life that we are concerned in what follows.

But we are not entirely alone in taking this approach. A focus on urbanism as a way of life has resurfaced in studies of globalisation in India, and the 'urban turn' proclaimed by Prakash and others testifies to a new body of literature that locates Indian cities at its centre (Prakash 2002). Much of this is concerned with the impact of global communication and information technologies on urban life, or with the nature of urban restruc-turing in the wake of liberalisation policies. As Fernandes has argued, the spatial restructuring of urban India reflects contemporary ways of imag-ining the global, the national and the local (Fernandes 2000; 2004). This new theorising of urban India is welcome but often based on generalised notions of 'Indian modernity' as an urban version of Euro-American metropolitan, middle-class lifestyles. Low has convincingly argued for the need to theorise the city more carefully and to deconstruct generalising assumptions about urban life, yet it is discouraging to see that her seminal reader on cities contains not a single case study from South Asia (Low 1999). The present volume hopes to correct this hiatus by presenting a new perspective on processes of place-making in urban South Asia and on how such processes reflect notions of the local, of culture and of identity.

Urban neighbourhoods in India

In this volume, we have chosen to focus almost exclusively on the neighbour-hood as a specific type of urban locality where politics and power struggles are *located* and *take place* on a day-to-day basis, or, as de Certeau put it, where social relations and values are shaped through the practices and 'tactics' of everyday life (de Certeau 1984). However, no discussion of a neighbourhood is ever limited to the unit so described, and all chapters in this volume illustrate how the social life of neighbourhoods is always affected by wider influences such as political and religious movements, state policies, economic transformations, and city-wide social and cultural change. Yet we are convinced that a focus on specific neighbourhoods, slums or suburbs makes good sense for a number of reasons.

First of all, localities are the concrete manifestation of spatial concepts, memories and practices that shape social relationships and are therefore relatively widely understood as loci for individual agency. Appadurai defines 'locality' as primarily relational and contextual, and 'neighbourhood' as 'the actually existing social forms in which locality, as a dimension or value, is variably realized' (1995: 204–5). Such a perspective on the neighbourhood emphasises how neighbourhoods constitute the actual locales where imaginations, representations and values of place are enacted and located.

One of the main characteristics of urban neighbourhoods is their role as sites for individual and collective memory. This role is particularly pertinent in instances where a history of displacement or state repression played a significant part in the formation of a locality (Ray 2002; Tarlo 2003). However, all urban neighbourhoods are places of remembered pasts and imagined futures, and are therefore shaped, monitored and given meaning through outside influences and politics. Whereas in the Hindu city of the past – to take one example of pre-colonial urbanism – these politics took the form of interaction between royal powers, castes and colonial authorities, today they are shaped by the actions and interventions of the Indian state. Simpson's chapter in this volume exemplifies how the attempt of the state to reconstruct neighbourhoods in the old town of Bhuj (Gujarat) after the earthquake brought out longstanding sentiments and identifications of caste, kingship and religion, which in Srinivas's felicitous words provide a 'landscape of urban memory' (Srinivas 2001).

Second, for their inhabitants, neighbourhoods are places of particular significance. To both insiders and outsiders, they represent the most imminent 'local' context within which histories, communities and differences are created and embedded in everyday practices. These practices range from gossip and informal meetings in the street to more organised activities such as schooling, medical care, and political and religious organisation. A discussion of such localities therefore enables us to link debates on political organisation, gender relations, labour movements and kinship to overarching expressions of religious, political and national identities (Chandavarkar 1994; Weiss 1998). They are frequently the places *in* and *through* which people gain access to resources and where they encounter the institutions and representatives of the state through schools, hospitals, mosques, government offices, political parties and unions. And above all, they constitute the locale where both individual and social identities are reproduced through shared ritual activity, economic co-operation and political mobilisation (Hansen 2001; Tarlo 2003). Neighbourhoods, therefore, have a distinctively communal quality to them, and their inhabitants often explicitly define them in terms of relatedness, interdependence, co-operation and conflict based on spatial proximity. As Donner in her chapter points out, even though its boundaries may be porous, its membership always ambivalent and its legal status contested, the neighbourhood is for most urban dwellers a social reality that has far-reaching effects on their lives. In providing a context for face-to-face relationships in social, political and cultural formations, the urban neighbourhood constitutes a parallel to the village. The neighbourhood as 'urban village' remains meaningful for its residents, even though people of different classes and genders may have differential access to and knowledge of it.

A third rationale behind our focus on neighbourhoods relates to their institutional and administrative relevance. Even in cases where there is little interaction among neighbours, as in highly individualistic suburbs, the neighbourhood, ward or slum remains a crucial mode of social organisation and classification that facilitates the state's intervention in the life of its citizens. Here, this is most clearly illustrated in the chapters by Chakrabarti and Simpson, where the ward and neighbourhood both shape and mediate interventions of state and political parties. Mines's contribution illustrates how the contemporary urban landscape of the city of Chennai is fashioned by social and spatial relations that modelled the city in pre-colonial and colonial times. Through a historical biography of the city, Mines charts how specific divisions within Chennai came about as part of caste-based collective identities, and how such divisions continue to determine the way in which city dwellers interpret and re-inscribe current urban developments.

Neighbourhoods lend themselves to the study of place and culture for at least two more reasons: one is conceptual, the other methodological. The neighbourhood is a space in-between *par excellence*, a locality that connects the direct experiences of households and families with their participation in wider networks of city, nation and the world. The question is not just how the neighbourhood builds bridges, but also how it mediates the national and the global in the local (Fernandes 2000). To the ethnographer, neighbourhoods are therefore intermediate places in the way McDowell describes 'communities' as intermediate (1999: 95). The neighbourhood is the place in which knowledge and experience of the wider world is articulated, and thus a prime location for the study of culture. Images and values of the wider world become meaningful only when translated into more localised narratives and practices located in such significant places of everyday interaction. It is precisely because of its mediating and translating role that the neighbourhood is an appropriate locale from where to start conceptualising the interconnectedness of places, peoples and cultures in a globalising world.

Furthermore, in spite of earlier calls for a holistic approach to the city, and in spite of the much hyped idea of 'multi-sited fieldwork', it still makes a great deal of methodological sense to focus on the neighbourhood as a place that researchers in fieldwork-based disciplines can come to 'know'. A pertinent question to ask is not whether the wider context of city or nation is relevant to localised lives – as it obviously is – but rather how to go about examining the connections between local settings and wider contexts in a rapidly globalising environment such as that of South Asian cities. The urban neighbourhood, we suggest, is a fertile place for the study of global-local interactions not because it is less complex than other terrains but because it is a space that emerges as a site of translation and contact between different spheres. We therefore advocate a perspective that does not only compare neighbourhoods within a single city, which is the approach chosen by some contributors to this volume, but also to compare neighbourhoods across cities. Such a perspective will ultimately provide insights into what is specifically urban and / or Indian about the localities we study, and improve our understanding of rapidly changing urban contexts and lifestyles.

The contributions in this volume

One of the most prominent themes in the study of urban spaces in South Asia is the role of *public spaces* in local politics, in which the neighbourhood as a site of everyday class, gender and caste relations takes a central place. Kaviraj's seminal account of the various historical transformations of Deshapriya Park in South Calcutta (1997) illustrates how ethnic and class identities are constructed as much through public spaces, including parks, squares and lanes, as through private ones. Once an extension of a Bengali middle-class residential neighbourhood, the park became the stronghold of post-partition refugees who set up a series of shacks and makeshift shops at its borders. The filth and disorder that this process of plebianisation entailed did not only alter the character of the park, but allowed the homeless refugees 'to symbolically establish their control over that space' (Kaviraj 1997: 107). Kaviraj shows that the park and its filth became the physical *and* conceptual place for struggles over class, access and entitlement. He aptly concludes that it is 'the site of the everyday, out of the surveillance of disciplines, that is usually turned into the place of small rebellion of the poor' (ibid. 110).

The chapters that follow similarly explore urban and public places as localities where processes of contestation and appropriation are at work. In public spaces such as wards, housing estates and neighbourhoods, the everyday politics of place are always closely intertwined with formal state and party politics. The first four papers of this volume examine such spatial politics and tactics that shape the worlds of the urban poor and the working classes.

In two case studies from urban Tamil Nadu, Geert De Neve and Hugo Gorringe explore the ways in which space is strategically used in the negotiation of changing caste and class relationships. Geert De Neve's ethnography reveals how members of a low but upwardly mobile caste in small-town south India, who benefited greatly from the economic liberalisation of the 1990s, mobilise space in the process of creating a new identity for themselves. The Vanniyars of Bhavani unite themselves in an attempt to reverse negative public representations of their community and relocate their factories to their own neighbourhood, Sengadu Thottam, located at the border of the town. De Neve shows how the ongoing relocation and concentration of Vanniyar factories in Sengadu Thottam, along with Vanniyars' self-representation as a close-knit moral community, point to a remarkable inclination to *consolidate* affinities of neighbourhood and caste at a time when modernity and globalisation are believed to bring about much more fluid and hybrid urban spaces. Liberalisation and economic restructuring do not necessarily translate into the rise of more heterogeneous urban spaces. They may well activate a politics of place in which upwardly mobile working-class groups (as well as Dalit groups, see Gorringe in this volume), in search of a new identity, opt for a politics of space that seeks to delineate clear boundaries and to consolidate in space newly acquired social positions.

Hugo Gorringe focuses explicitly on such practices of boundary marking in his chapter on Dalit politics around Melavassel, a housing estate mainly occupied by Dalit municipal employees in Madurai. Just as the *cheris* or Dalit hamlets found in the surrounding villages testify to a long history of caste-based discrimination and segregation, the housing estates of urban India largely reproduce the social and spatial exclusion that marked rural life. Gorringe presents an incisive analysis of Dalit Panther movement activity around the estate of Melavassel, a movement that seeks to establish or redefine territories precisely through a process of boundary marking. Locality is produced and territory is established not in a once-and-for-all manner, but through a constant process of activity, revision and contestation. Wall paintings, posters, graffiti and flagpoles have become the powerful symbols of a defended neighbourhood and a vibrant political movement. Through such symbols and performances, the residents of Melavassel are not only marking the boundaries of a Dalit locality but they are simultaneously publicising their affiliation to the wider Dalit Panther Movement. As in the case studies of De Neve and Vera-Sanso (see later), Gorringe shows how changing caste and class relations are articulated through a politics of space that often (re)creates rather than dissolves boundaries and localities.

Indranil Chakrabarti turns to a different sort of politics. He presents a fine analysis of neighbourhood organisations in two *bustees* (slums) of Calcutta, Dover Terrace and Swinhoe Lane. In particular, he explores the critical role of neighbourhood activism in improving the performance of local health care officials and ensuring better access to basic services. Chakrabarti found that while in Swinhoe Lane neighbourhood groups were active in monitoring the role of local health officials, in Dover Terrace residents remained passive in view of poor health service delivery. Having shown that both localities are equally heterogeneous and socially divided, Chakrabarti successfully debunks two common assumptions in development's decentralisation theory. First, residential communities or neighbourhoods do not always represent consensual units for collective action and, second, social and ethnic heterogeneity of urban neighbourhoods does not necessarily prevent their inhabitants from engaging in collective action, as illustrated in the case of Swinhoe Lane's dynamic neighbourhood organisations. What explains the difference between these localities, Chakrabarti argues, is that in Swinhoe Lane a left-wing political party, the CPI(M), played a vital role in encouraging the proliferation of 'mass front organisations' (grassroots party-related organisations), while in Dover Terrace, a Congress Bastion, a low-level organisational network was never developed. It was the particular historical and political contexts of party organisation that made neighbourhood organisations thrive in Swinhoe Lane and prevented their emergence in Dover Terrace.

The crucial role of wider political influences and historical formations on contemporary urban landscapes is even more central to the contribution of Mattison Mines, who examines how the great merchant traders of Madras City have left their imprint on the city today. Mines demonstrates how the Beeri Chettiars and the Komatis, two leading merchant castes of Madras City, constructed their neighbourhoods in quite different manners, reflecting their contrasting integration into south Indian society as well as their respective relationships with the English East India Company. While the Beeri Chettiars (a left-hand caste) portrayed themselves as a kingly caste and as trustees of major temples, the Komatis (a right-hand caste) followed the style of *karmayoga*, correct action expressed as piety and charity, and presented themselves as patrons of charity and education. These different public styles were reflected in the development of separate residential areas and different social activities in the Petta or Black Town of Madras, known today as George Town. Mines not only provides us with a rich description of the physical development of Black Town, but also with a detailed analysis of a history of riots and arguments between two social groups that left its imprint on the urban landscape as we know it today. The changing fortunes of these castes during the twentieth century resulted in the Komatis moving out of the Petta west towards Poonamallee High Road where palatial garden houses were built, leading to a new phase of urban development. Mines thus provides us with a wonderful illustration of how the social dynamics and public arguments of a city's past are reflected in its contemporary landscape – its streets, temples and neighbourhoods.

Any town or city, however, reflects more than past divisions and politics: it also mirrors the inhabitants' memories and their current imaginations. Emma Tarlo's work on the politics of the Emergency in a resettlement colony in East Delhi, for example, illustrates how memories of the disruptive government policies of 'resettlement' and 'family planning' shape people's current 'sense of place' as well as contemporary narratives of the Emergency, which combine reflections both on places and bodies (Tarlo 2003). Yet imaginations and expectations also fashion urban landscapes, and this is addressed in this volume by Jeffery *et al.* who explore an 'educational environment' that has emerged in Bijnor, a small town in Uttar Pradesh. The educational environment that spreads along the main roads in North West Bijnor, and consists of schools, colleges, playgrounds and residences, forms an interesting urban space, quite different from the old town *mohallas* (neighbourhoods) or the new suburban *colonies*. Jeffery *et al.* unpack this educational environment as an institutional *and* discursive space – that is, as a place where people acquire education and as a space that they can inscribe with meaning and identity. The educational environment of North West Bijnor, the authors argue, constitutes an important site through which the residents are able to imagine and express a 'provincial modernity', their own version of the Nehruvian vision of progress. Yet, while the institutions and the flows around them provide the urban elite with models of imagined futures and opportunities, they also tend to exclude others, including the surrounding rural population, Muslim and Scheduled Caste youth. Jeffery *et al.* not only demonstrate how meanings of modernity and success are attached to this particular public space but also how such meanings are continuously contested and undermined by those sections of the population that have been pushed to the margins of this modernity. The urban landscape reflects the politics of its residents as much as it helps to shape it.

Whereas the first chapters of this volume examine the politics of the urban working classes and the urban poor, Mines's and Jeffery *et al.*'s contributions shift the focus onto the middle classes and their impact on the urban environment. Henrike Donner's paper also highlights this through a discussion of gendered spatial practices among middle-class inhabitants of a heterogeneous neighbourhood of Central Calcutta. Donner explores how spatial concepts and practices are drawn upon in people's everyday interactions to (re-)produce hierarchies of gender, ethnicity and class. In particular, Donner analyses middle-class women's views and experiences of the urban neighbourhood and their mobility in the public spaces that belong to it. She shows how women's experiences are shaped by gender-specific discourses on the public-private distinction, but draw on communal histories and class-based notions of respectability. The more general point that emerges from this material is that, while space is socially constructed, social distinctions (such as those of gender and class) are themselves produced with reference to spatial concepts and boundaries that are gender-specific.

Like Donner, Kathinka Frøystad explores expressions of class and gender in public places. Frøystad looks at class positioning of strangers in public spaces and the forms of social distancing that this positioning brings about. Exploring new spaces of consumption in Kanpur, Uttar Pradesh, Frøystad describes how people label strangers when encountering them in public spaces as 'good people', 'bad people', 'small people' and 'big people'. This labelling is based on outside markers of ethnic and class identities, such as clothing, complexion, movement and speech, in which caste and class connotations are often conflated. Frøystad argues that, in this context, markers of class difference routinely draw on implicit assumptions about caste – for instance, where a wealthy person is generally assumed to belong to a high caste. Such labelling eventually results in forms of social distancing – particularly relevant to women – enhanced through the emergence of 'practices of enclosure' that restrict access to specific venues to those who are perceived to be of the same social background. Such practices of enclosure can take different forms such as withdrawal from public spaces, as is often the case for women, the use of private transport or the temporary appropriation of public spaces, such as parks or streets, by members of a specific group (see also Kaviraj 1997). Donner's and Frøystad's chapters thus go some way to explain what is particularly Indian about urban neighbourhoods in India by showing how strategies of class labelling and public distancing are strongly informed by assumptions of caste, even if the public discourse is expressed in terms of class.

This moves the discussion of urban places beyond the residential neighbourhood and demonstrates that class, gender and ethnicity are produced and reinforced in the many public arenas in which urban life unfolds. As such, public spaces are shaped by communal histories and historically specific moralities as much as they are being refashioned by increasingly pervasive cultures of consumption.

Penny Vera-Sanso and Edward Simpson engage – in comparable ways – with the impact of wider ideologies and discourses on the formation and reconstruction of particular localities. These ideologies are not merely state discourses (whether regional or national) but draw on a variety of culturally specific ideologies that pervade state action and public intervention. Focusing on two heterogeneous neighbourhoods in Tamil Nadu, Vera-Sanso explores how changing Tamil/Dravidian nationalist discourses are mobilised in the formulation of neighbourhood identities and interactions in heterogeneous urban settlements. In particular, Vera-Sanso discusses how during her 1990–2 fieldwork in Chennai, people drew on an anti-Hindi, anti-North Indian Dravidian discourse that 'emphasised a common Tamil identity based on essentialised Tamil values of female chastity, valour, motherhood and love of the Tamil language'. People living in poor heterogeneous areas used this framework of norms and values to assess the reputation of other families and to define which families 'really belonged' to their neighbourhood. By 2000, however, this Tamil nationalist discourse had been undermined in significant ways. Tamil identity had been fragmented by the opening up of the Indian economy, the new consumerism and the normalisation of Hindutva ideology. In a new, gentrifying neighbourhood of a town near Coimbatore, this meant that local neighbourhood relations were now guided by a more 'common-sense' (middle-class) discourse about decency and respectability that – while still focusing on female chastity – referred much less to a specifically Tamil identity. In both cases, however, the principle remains the same: regional ideologies permeate the neighbourhood and mould the interactions among its residents.

In moving from Tamil Nadu to Gujarat, Simpson presents us with an intriguing discussion of the politics and rituals of neighbourhood reconstruction after the Gujarat earthquake of 2001. In the town of Bhuj, local politics of rebuilding are infused with wider religious and nationalist discourses in as much as they are fashioned by local disputes. Simpson's sensitive ethnography of neighbourhood reconstruction, or of 'place-making' in the literal sense of the word, moves from the human experiences of reconstructing lives after devastation to the formal politics of reconstructing homes and neighbourhoods. While reconstruction largely happened in a haphazard manner, there was nevertheless a dominant discourse on how the area should be reconstructed: a discourse that was not derived from religious scripts but nevertheless replete with Hindu nationalist imagery of reconstruction. In the many consultation exercises and rehabilitation committees in the neighbourhood of Soniwad, elite Hindus were over-represented, which in turn facilitated the performance of Hindu public rituals and the revamping of myths and memories that aimed to resurrect the structures of the long-lost Hindu kingdom of Kachchh. Simpson points out how the reconstruction efforts were mirroring a wider Hindu nationalist discourse on the construction of India as a land that befits its Hindu population. In the process, the Muslim population of Soniwad was not only being marginalised but the Hindu nationalist discourse was deepening its imprint on the spatial and social make-up of the newly built urban landscape.

In her discussion of the Islamic city, Janet Abu-Lughod asks whether there is an 'Islamic city', and whether or not one would 'expect Islamic cities to be similar and in what ways' (1987: 160). The same questions could be asked with reference to the Indian city, its determining features and regional variations. Much of the material presented in this volume highlights the way in which the history of the Indian state as well as changing economic and social relations have shaped the urban landscape. While a detailed comparison with other urban formations falls beyond the scope of this volume, the contributors emphasise local, regional and national forces that impact on the development of the urban, and that bring about specifically Indian urban spaces. The outcome, we believe, is a set of fascinating arguments about the heterogeneity and fluidity of urban space, which highlight trends, similarities and differences and invite further work on the urban in its South Asian form.

Acknowledgements

We thank the anonymous reviewer for constructive comments on an earlier draft of this chapter.

References

Abu-Lughod, Janet (1987) 'The Islamic city – historic myth, Islamic essence, and contemporary relevance' 19(2) *International Journal of Middle Eastern Studies* 155–76

Appadurai, Arjan (1981) *Worship and Conflict Under Colonial Rule: A South Indian Case*, Cambridge: Cambridge University Press

——(1990) 'Disjuncture and difference in the global cultural economy', in Featherstone, Mike (ed.), *Global Culture: Nationalism, Globalization and Modernity*, London: Sage Publications

——(1995) 'The production of locality', in Fardon, R. (ed.) *Counterworks*, London: Routledge

Ballhatchet, Kenneth and Harrison, John (eds) (1980) *The City in South Asia: Premodern and Modern*, London: Curzon

Banga, Indu (ed.) (1991) *The City in Indian History: Urban Demography, Society, and Politics*, New Delhi: South Asia Publications

Berreman, Gerald D. (1979) *Caste and Other Inequities*, Meerut: Folklore Institute

Béteille, André (1992) *The Backward Classes in Contemporary India*, Delhi: Oxford University Press

Bose, Nirmal K. (1968) *Calcutta 1964: A Social Survey*, Calcutta: Lalvani Publishing House

Castells, Manuel (1996) *The Information Age: Economy, Society and Culture, Vol I: The Rise of the Network Society*, Cambridge, MA: Blackwell Publishers

Chandavarkar, Rajnarayan (1994) *The Origins of Industrial Capitalism in India: Business Strategies and the Working Classes in Bombay, 1900–1940*, Cambridge: Cambridge University Press

de Certeau, Michel (1984) *The Practice of Everyday Life*, Berkeley, CA: University of California Press

Dirks, Nicholas (1987) *The Hollow Crown: Ethnohistory of an Indian Kingdom*, Cambridge: Cambridge University Press

Dirlik, Arif (2001) 'Place-based imagination: globalism and the politics of place', in Praznaik, Roxanne and Dirlik, Arif (eds), *Places and Politics in an Age of Globalization*, Lanham: Rowman and Littlefield

D'Souza, V. (1975) 'Scheduled castes and urbanization in Punjab: an explanation' 24 *Sociological Bulletin* 2–12

Dupont, Veronique, Tarlo, Emma and Vidal, Denis (eds) (2000) *Delhi: Urban Space and Human Destinies*, Delhi: Manohar

Escobar, Arturo (2001) 'Culture sits in places: reflections on globalism and subaltern strategies of localization' 20 *Political Geography* 9–174

Featherstone, Mike (ed.) (1990) *Global Culture: Nationalism, Globalization and Modernity*, London: Sage Publications

Ferguson, James (1999) *Expectations of Modernity: Myths and Meanings of Urban Life on the Zambian Copperbelt*, Berkeley, CA: University of California Press

Fernandes, Leela (2000) 'Nationalizing "the global": media images, cultural politics and the middle-class in India' 22(5) *Media, Culture and Society* 611–28

——(2004) 'The politics of forgetting: class politics, state power and the restructuring of urban space in India' 41(12) *Urban Studies* 2415–30

Foucault, Michel (1975) *Discipline and Punish: The Birth of the Prison*, New York: Vintage

Fox, Richard G. (1980) 'Rationale and romance in urban anthropology', in Press, I. and Estellie Smith, M. (eds), *Urban Places and Processes: Readings in the Anthropology of Cities*, New York: Macmillan

Frykenberg, Robert E. (1986) *Delhi through the Ages: Essays in Urban History, Culture and Society*, Delhi: Oxford University Press

Gans, Herbet (1962) *The Urban Villagers: Group and Class in the Life of Italian-Americans*, New York: Free Press of Glencoe

Giddens, Anthony (1990) *The Consequences of Modernity*, Cambridge: Polity Press

Gooptu, Nandini (2001) *The Politics of the Urban Poor in Early Twentieth-Century India*, Cambridge: Cambridge University Press

Gupta, Akhil and Ferguson, James (eds) (1997) *Culture, Power, Place: Explorations in Critical Anthropology*, Durham, NC: Duke University Press

Hansen, Thomas Blom (2001) *Wages of Violence: Naming and Identity in Postcolonial Bombay*, Princeton, NJ: Princeton University Press

Hansen, Thomas Blom and Stepputat, Finn (eds) (2001) *States of Imagination: Ethnographic Explorations of the Postcolonial State*, Durham: Duke University Press

Harvey, David (1990) *The Condition of Postmodernity: An Enquiry into the Origins of Cultural Change*, Cambridge, MA: Blackwell

Haynes, Douglas E. (1991) *Rhetoric and Ritual in Colonial India: The Shaping of a Public Culture in Surat City, 1852–1928*, Berkeley, CA: University of California Press

Karlekar, Malavika (1982) *Poverty and Women's Work: A Study of Sweeper Women in Delhi*, New Delhi: Vikas

Kaviraj, Sudipta (1997) 'Filth and the public sphere: concepts and practices about space in Calcutta' 10(1) *Public Culture* 83–113

Khare, Ravindra S. (1985) *The Untouchable as Himself: Identity and Pragmatism among the Lucknow Chamars*, Cambridge: Cambridge University Press

Low, Setha M. (ed.) (1999) *Theorizing the City: The New Urban Anthropology Reader*, New Brunswick, NJ: Rutgers University Press

Low, Setha M. and Lawrence-Zúñiga, Denise (2003) 'Locating culture', in Low, Setha M. and Lawrence-Zúñiga, Denise (eds) *The Anthropology of Space and Place: Locating Culture*, Malden: Blackwell

Lynch, O. (1969) *The Politics of Untouchability: Social Mobility and Social Change in a City of India*, New York: Columbia University Press

Massey, Doreen (1994) *Space, Place and Gender*, Cambridge: Polity Press

McDowell, Linda (1999) *Gender, Identity and Place: Understanding Feminist Geographies*, Cambridge: Polity Press

Mitra, Sanjay (2002) 'Planned urbanisation through public participation: the case of New Town, Kolkata' *Economic and Political Weekly*, 16 March

Nair, Janaki (1999) *Miners and Millhands: Work, Culture and Politics in Princely Mysore*, Walnut Creek, CA: AltaMira Press

Nandy, Ashis (2001) *An Ambiguous Journey to the City: The Village and Other Odd Ruins of the Self in the Indian Imagination*, Delhi: Oxford University Press

Parry, Jonathan P. (1999) 'Ankalu's errant wife: sex, marriage, and industry in contemporary Chhattisgarh' 35(4) *Modern Asian Studies* 783–820

——(2003) 'Nehru's dream and the village "waiting room": long-distance labour migrants to a central Indian steel town' 37(1,2) *Contributions to Indian Sociology* 217–51

Patel, Sujata and Thorner, Alice (eds) (1996) *Bombay: Mosaic of Modern Culture*, Delhi: Oxford University Press

Pinney, Christopher (1999) 'On living in the *kal(i)yug*: notes from Nagda, Madhya Pradesh' 33(1,2) *Contributions to Indian Sociology* 77–106

Prakash, Gyan (2002) 'The urban turn', in Vasudevan, R. *et al.* (eds), *Sarai Reader 02: The Cities of Everyday Life*, Delhi: Rainbow Publishers

Press, Irvin and Smith, Estellie M. (eds) (1980) *Urban Places and Processes: Readings in the Anthropology of Cities*, New York: Macmillan

Ramachandran, Ranganathan (1989) *Urbanization and Urban Systems in India*, Delhi: Oxford University Press

Rao, M.S.A. (ed.) (1986) *Studies in Migration*, Delhi: Manohar Publications

Ray, Manash (2002) 'Growing up refugee' 53(1) *History Workshop* 149–79

Sassen, Saskia (1996) 'Whose city is it anyway? Globalization and the formation of new claims' 8 *Public Culture* 205–23

Sandhu, Ravinder S. (ed.) (2003) *Urbanization in India: Sociological Contributions*, Delhi: Sage Publications

Searle-Chatterjee, Mary (1981) *Reversible Sex-Roles: The Special Case of Benares Sweepers*, Oxford: Pergamon

Sharma, R.N. and Sita, K. (eds) (2001) *Issues in Urban Development: A Case of Navi Mumbai*, Jaipur and New Delhi: Rawat Publications

Siddique, Mohammed K.A. (ed.) (1982) *Aspects of Society and Culture in Calcutta*, Calcutta: Anthropological Survey of India

Singer, Milton (1972) *When a Great Tradition Modernizes*, New York: Praeger

Singer, Milton and Cohn, Bernard S. (eds) (1968) *Structure and Change in Indian Society*, Chicago, IL: Aldine

Sinha, Surajit (ed) (1972) *Cultural Profile of Calcutta*, Calcutta: The Indian Anthropological Society

Soja, Edward W. (1989) *Postmodern Geographies: The Reassertion of Space in Critical Social Theory*, London: Verso

Srinivas, Smriti (2001) *Landscapes of Urban Memory: The Sacred and the Civic in India's High Tech City*, Minneapolis, MN: University of Minnesota Press

Subrahmanyam, Sanjay (1990) *The Political Economy of Commerce: Southern India 1500–1650*, Cambridge: Cambridge University Press

Subramanian, Lakshmi (1996) *Indigenous Capital and Imperial Expansion: Bombay, Surat and the West Coast*, Delhi: Oxford University Press

Tarlo, Emma (2003) *Unsettling Memories: Narratives of the Emergency in Delhi*, London: Hurst

Vatuk, Sylvia (1971) *Kinship and Urbanisation: White Collar Migrants in North India*, Berkeley, CA: University of California Press

Weiss, Anita M. (1998) 'The gendered division of space and access in working-class areas of Lahore' 7(1) *Contemporary South Asia* 71–89

Wirth, Louis (1938) 'Urbanism as a way of life' 44(1) *American Journal of Sociology* 1-24

2

ECONOMIC LIBERALISATION, CLASS RESTRUCTURING AND SOCIAL SPACE IN PROVINCIAL SOUTH INDIA

Geert De Neve

Since the 1990s, the politics of place has attracted renewed interest in the social sciences and, albeit with some delay, in anthropology too. The influential work of Gupta and Ferguson (1997) has been pivotal in setting an engaging agenda for research into the politics of place, while ousting once and for all the assumed isomorphism of place, culture and community. Processes of place-making and politics of space have become the focus of recent ethnographic research that probes into the ways that space is socialised and social relations are spatialised (Massey 1994).

In this renewed engagement with place, the dominant approach has been to uncover the ways in which extra-local, often national and global, transformations and discourses have affected the configuration of specific localities and the social relations of which they are made up (Weiss 1998; Appadurai 2000). In the context of South Asia, as in many other parts of the world, processes of globalisation – in the form of migration, relocation, de-territorialisation and other movements – are often seen as a vital engine of social change at the local level, and as a major cause of the ongoing uncoupling of place and community.[1] Globalisation, the adage goes, destabilises social and cultural boundaries, and deconstructs boundaries of difference not least by providing new pathways of economic opportunity and new styles of consumption that are open to increasing numbers of people (Fernandes 2000a; 2000b).

This chapter, however, considers the possibility that 'space', as a dynamic force in the creation of identities, can reproduce social differences by realigning caste, class and spatial positions. Or, put differently, if the politics of space allows for the disconnecting of locality and community, it allows as much for the reconnecting of identities and localities under particular circumstances. Such processes of place-making and the use of space to consolidate community and class identities are the concern of this chapter. I will describe how members of an upwardly mobile caste in small-town south India, who benefited greatly from the economic liberalisation of the

1990s, mobilise space in the process of creating a new identity for themselves.

While this chapter illustrates the spatial dimension of the mobility of a lower ranking caste through opportunities offered by economic liberalisation, renewed processes of boundary marking are not unique to this section of society. Recently, similar processes have been described for Dalit communities as well as for the new Indian middle classes. Gorringe, for example, discusses how Dalit movements in contemporary Tamil Nadu attempt to establish and redefine territory precisely through a process of boundary marking and the creation of caste-exclusive spaces around an urban estate in Madurai (Gorringe 2005 and this volume). For the middle classes, Fernandes has described how the production of urban middle-class identity is linked to a new politics of spatial purification which 'centres on middle-class claims over public spaces and a corresponding movement to cleanse such spaces of the poor and working classes' (2004: 2416; see also Kaviraj 1997). Using the example of Mumbai, Fernandes reveals how both the state and the new middle classes use spatial tactics of urban purification and beautification to further marginalise and displace the poor and the working classes within the dominant national political culture (ibid. 2421–2).

When conceiving of space as a site of politics, it is easy to see that places can indeed act as powerful tools in the reconfiguration of differences of caste and class under economic liberalisation. Recent discussions of such social and spatial reconfigurations, however, have mainly focused on those groups known as the 'cosmopolitan elite' (Gupta 2000) or the 'new Indian middle classes' (Varma 1998; Fernandes 2000b; 2004) who live in India's largest cities. This perspective has unfortunately ignored a vast world of more provincial urban communities, often dominated by agrarian capitalists, new business groups and export manufacturers, spread across the smaller towns of the subcontinent (Gidwani and Sivaramakrishnan 2003; Chari 2004 and Jeffery et al. in this volume). Although such social groups do not belong to India's new cosmopolitan elite, and are unlikely to describe themselves in such terms, their lives have nevertheless been directly affected by recent policies of economic liberalisation, deregulation and privatisation from which many of them have benefited greatly. Gidwani and Sivaramakrishnan call these groups 'rural cosmopolitans' and, focusing on circular rural-urban migrants, they suggest that 'the rural cosmopolitan is that ambivalent and largely invisible figure', who does not always produce progressive agendas, and who may well 're-inscribe and consolidate traditional [spatial] arrangements, rather than undermine them' (Gidwani and Sivaramakrishnan 2003: 362). It is on such a social group that this chapter focuses, and on the process by which their socio-economic mobility has led to the reification of bounded spatial arrangements and representations in which caste, class and locality have once again come to overlap.

The case of the upwardly mobile Vanniyars of Tamil Nadu illustrates a process that affects an increasingly large number of lower- and middle-caste groups living in India's provincial towns today (Templeman 1999). With the boom in the export industry under trade liberalisation, the Vanniyars of the Bhavani Taluk (Erode District) have been able to capture a niche in the local textile industry, in which they have successfully come to dominate the dyeing sector as workers and more recently as factory owners and traders. Their socio-economic mobility from workers to manufacturers and traders has led to a spatial reconfiguration of social and economic relations in the area. Whereas, until recently, dyeing factories were spread across the twin towns of Bhavani and Kumarapalayam, since the mid-1990s Vanniyar factory owners have begun to relocate and centralise their dyeing factories in Sengadu Thottam, a Vanniyar neighbourhood at the borders of Bhavani, where this caste has its roots and where land and labour are readily available. By relocating their newly acquired factories to their 'own' neighbourhood, Vanniyars seek to mobilise urban space to reconnect community, identity and locality. While the strengthening of neighbourhood boundaries is the spatial reflection of shifting configurations of class following economic restructuring, Vanniyars are also contesting negative public representations of their neighbourhood and community (see also Chari 2004; Vera-Sanso in this volume). On the one hand, outsider representations of this neighbourhood reproduce a stigmatising discourse about Vanniyar immorality, violence and backwardness but, on the other hand, Vanniyars' new affluence, produced by structural shifts in the economy, has also led to new expressions of public resentment by other communities, a resentment that continues to be expressed in the idiom of caste (see Frøystad in this volume). Here, as in other parts of Tamil Nadu, the resulting antagonism between Vanniyars and others is as much the outcome of shifting configurations of class as of older perceptions of caste and morality.

I thus argue that the ongoing relocation and concentration of Vanniyar factories in Sengadu Thottam along with Vanniyars' self-representation as a close-knit moral community point to a remarkable inclination to *consolidate* affinities of neighbourhood and caste at a time when modernity and globalisation are believed to bring about urban spaces that are much more fluid and hybrid. Liberalisation and economic restructuring do not necessarily translate into more heterogeneous urban spaces. They may well activate a politics of place that produces social spaces in which reconfigured caste, class and community identities once again overlap.

In what follows, I first introduce the neighbourhood and some encounters that illustrate the ways in which neighbourhood boundaries are actively reproduced in everyday interactions around living space. I then present the prevailing public representation of Sengadu Thottam and the Vanniyar community in Bhavani, as well as Vanniyars' self-representations through which they seek to counter a negative public image. Those self-representations emanate first from their experience of the neighbourhood as *ur* (home) connected to a wider network of Vanniyar villages; second, from their experience of work as a source of pride, currently shored up by the community's upward mobility; and, third, from discourses about the morality of the body, because talk of kidney sales is a recurrent idiom through which Vanniyars express their community's solidarity and morality in contrast to the lack of morality of others. The final section of the paper turns towards Vanniyars' recent upward mobility in the wake of trade liberalisation and booming export markets, and discusses the processes of industrial relocation and neighbourhood consolidation in provincial neoliberal India – the crucial point being that, in the context of a neoliberal regime, Vanniyars' self-representation as a bounded community as well as their renewed spatial concentration bring about remarkably homogeneous urban spaces in India's provincial towns.

More broadly, the analysis draws on Lefebvre's (1991) work on the production of social space. Lefebvre conceives of space as having material, perceived and lived dimensions. Space, he argues, is produced through a triad of (1) *spatial practices*: the particular locations and spatial forms of production and reproduction, which constitute the material basis of space; (2) *representations of space*: the conceptions of spatial environments, which tend towards a system of verbal signs and codes, often controlled and imposed; and (3) *representational spaces*: the everyday lived spaces of inhabitants and users, their often hidden symbols and codes (1991: 26–53). In the following sections, I present a discussion that combines the material, perceived and lived dimensions of space without reducing the construction of space to any single one of these.

Sengadu Thottam and the Vanniyar legacy

In Sengadu Thottam, the material aspect of space refers to the physical environment of the neighbourhood with its houses, factories and streets; the perceived aspect relates to the conflicting representations of the neighbourhood by outsiders and insiders, and the lived dimension is reflected in the experience of the locality as *ur* (home) and as the site of work. Each of these dimensions will be unpacked in what follows.

My initial encounter with Sengadu Thottam took place when I started fieldwork in India for the first time in 1995. I found a house to rent at the eastern border of this semi-urban neighbourhood situated in the north-western corner of the town of Bhavani in Erode District, Tamil Nadu (see Map 2.1). As I was soon to realise, Sengadu Thottam was a strikingly homogeneous working-class area of Bhavani, where better-off people who do not belong to the community of Vanniyars or who were not born in the locality would not choose to live or, as the case below shows, be allowed to do so.

Class, however, is not the only barrier to entry in the neighbourhood – religion plays an important role too. During the first months of my stay in this house at the border of Sengadu Thottam, a major dispute arose between

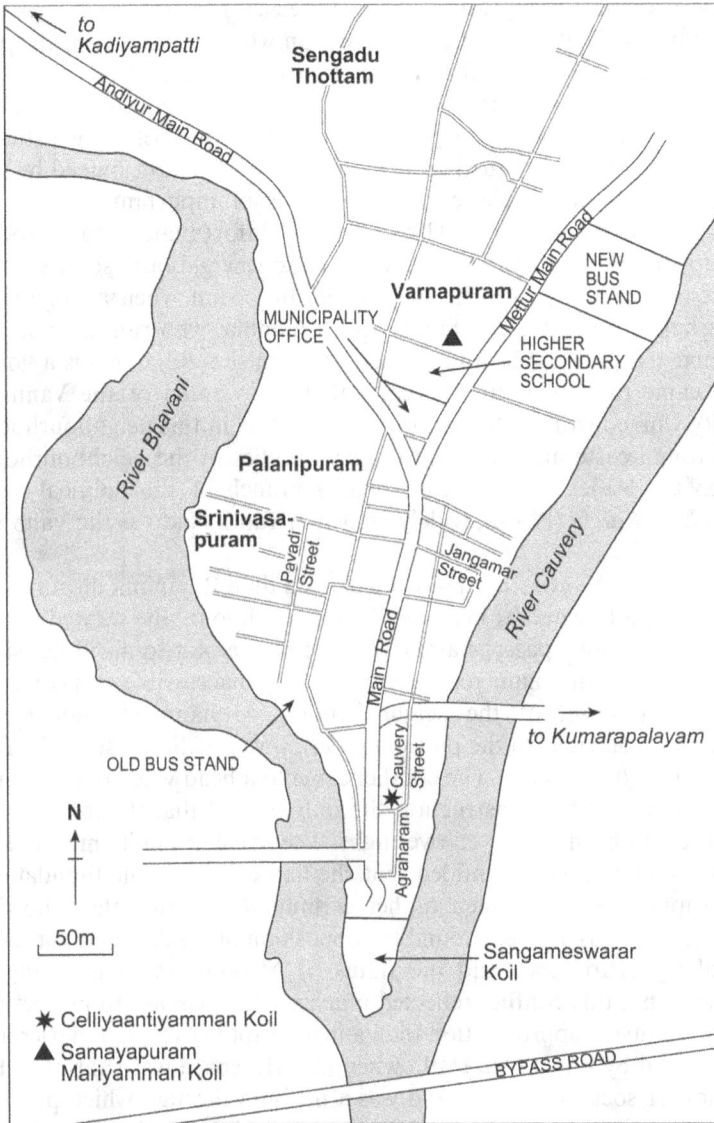

Map 2.1 The town of Bhavani and the neighbourhood of Sengadu Thottam

the people of the neighbourhood, led by a local woman called Rajamma, and a Muslim family who were about to construct a new house on a plot of land that they had purchased on the street where I lived. When I attended the foundation prayer (*kadagal puja*), Mohammed, the owner, explained to me that they had done 'their own [Muslim] *puja*' before but that, because the construction workers were Hindu, they wanted to perform their *puja* too. The foreman along with the other construction workers performed the *puja* around a statue of Ganesha. Reflecting on this Hindu ritual performed by the workers, Mohammed uttered to me: 'We Muslims, and also the Christians, are very tolerant. Although this *puja* is not part of our beliefs, we still let them perform it. We are adjusting to their culture.' Tolerant indeed he was in the face of a Hindu foundation ritual that was an important symbolic re-appropriation of his plot as a Hindu space. Unfortunately, this process did not stop there, and relations with the Hindu neighbours soon soured. The construction of the new house had hardly begun when a huge fight broke out between the Muslim family and Rajamma, who runs a small but very popular tea stall just behind the construction site. Rajamma is a 'local' and, as I came to realise later, a very influential woman of the Vanniyar community who constitute the majority of residents in this neighbourhood.[2] Linked through caste and kinship to many families in the neighbourhood, she is also the leader of the local women's branch of the political party *Pattali Makkal Katchi* (PMK), widely known in Tamil Nadu as the Vanniyar party.

No sooner had the construction work started than Rajamma disputed the borders of the plot owned by her new Muslim neighbour. She wanted him to leave a two-foot public passage along the side of the plot to avoid her shop being cut off from the main road and becoming inaccessible to people on their way in and out of the neighbourhood. Mohammed's documents confirmed his legal right to the plot but soon proved of little use in the face of neighbourhood resistance. The conflict came to a head when one morning the owner arrived at the construction site only to find that the foundations of his house had been destroyed overnight. The Muslim family moved else-where, and Rajamma later confided that she had destroyed the foundations with the support of a few men of her community. During the following months, conversations evolved around the opposition of insiders and outsiders, differential rights to space and the status of Muslims more generally. It became clear that this conflict reflected much more a passion to protect the locality from outside appropriation than a mere dispute over boundaries and passages started by a local tea stall owner. Clearly, space was central to the construction of social difference and was a medium through which physical as well as communal boundaries could be reproduced. I found this passionate instance of boundary marking intriguing, especially given that many other neighbourhoods in town were remarkably heterogeneous yet relatively free of antagonism between castes and religious communities (see also Vera-Sanso in this volume).

Although communal boundaries were important in this instance, everyday opinions about neighbourhood, community and morality were even more prominent in local discussions of caste. Muthukaruppan, a Nadar, did not hide his contempt for the Vanniyars living in this neighbourhood. When I first met him, he mentioned that members of this caste were aggressive and always stuck together when a problem arose. Muthukaruppan himself was born in Tiruchengodu and moved to this locality after making heavy losses in a salt business in Coimbatore. In Sengadu Thottam, he started a small shop and rented a house from a Vanniyar landlord. However, soon after his arrival, he and the landlord started to argue and he was asked to vacate the house immediately. 'Once they began to throw stones at me, I realised that I had to leave', Muthukaruppan explained. As he was the only Nadar in the area, he had nobody else to rely on and had to give in. In this first conversation, he added a warning that I had better be careful in this area given that 'Until three months ago they were approaching people with a knife near the bus stand and took their money. Luckily, the police managed to catch them.'

When I told friends and middle-class informants living in other parts of town that I lived in Sengadu Thottam, they often replied, 'Oh, how brave of you!', 'How dare you to live there?' and 'Do you know how dangerous (*abayam*) and violent those people are?' In a typical example, a friend commented on the assumed qualities of the Vanniyars of this locality by saying:

> They are always ready to fight. If a problem arises, all of them will get together and fight. And even when there are no problems, they will create one. They can easily be organised and incited to realise something, but even more easily to destroy something. It is better to stay away from them.

After a few months in the field, an older man, belonging to the Vellalar Gounder caste of landowners and cultivators, called me to his house and vigorously told me off for moving around so freely with members of the Vanniyar caste and even inviting them into my house. He stated, 'They will teach you to smoke, drink, use drugs and all other kinds of bad behaviour! Have you ever seen us mingling with them or going over there?' When asked *why* they were so dangerous, he explained: 'It's their caste! (*avangu jati taan*)' and he recalled many fights to support his point.[3] The violent reputation of Vanniyars is closely tied to the memory of the state-wide Vanniyar uprisings of the mid-1980s when their caste-based association, the *Vanniya Sangam* (Vanniyar Association), gained popularity. During that time, violence broke out across Tamil Nadu and many militant rallies and demonstrations were staged to draw the attention of the central and state governments to the situation of the impoverished Vanniyar caste. During these agitations, orchestrated by Vanniyar leaders, Vanniyars resorted to the felling of trees on main roads in order to obstruct traffic and create disorder. Many of these demonstrations led to violent clashes with the police and in Bhavani these public protests took the form of street violence on the main road (Radhakrishnan 2002, 2003).

But violent behaviour is not the only legacy attached to the Vanniyars' name. As a Tamil caste of agricultural labourers and small cultivators,[4] they used to be employed by landowners and many have a history as *pannaiyals* or bonded farm labourers (Mencher 1978: 126–59). From at least the 1950s onwards, Vanniyars started to migrate to the towns, and it is also since that time that their numbers have soared in Bhavani. Around the middle of the century, Bhavani had a population of 12,133 (Census of 1951), while by the early 1990s this number had risen to 35,198 (Census of 1991). Among the many Vanniyars who took up carpet weaving, most worked as daily wage labourers on the looms of wealthier Mudaliyar or Devangar Chettiyar manufacturers. Today, in and around Bhavani, the Vanniyars constitute a major section of the workforce in handloom weaving, dyeing factories and power-loom workshops, and are increasingly found in the mill industry. Many more earn a living as vendors, cart drivers, fitters, oil-pressers, bricklayers and masons. As a caste, Vanniyars are generally looked down upon with distrust by members of other castes: Vellalar landowners remember them as belligerent agricultural workers, while Mudaliyar and Devangar Chettiyar factory owners frequently stereotype them as the unreliable and uncontrollable workers in their workshops. A locally influential factory owner and employer expressed a common view when he commented that:

> The Vanniyars are people who are willing to follow good advice, but even more willing to follow bad advice and be violent. The earlier leaders of the PMK party made use of precisely this aspect of their character and they encouraged violence against public property to consolidate their party.

More often than not, the 'labour problem' in town is equated with the problem of controlling Vanniyar workers. Thus, employers' discourses commonly represent them as strong but argumentative workers, who are difficult to control and who seek confrontations (see later and De Neve 2005).

This public image of Vanniyars builds on centuries of stigmatisation of this non-untouchable group of low socio-economic standing and ritual status. Their rough and violent behaviour, their non-vegetarian cuisine, their involvement in manual and defiling labour and their worship of minor deities, for which they perform sacrifices of all kinds (blood sacrifices, *alaku* (piercing) sacrifices, fire walking, etc.) ascribe them a status only marginally higher than that of untouchable communities. While this reflects the public perception of Vanniyars across Tamil Nadu, in Bhavani it is a representation that is particularly associated with this neighbourhood, which is almost exclusively made up of Vanniyar households. Such outsider *representations of space* are tenacious, yet not uncontested, and perhaps the most compelling contestation lies in the powerful counter-discourses that Vanniyars have constructed for themselves.

The neighbourhood as a moral community

How, then, do Vanniyars represent themselves in the light of disparaging public representations? Vanniyars' self-representation is rooted in a number of lived experiences through which they represent themselves as a cohesive moral community. Lefebvre referred to such lived experiences as *representational spaces* (1991: 39) and they relate, first, to their experience of *ur* or home / place as a cohesive moral community connected to a wider network of Vanniyars beyond the neighbourhood; second, to their everyday experience of work as employers and workers in the dyeing industry of the area; and, third, to a concept of the body as reflecting community morality. This self-representation as a moral community contrasts sharply with the public images of them presented earlier.

Until a few decades ago, this was a small and scarcely populated settlement situated among the open fields between Bhavani and the village of Kadayampatti, about two miles to the north-east of the town. With the expansion of Bhavani towards the north, Sengadu Thottam was gradually incorporated into the municipality and turned into an urban neighbourhood (see Map 2.1). Until the early 1990s, however, the area consisted of huts and a few brick houses, and it is only recently that the economic success of some community members has led to the construction of larger dwellings and workshops in the area. At the time of my fieldwork in 1995, the area had a distinctly rural feel to it and even today the northern and western borders of Sengadu Thottam consist of open fields.

The experience of ur

In and around Bhavani, the Vanniyars are made up of various sub-groups of which the *Yelu Ur* Vanniyars, or Seven Village Vanniyars, are locally the largest in number. This Vanniyar sub-caste was traditionally found in *yelu ur* or the seven villages around Bhavani (including Sengadu Thottam) in which they were the dominant community.[5] Although today some of them have obviously moved out of these villages, this spatial network is still meaningful to the caste's social organisation. Up to a generation ago, marriage partners were always selected from within the *yelu ur* area and marriages outside the area were socially stigmatised and could even be subject to fines or cause excommunication. Similarly, marrying outside the sub-caste was generally frowned upon. In Bhavani, the Vanniyars emphasise that it was through the *Vanniya Sangam* and later the PMK party that a sense of unity emerged among them. Their leader, Dr Ramadoss, played a crucial role in consolidating the Vanniyar community and creating a sense of unity. The encouragement of marriage across sub-castes was central to this project. Today, better-off Vanniyars look for marriage partners further afield and sub-caste endogamy is no longer enforced by the community. Nevertheless, within the *yelu ur* area, sub-caste endogamy is still the ideal and at weddings between partners from different sub-castes comments are made about the incompatibility of rituals, the differences in *kuladeyvam* (lineage deity) and indeed the hierarchical ranking of sub-castes. Among poorer Vanniyars, and especially those who lack the social connections to find suitable partners from outside the area, marriage within the *yelu ur* area is still the most common and preferred arrangement, in combination with cross-kin preferences. As a result, the majority of Sengadu Thottam residents still marry within this circle of seven villages and today they continue to use the same area as a first point of reference in their search for marriage partners for their children.

While at one level the Vanniyars of Sengadu Thottam make up a fairly bounded neighbourhood, at another level their social and territorial organisation across the *yelu ur* connects them to a wider community of caste, kin and relatives, which extends neighbourhood relationships into the surrounding area. Valentine Daniel has described how the Tamil notion of *ur* 'can and does vary according to any given person's changing spatial orientation' (1984: 65). Unlike the Tamil term *graamam*, which by and large refers to the bounded administrative unit of the village, the culturally significant concept of *ur* (place, territory, home) does not have a clearly delineated boundary; both its boundary and meaning shift according to context. While in some contexts Vanniyars' use of *ur* refers to the particular neighbourhood of Sengadu Thottam, in other contexts it refers to the wider *yelu ur* (seven villages) area to which they belong. Connections within this wider territory are primarily maintained and reproduced through weddings, festivals and other rituals, when families leave the neighbourhood to celebrate festivals in their natal villages, or when relatives from the villages join their kin to live in town. The annual celebrations of the lineage deity, for example, bring together kin from across the *yelu ur* area to the ancestral house or village where the *kuladeyvam* is located. Similarly, kin and acquaintances within the area are the first ones to be mobilised when a family searches for a marriage partner for a son or daughter. Following the cross-kin preference, it is not uncommon for a woman to marry into a village that is also her mother's natal place. As a result, in Sengadu Thottam most households are related to several other households both within the neighbourhood itself and in the other *yelu ur*. Visits back and forth between kin in the *yelu ur* area take place throughout the year and help maintain close social and economic ties.

Public images of the neighbourhood as a rough place to be avoided by outsiders are countered by Vanniyars' own representations of their *ur* as a cohesive moral community of close kin in which mutual support, shared values and close relationships make even the everyday life of the poorest residents bearable. This sense of community is closely related to the Vanniyars' concept of *ur*, which they use interchangeably to refer to the neighbourhood or to the wider network of seven Vanniyar villages.

The experience of work

A sense of pride in their own locality is also rooted in Vanniyars' everyday experiences of work, over which they have recently gained an unprecedented amount of control following their success in the local industry (see below).

Dyeing in and around Bhavani developed as an ancillary industry to the handloom and powerloom industry.[6] Initially, the first factories were situated in Kumarapalayam, at the opposite side of the Cauvery river, and run by higher caste owners of powerloom factories, who used to manage their own dyeing units, for which labour was provided by the low-caste Vanniyar and Scheduled Caste communities (SC), such as Paraiyar and Chekkliyar. Work in a yarn-dyeing unit is particularly dirty and exhausting, and this is why lower caste Vanniyars constitute a high proportion of the workforce in this industry (De Neve 2005). All yarn dyeing in the area is manual work. Workers stand in water basins filled with bleach or dyes for hours at a stretch, while the chemicals are splashed all over their bodies. 'This is very dirty work, only we Vanniyars will do it and only we are physically strong enough to work in it' is a commonly heard statement. Vanniyars often explain their physical abilities with reference to their history as agricultural labourers. One Vanniyar owner of a dyeing unit explained:

Only the Padaiyatchi (local term for Vanniyars) can tolerate physically hard work, the heat of the tanks and the dirt (*alukku*) of the dyes. When dyeing the yarn, they are wearing black and dirty clothes and get dirty all over their arms and legs. Only they can do it. They have been used to hard work and it is only when one has done lower jobs (*kile veelai*) that one can also do higher jobs (*meele veelai*). So, the Devangar Chettiyars who have always been used to weaving cannot come to this lower job and work here, even if they could earn more money in dyeing yarn.

Vanniyars themselves recognise a close and unavoidable link between their poverty, their traditional involvement in manual labour and 'lower jobs', and their lack of choice. Although a certain fatalism is definitely present in the way they talk about their work in the looms and factories, Vanniyar workers never fail to express their pride too: they are not only the ones who *have to* do hard work, they are in fact the only ones who *can* do such work, since they have been bestowed with the necessary physical power and mental strength.[7] They are always keen to point out the source of this strength in their alleged descent from the army of the Pallava kings. And they keenly demonstrate that *uzhaippu* (hard work, toil) has paid off, at least for some of them. An ever-increasing number of Vanniyars have successfully managed to come up within the industry, and over the last odd 20 a good number of them have moved up from worker to *maistry*,[8] leaseholder and, more recently, owners of dyeing factories[9] (see later). While *uzhaippu* is a core element of Vanniyar identity (male and female), it is not stigmatised in negative terms. Rather, it is presented as a valuable means through which they are able to improve their position in the local society and industry.

The morality of the body

A neighbourhood that outsiders perceive as dangerous and socially disruptive is by insiders experienced as a locality of mutual support, solidarity and protection. This sense of solidarity became especially clear to me when enquiring about rumours of workers selling their kidneys for money. Rumours of kidney sales as a way to pay off debts were rampant in the area, and stories were told about people being lured to Madras or Bangalore to have a kidney removed. Given my interest in debt relationships, I interviewed a number of informants in the powerloom factories of Kumarapalayam, where workers are massively indebted to their employers due to the large advances (*baki*) that are handed out at the time of recruitment (De Neve 1999).

From interviews with both factory owners and powerloom workers in Kumarapalayam, it soon transpired that kidney sales are not uncommon among impoverished and debt-bound workers in the powerlooms. In 2000, one factory owner claimed that an estimated 10–15% of his workers had sold a kidney. The story goes that it all started in 1993 with a man who went to Bangalore after being told that he could get Rs 100,000 by selling a kidney. It was fear of an aggressive Gounder factory owner, who was pushing him to repay an outstanding debt of more than Rs 50,000 and who threatened him with violence, that pushed him into taking the risk. Having no alternative means of repaying the employer and being unable to move to another factory, he left for Bangalore where his kidney was removed in return for the promised money. He paid off his debt, was able to move to another factory and ended up with some spare cash. Since then, the practice has become widespread but, whereas selling a kidney in order to survive is to some extent seen as acceptable, the practice is certainly condemned when this is done for the purpose of conspicuous consumption, or *nagarikam* (urban life style) as it is locally referred to. Again, representations of caste play a key role in such moral assessments, as Gounder factory owners emphasised that it is primarily Vanniyars who sell kidneys.

When I turned to friends in Sengadu Thottam and enquired about the sale of kidneys by those living in the neighbourhood, their responses were strikingly different. In Sengadu Thottam, the sale of kidneys was presented as a matter of community morality, which was in turn expressed through notions of solidarity and protection. Shivaji, a well-known factory owner and a 'big man' in the neighbourhood, was outraged at my suggestion that Vanniyars in this area would sell their kidneys for money. He exclaimed:

We Vanniyars give each other support and we would shout at anyone who would want to sell a kidney. We help each other's families to repay loans and will ask them: why do you have a *mama* [maternal uncle] or a *cittappa* [paternal uncle]? Tell us about your debts and we will help you to settle them. No Vanniyars in Sengadu Thottam have sold their kidneys. It is the Mudaliyars and Chettiyars who do such things.

Shivaji further explained that better-off Vanniyars (usually those who now have dyeing units of their own) go directly to the hospital or shop to settle the bills of their workers:

We then retain part of their weekly pay in return for the money we spent on their behalf, but they won't even ask about it [such pay reductions] as they know they can always come to us when they are short of money. Often, even the wife of a worker will come and ask for Rs 100 or Rs 200 and we will give it to them and then deduct it from their weekly payment.

This discourse of community solidarity and morality has to be understood in relation to the fact that in Sengadu Thottam's factories most workers and employers are Vanniyars and indeed closely linked through kinship and neighbourhood networks. In contrast, in the Kumarapalayam powerloom factories, where getting into debt through *baki* (advance payments) frequently occurs, employers and workers not only belong to a variety of communities but also live in different parts of town and often hardly interact beyond the shop floor. For them the world of work and life is separated by caste and kinship as much as it is by space.

In the discourse of Vanniyar labourers, images of exploitation, violence and deception presented an image of Kumarapalayam and its people that stood in sharp contrast to representations of their 'own' locality. Indeed, the picture presented of Sengadu Thottam was that of a moral community consisting of neighbours, employers, workers and kin who were engaged in morally acceptable relationships in which labour, money and care were mutually exchanged. One might suggest that this is surely the discourse of employers keen to present themselves as patrons and benefactors, but there is more to it. Workers in Sengadu Thottam themselves are always keen to tell how their employers and neighbours are 'looking after' them or helping them out. Sundaram, a cousin and worker of Shivaji made the following comment about Shivaji:

He's very helpful and not only to those families who work for him, but to all families in "that line" [main road of Sengadu Thottam]. I myself got Rs 16,000 from him for the wedding of my younger sister and I have paid back all but Rs 4,000.

Kin and caste ties closely overlap and, although I would not argue that exploitation is absent in Sengadu Thottam, a powerful sense of community generates ties and responsibilities that few employers can defy.

While the extent of employers' involvement in kidney sales in Kumarapalayam is difficult to establish, the point I want to emphasise here is that the residents of Sengadu Thottam present themselves as a community that protects its members from this sort of bodily harm found elsewhere. In Sengadu Thottam, even the more vulnerable workers are not only protected from violence, which takes the form of recurrent hassling, threats and physical attacks committed by employers against their workers elsewhere, but also from the harm that the poorest are often forced to inflict on their own bodies. Both forms of violence were strongly denounced in Sengadu Thottam and seen as signs of a more deep-rooted power imbalance between employers and workers in other localities. The reciprocity and mutual care described to me in Sengadu Thottam is also a source of pride to the Vanniyars. It is an important symbolic marker through which they claim moral high ground and integrity, and seek to counter the public image of their caste. This is especially obvious in opposition to Gounders, whom they characterise as violent, deceptive and uncaring. Vanniyars thus seek to reverse stereotypes of themselves as violent and untrustworthy, and to replace them with self-representations of a supportive moral community. Talk about kidney sales is central to these wider discourses on the nature of caste and class relations, and contributes to the consolidation of moral and spatial boundaries.

The neighbourhood as industrial locality

Spatial and community boundaries have also been consolidated in a different way – that is, through the physical relocation of factories to Sengadu Thottam, which reflects changes in the material dimension of space, or in what Lefebvre called *spatial practices* (1991: 33). While Sengadu Thottam has a long history as a Vanniyar settlement, the neighbourhood has since the late 1980s gained particular importance as a site of work, industry and social mobility. Until the middle of the 1980s, the locality was primarily a residential area whose inhabitants worked outside the locality or undertook some agricultural work in the surrounding fields. The Vanniyars of Sengadu Thottam mainly worked as handloom weavers in workshops owned by Mudaliyars and Devangar Chettiyars in Bhavani, or they were employed as powerloom operators and dyeing factory workers by Gounder, Mudaliyar and Chettiyar workshop owners in Kumarapalayam. The rapid expansion of the powerloom industry during the 1970s and 1980s, however, led to a worker-employer crisis in Kumarapalayam. The crucial outcome of this crisis was a number of major changes in the organisation of the industry.

Mudaliyar and Chettiyar manufacturers, who owned dyeing units and powerloom factories, increasingly felt incapable of managing all their units on their own. Factory owners who lacked support of brothers or extended kin were particularly keen to farm out the management of some of their units. The preferred form of sub-contracting was a short-term lease, and the preferred workshops to lease out were the dyeing units because it was here that the Vanniyars formed the bulk of the labour force. A leasehold allows the manufacturers to hold on to their units and retain some control over the way they are run, while being freed from the day-to-day management of production and labour. It also allows the owners to focus on their power-loom workshops where they make the most significant investments, where profits margins are largest and where their direct involvement is essential for the maintenance of quality standards. Hence, from the mid-1980s, dyeing units were gradually handed over to former workers, usually to *maistries* (foremen; technicians) or managers who had worked for the manufacturers in the past. In most cases, these leaseholders were Vanniyars, who, with their longstanding experience in dyeing, were able to run the units successfully. As the workers were largely recruited from among their own kin and caste, the management of labour by Vanniyars did not constitute a problem, in contrast to the experiences of the Mudaliyar and Chettiyar owners in Kumarapalayam.

The lease of dyeing workshops opened up unprecedented opportunities for Vanniyars in the area, probably far more than the manufacturers ever intended to devolve to them. The profits of the dyeing units became substantial and leaseholders managed to accumulate assets very quickly as the export boom continued throughout the 1990s, albeit with ups and downs. By the early 1990s, two further developments transformed the industry once more. The first was the process in which Vanniyar leaseholders began to buy out the dyeing units while continuing with job-work for the manufacturers, and the second was the process in which Vanniyars started up new units from scratch.[10] Irrespective of how Vanniyars acquired workshops, the crucial point is that they soon began to move their dyeing units away from Kumarapalayam and towards Sengadu Thottam. The relocation of the dyeing industry was well under way during my fieldwork in 1995–6, and in 1999–2000 hardly a month passed without a dyeing workshop being shut down in Kumarapalayam to be re-opened as a new unit in Sengadu Thottam. Thus, a quiet residential neighbourhood was rapidly transformed into an industrial area in which houses, tea stalls and workshops can be found side by side.

The Vanniyars had good reasons to relocate their factories 'closer to home'. The first was that in Sengadu Thottam land and water were easily available. The ownership of a small plot of land is usually sufficient to build a dyeing unit, and a good number of families already owned small plots on which they had built a house or which was used for cultivation. Others were able to acquire some land from close relatives who would often join in the new venture. Land in Kumarapalayam, by contrast, is expensive and hard to get, and access to water is often a major problem with several units being dependent on water brought to them each day by lorry. Apart from the land, setting up a dyeing unit requires only limited capital investment. The factories consist of three walls constructed from concrete or bricks and covered with sheets of corrugated iron. Towards the back of the factories, yarn is dried in the open, while in some units a shed, made of wood and coconut leaves, has been erected to allow drying during the rainy season. Once land is available, it is only a matter of weeks until a unit is up and running. As Sengadu Thottam is situated near the Bhavani river, water can easily be brought to the surface with a simple pump and, apart from the dyeing tanks, little else is found on the factory grounds.

However, it was not only the availability of land and water that made Sengadu Thottam an attractive place for the relocation of factories. The support of kin and the presence of labour were major pull factors too. Most Vanniyars never moved to Kumarapalayam. Even though many older men worked a lifetime as daily wage labourers in the factories of Kumarapalayam, few settled there permanently. Most workers commuted between the workshops of Kumarapalayam and their homes in Sengadu Thottam or any of the other *yelu ur* villages. Kumarapalayam was seen as the place where work was available, wages could be earned and skills learned. Home, on the other hand, lay elsewhere. It is not surprising, therefore, that once the opportunity arose to set up factories of their own, Vanniyars seized the chance to move closer to home where they do not face discrimination from other communities. In Sengadu Thottam they can work independently from members of other castes and thus avoid the demeaning treatment to which they are subjected in other places.

The relocation of factories to a familiar neighbourhood has allowed many of the young owners to benefit from existing networks of kin and caste, and to build synergies that are cost-effective and facilitate expansion. There is often a cousin or brother around who can be called upon to finish an urgent order or to put in an extra day of work, and the practice of giving cash advances (*baki*) to attract workers has never been necessary in this environment.[11] Examples of factory owners passing on orders between themselves, or sharing water, tanks, chemicals or drying space abound. Less tangible, but as important, are the transfers of skill and advice between relatives and neighbours. Shivaji, whom I mentioned earlier, has two of his neighbouring cousin-brothers employed in his factory, while he himself maintains close connections with his *mama* (maternal uncle) who runs a unit across the road. They jointly constructed an effluent treatment tank, the use of which has been a major money saver to both of them as used water from both factories is purified in the tank.

Neighbourhood cohesion has been further bolstered as factory owners have organised themselves to respond to government action regarding environmental pollution in the 1990s. New government regulations regarding the disposal and treatment of polluted water have led to increased co-operation and joint action among the factory owners of the area. Many informants still located in Kumarapalayam mentioned the pollution problem as one of the main reasons for wanting to move to Sengadu Thottam. All factories are now asked to build and use an effluent treatment tank to purify the water that is released from their units. As most Vanniyars in Kumarapalayam produce under leasehold, neither they nor the owners of the units are willing to release Rs 300,000–400,000 for the construction of an effluent treatment tank. Moreover, in the densely populated centre of Kumarapalayam where units already suffer from a lack of space, there is little spare room to build tanks, while vacant land is neither available nor affordable. In Sengadu Thottam, on the outskirts of Bhavani, however, such tanks can be accommodated more easily. But practicalities are not the only issue. In Kumarapalayam, dyeing factories are dispersed throughout the town and, when an inspector calls to check which treatment facilities are in place, his orders or threats are often difficult to contest by a leaseholder who lacks the support of others around him. In places such as Sengadu Thottam, on the other hand, where factories have been built side by side, the owners are much better placed to take joint action or to challenge the sudden imposition of government regulations. Physical closeness facilitates collective action among those who struggle to develop their industries and protect common business interests.[12]

The ongoing relocation and concentration of Vanniyar factories in and around Sengadu Thottam thus points to a remarkable inclination to consolidate affinities of neighbourhood and caste at a time that modernity and globalisation bring about much more fluid and hybrid urban spaces. The acquisition and re-location of factories by Vanniyars is itself the direct outcome of industrial restructuring at the regional level, facilitated by national trade liberalisation policies and increasingly global export markets.

Many of the new owners experience a degree of social mobility and, since the mid-1990s, new and impressive bungalows made from concrete and finished with teakwood and marble floors, have sprung up amid the workers' brick houses and dyeing units. Constructed by Vanniyar factory owners, they reflect most visibly the current upward mobility of the community as a whole. While some workers may comment critically on them, they are generally referred to as markers of the Vanniyars' economic potential and increasing social mobility, to which most community members aspire. But houses are not the only sign of mobility – another is the increased preoccupation with education in Sengadu Thottam. I had unsolicited conversations with many factory owners about primary schools, the quality of secondary education and the choices of university degrees. Even among the workers, there is an awareness that government schools are best avoided and that it is only through further education that their children will be able to escape a future in the dyeing industry.

However, not all Vanniyars in Sengadu Thottam have been able to benefit equally from the opportunities at hand, and new differentiations have arisen within the community and locality. The families who already owned land in the neighbourhood were certainly better placed to start units of their own, and fortunes were made by those who set up their factories early in the 1980s and benefited from the 1990s' boom. Given the current level of competition, it is now much harder to open a new factory and get sufficient orders to survive. In addition, the pollution caused by the factories has led to intensified government control and regulation. The increased need for investment in effluent treatment tanks makes starting up a new factory considerably more expensive.

In the process of upward mobility, class differentiations emerged not only within the neighbourhood and the community but also within extended families. Some workers became factory owners while their fathers and brothers were still employed as daily labourers. Some men were successful while their brothers or cousins suffered from repeated setbacks. Relationships between workers were transformed into worker-employer hierarchies as new employers began to recruit their former workmates. This is further compounded by an uncomfortable inversion of age hierarchies as it is often younger men who manage to establish themselves as *mudalali* (employer/ owner) and now recruit older men, whose apprentices they may have been before. Whereas previously the difference between Vanniyars and, for example, Chettiyars was also a difference of class, class differentiation is now increasingly marking differences within the locality and community of Vanniyars themselves. It is difficult to guess at this stage what its impact will be on long-term community cohesion and morality in the neighbourhood. Yet a few trends are already apparent and, not surprisingly, these transpire most clearly in discourses on marriage. As soon as a family reaches a certain level of success, their willingness to marry poorer kin is usually re-assessed, which is in turn strongly resented by those affected.

Boundaries of neighbourhood, home and workplace

Yet, what is the nature of boundaries within the neighbourhood itself? A striking feature of the workshops in this neighbourhood is that there are no compound walls or fences to separate the factories from the street. The dyeing factories in Sengadu Thottam are located along the main road, interspersed with houses and fields. The newly constructed bungalows of the owners and the lines of workers' houses, made of brick with tiled roofs and consisting of one or two rooms, can be found side by side. People working in the factories run back and forth between the *patrai* (factory) and the tea stall or their own house. Inversely, neighbours, suppliers or family members drop in on each other in the factory on their way to other destinations. Indeed, the contrast with the factories in Kumarapalayam is striking. Here, dyeing factories are fenced off, gates are always closed and a guard is sometimes placed at the entrance to monitor movements in and out of the factory. And despite the fact that gates are locked at night, theft is rampant and factory owners are often at a loss about how to prevent crime of all sorts.

38

In Sengadu Thottam, men and women move around freely and without much restriction. After work men rarely 'go home', but prefer to hang around the tea shop that is located at the centre of the main road opposite a small temple dedicated to Vinayaka (Ganesha). During their break, men get together on the steps in front of the shrine, where they chat, read the local papers and drink tea. Alternatively, men 'disappear' after work only to return home drunk after a few hours. In the evenings, men and women gather in front of the TV in the tea stall, because a TV is still a commodity that very few workers are able to afford. Women have little spare time and go home to start their chores of washing, cleaning and cooking immediately after finishing their work. Whereas men are the dyers, women are mainly employed in the workshops to dry and bundle the yarn. The men of the neighbourhood work either locally or cycle to Kumarapalayam; in contrast women prefer to work locally. Living next to the factory saves on travel time, allows them to move back and forth between home and factory during their breaks and, importantly, facilitates combining childcare and work. Children and babies are brought into the factory where they play around or sleep in a corner or on a bundle of yarn. Boundaries between workplace and home are further blurred in the case of those women who take material out of the factory to bundle yarn in front of their own houses on the street side while they chat with neighbours. Given the levels of trust among workers and their employers, the latter never object to such practices.

The position of factory owners' wives is also revealing. With the exception of the wealthiest employers, whose wives usually withdraw from paid work altogether, the wives of owners in smaller units help with the work. Here, the owner is involved in the management and acts as *maistry* or even dyes yarn himself. His wife is usually employed bundling yarn and works alongside other women. In most units, I was unable to spot the owner's wife as she came and went along with the other workers, and she seldom stands out in terms of dress or movement within the factory. Interestingly, the owner's wife (as she is usually referred to) is often also paid just like the other women. Her name is written in the account books next to those of other workers and she receives a wage for the days worked. In terms of her time, mobility and work, the wives of employers occupy a class position in the locality that is remarkably similar to that of women workers. Only once an employer can afford to run the unit without his wife's labour does the latter's position in the locality begin to change.

While the internal boundaries between home and work or street are to a large extent blurred within the neighbourhood, so are its external physical boundaries. Towards the north, the neighbourhood opens up onto fields, and towards the west it meets with the adjacent village of Kadaiyampatti, which is also one of the *yelu ur*. In the south, the neighbourhood merges with an SC colony without any clear boundary, while in the east it gradually changes into the heterogeneous middle-class area of Varnapuram where people of various caste and occupational backgrounds form an altogether different locality. However, while its physical boundaries are blurred and the inhabitants freely enter the adjoining neighbourhoods to go to work or to the shops situated along the main road of Bhavani, few 'outsiders' enter Sengadu Thottam without good reason. Given that everyone belonging to the neighbourhood is familiar with each other, an 'outsider' is quickly noticed and usually approached by a 'local' keen to ascertain the purpose of the visit.

Conclusion

India's national policies of trade liberalisation and the global removal of trade barriers have had significant impacts on urban spatial configurations that reach well beyond the cosmopolitan cities so central in contemporary writing on urban social change. In many cases, rural and small town businessmen, manufacturers and even workers have also benefited, albeit often in very unequal ways, from new opportunities and restructured industries, as illustrated by the upwardly mobile Vanniyars of Tamil Nadu. Following their success in a niche of the local textile industry, Vanniyars of Bhavani began to relocate their newly acquired factories to the neighbourhood from which they originated, effectively using this spatial relocation as a means to reconnect community and place in the process of reconstructing a new class identity. This ongoing relocation of Vanniyar factories in and around Sengadu Thottam therefore points to a remarkable trend to consolidate affinities of neighbourhood and caste at a time when modernity and globalisation are assumed to bring about urban spaces which are much more fluid and hybrid. The ongoing process of neighbourhood consolidation, instigated by Vanniyars, would not have been possible without their recent economic success, which allowed them unprecedented independence from other communities on whom they were until recently dependent for their livelihoods.

However, the spatial consolidation of their community is also a reaction against public representations of their caste that they are increasingly eager to refute. In order to thwart persistent representations of Vanniyars as degenerate and violent, and of their neighbourhood as a seat of urban trouble, Vanniyars now seek to present themselves as a moral community that treasures hard work, networks of caste and kinship, community support and economic co-operation. As demonstrated, space plays a key role not only in such politics of representation, but also in the ways in which successful communities seek to construct a new class identity for themselves in the process of upward mobility. Indeed, although caste features centrally in discourses about neighbourhoods, their qualities and their residents, such discourses of caste increasingly act as a proxy for discussing rapidly transforming class relations in neoliberal India.

Using the three spatial dimensions outlined by Lefebvre (1991), I have illustrated the processes through which a neighbourhood is reproduced and consolidated as a homogeneous and exclusive space by an upwardly mobile caste. In this context, Lefebvre's *spatial practices* include the physical relocation and concentration of factories within the neighbourhood, and the co-operation of factory owners within the locality. Such practices have considerably enhanced the identity of the neighbourhood as an industrial locality. Second, the *representations of space* comprise both outsider perceptions of the neighbourhood as a place of violence and immorality and insider counter-discourses that emphasise community cohesion, solidarity and dignity. The latter discourses present the neighbourhood as *ur* (home) – that is, as a place of belonging featuring qualities of solidarity and reciprocity, and as a safe place that protects its inhabitants from various forms of violence, not least those inflicted on the body through such practices as organ donation. Such Vanniyar representations have been backed up by their newly gained wealth and by economic co-operation, which in turn has shored up their confidence and dignity as a social group. Finally, *representational space*, or the lived experience of space, includes the everyday experience of work in the factories and the day-to-day exchanges that shape life in the neighbourhood among kin, neighbours, workers and employers who almost all belong to the same caste. These experiences increasingly reflect a level of confidence and pride in a localised community that has seized upon new market opportunities.

Yet, new opportunities produced by neoliberal policies and opening markets also entail new uncertainties and risks. Vanniyars' spatial concentration in an urban neighbourhood, where they enjoy the support and protection of caste and kin networks, is also a way of protecting themselves as an upcoming but apprehensive group against the ups and downs of unpredictable economic fortunes. Clearly, the ongoing spatial and class reconfigurations have not resulted in more heterogeneous urban spaces nor in the gradual blurring of boundaries. They have led to a rather unexpected reproduction of homogeneous spatial arrangements and representations in which caste, class and locality have once again come to overlap.

Acknowledgements

Earlier versions of this chapter were presented at the urban neighbourhoods workshop, held at the University of Sussex (2002), and at the Association for Asian Studies Annual Meeting in Chicago (2005). I am grateful for comments by the participants and in particular for a critical reading of the paper by Henrike Donner, Mattison Mines, Filippo Osella, Penny Vera-Sanso and Grace Carswell.

Notes

1 For a critique of this imbalance in representations of the local and the global, see Dirlik (2001).

2 The Vanniyars were agricultural labourers and small cultivators but have now entered other occupations, such as handloom weaving, powerloom work and dyeing work.

3 The Vanniyars are also known locally as Padaiyatchi (lit. troops of the king), a term which they use to emphasise their physical strength and bravery.

4 Today Vanniyars constitute more than 70% of the labour force in the dyeing factories of Bhavani and Kumarapalayam.

5 The seven settlements are Sengadu Thottam, Kadiyampatti, Kuruppanaicken-palayam, Seringrayanpalayam, Cittapalayam, Periyamolapalayam and Cinnamol-apalayam (interview with Ur Gounder, Kuruppanaickenpalayam, 30 September 1996).

6 The ethnography presented here results from fieldwork conducted in 1995–7 and 1999–2000 in the dyeing factories of the twin towns, Bhavani and Kumarapalayam, located on the opposite sides of the river Cauvery in Tamil Nadu, south India. The data on which this chapter is based were collected through standard ethnographic methods of interviewing, observation and participation on the shop-floor.

7 It is a well-documented feature of lower castes to represent their own inferior position in positive terms as a source of strength, capability and even dignity (see, for example, Deliège 1993).

8 A maistry is a skilled dyer who is primarily engaged with product quality but who often also functions as a sort of foreman involved in labour recruitment and disciplining on the shop-floor.

9 The reasons for the upward mobility of the Vanniyars cannot be discussed at length here, but they relate to successful union activity, expanding export markets, inability of the other communities to run their dyeing units and increasing political consciousness among the members of this community.

10 In the 1990s, a handful of Vanniyars also began to take over powerloom units. However, few of them were able to enter manufacturing (of cloth) directly given the substantial capital outlay that was needed to purchase looms. By 2000, however, an increasing number of Vanniyars were able to invest profits from the dyeing industry in powerlooms.

11 Elsewhere I have discussed the limits to kin support and kin morality (De Neve 2005).

12 For a much more detailed discussion of co-operation between factory owners, see De Neve (2005).

References

Appadurai, A. (2000) 'Spectral housing and urban cleansing: notes on millennial Mumbai' 12(3) *Public Culture* 627–51

Chari, S. (2004) *Fraternal Capital: Peasant-workers, Self-made Men, and Globalization in Provincial India*, Stanford, CA: Stanford University Press

Daniel, E.V. (1984) *Fluid Signs: Being a Person the Tamil Way*, Berkeley: University of California Press

Deliège, R. (1993) 'The myths of origin of the Indian untouchables' 28 *Man* (N.S.) 533–49

De Neve, G. (1999) 'Asking for and giving baki: neo-bondage, or the interplay of bondage and resistance in the Tamilnadu power-loom industry', in Parry, J.P., Kapadia, K. and Breman, J. (eds), *The Worlds of Indian Industrial Labour*, New Delhi: Sage Publications

——(2005) *The Everyday Politics of Labour: Working Lives in India's Informal Economy*, Delhi: Social Science Press

ECONOMIC LIBERALISATION

Dirlik, A. (2001) 'Place-based imagination: globalism and the politics of place', in
Prazniak, R. and Dirlik, A. (eds), *Places and Politics in an Age of Globalization*,
Lanham, MD: Rowman and Littlefield
Fernandes, L. (2000a) 'Nationalizing the "global": media images, cultural politics
and the middle class in India' 22(5) *Media, Culture and Society*, 611–28
——(2000b) 'Restructuring the new middle class in liberalizing India' 20(1,2)
Comparative Studies of South Asia, Africa and the Middle East 88–112
——(2004) 'The politics of forgetting: class politics, state power and the restructuring
of urban space in India' 41(12) *Urban Studies* 2415–30
Gidwani, V. and Sivaramakrishnan, K. (2003) 'Circular migration and rural
cosmopolitanism in India', in Osella, F. and Gardner K. (eds), *Migration, Moder-
nity and Social Transformation in South Asia*, Delhi: Sage Publications
Gorringe, H. (2005) *Untouchable Citizens: Dalit Movements and Democratization in
Tamil Nadu*, Delhi: Sage Publications
Gupta, A. and Ferguson, J. (eds) (1997) *Culture, Power, Place: Explorations in Crit-
ical Anthropology*, Durham, NC: Duke University Press
Gupta, D. (2000) *Mistaken Modernity: India between Worlds*, New Delhi: Harper
Collins Publishers
Kaviraj, S. (1997) 'Filth and the public sphere: concepts and practices about space in
Calcutta' 10(1) *Public Culture* 83–113
Lefebvre, H. (1991) *The Production of Space*, Oxford: Blackwell Publishing
Radhakrishnan, P. (2002) 'Vanniyar separatism: nebulous issues' XXXVII(32) *Economic
and Political Weekly* 10–16 August
——(2003) 'Vanniyars and social mobility' *The New Sunday Express* 2 February
Massey, D. (1994) *Space, Place and Gender*, Minneapolis, MN: University of
Minnesota
Mencher, J. (1978) *Agriculture and Social Structure in Tamil Nadu*, Delhi: Allied
Publishers
Templeman, D. (1999) *The Northern Nadars of Tamil Nadu: An Indian Caste in the
Process of Change*, Delhi: Oxford University Press
Varma, P. (1998) *The Great Indian Middle Class*, New Delhi: Viking
Weiss, A.M. (1998) 'The gendered division of space and access in working-class areas
of Lahore' 7(1) *Contemporary South Asia* 71–89.

3

'ESTABLISHING TERRITORY'

The spatial bases and practices of the DPI

Hugo Gorringe

Palani Kumar is a local organiser of the Dalit Panther *Iyyakkam* (Movement) (DPI). He lives in the Melavassel housing estate in Madurai and is constantly visited by a stream of people seeking help, advice or news of the movement. In July 2002, he spoke of the Melavassel Riot:

> In 1995 – shortly after I finished college – I was asked by some DPI lads to address a meeting / festival they were having. I was reluctant, but they wanted me to talk about college and encourage the young-sters and so I agreed . . . There was a moderate crowd but when it was my turn to speak there was a drunkard making a nuisance. I said to him, 'Subramani, stop reeling about when we are trying to have a meeting, go inside and sleep it off.' He refused and there was a bit of a row before some lads . . . knocked him about and told him to push off. Now this Subramani . . . went off, got a policeman and told him that he had been roughed up and they came back together. The thing was the policeman was off duty, he was in 'mufti' [plain clothes] and not in uniform. So he came up to us and said: 'Who is Palani Kumar?' and I stepped forward and with no explanation or anything he hit me across the face. The next minute could also be said to have sealed my fate [i.e. made him a movement activist], because the man who hit me was being thrashed by 40 or so people.

H: They knew he was a policeman and still beat him up?

PK: Even as they hit him he was saying 'I'm a policeman', but they said: 'So what! Be who you like, who asked you to come and assault our speaker?' . . . But of course he ran off to the nearest police station and came back with his colleagues. When five or six of them in uniform came towards us everyone dispersed, but I stayed to face them. . . . I do not know why or how I was able to remain there calmly and wait for them, but I waited for them to tell them the

44

story and set things straight. Instead, they just hit me and dragged me off to the station ... the inspector cross-questioned me and asked which organisation I belonged to and so on. But while this was happening I could hear noises outside and the police were looking scared and retreating into the building, and one of them came in to call for reinforcements because there was a 'riot' outside. It seems the 40 lads had dispersed and rustled up a crowd of hundreds of people from round the city and they had come and were demanding my release. They had faced up to the police and driven them back and were demolishing the police station compound. So riot police turned up with all their gear and charged at the crowd and fired tear gas but there were buses and shops burnt and people were clamouring for me to be let out.

H: All this for ordinary Palani Kumar who was not even a member of the DPI?

PK: I know, I could not believe it. All this time I was inside and I did not understand when the police were asking who I was and what organisation I was in ... At this stage there were crowds of people milling around in the station compound and calling for my release; they were not letting anyone in or out. Even the movement lawyers could not get in but were threatened, beaten and chased off because they were not known to the people.

H: Ha Ha, the DPI lawyers were chased away? So then, who organ-ised the demo?

PK: It was those lads only, but the people taking part were from our area. Anyway finally the chief inspector said that he accepted my story ... Then I came out from the station and the crowd started cheering and they lifted me up on their shoulders and carried me off to Melavassel. I did not know what to do with myself, it was sort of embarrassing but also elating at the same time. What a day! Have you seen the news reports for that day? They make some reading. See the headlines: 'Riots in Madurai'.

Introduction

Madurai is the 'Temple City' at the heart of Tamil Nadu, the southernmost state in India, where I spent one and half years between 1998 and 1999 researching Dalit Movements.[1] One issue that recurred repeatedly was that of space and place, highlighting the fact that social space is central to Dalit identity in a number of interrelated ways. First and foremost is the 'traditional' confinement of Dalits to *cheris* (Untouchable settlements) on the outskirts of the village proper (*oor*). Many Dalits in rural Tamil Nadu still live in such outlying settlements and Dalit movements refer to urban slums and estates as *cheris* in a rhetorical assertion of continuing inequality. One of the most prominently cited reasons for Dalit protest is the perceived repression of *cheri*-dwellers. Such rhetoric establishes a link between the contemporary experience of social exclusion and prior forms of inequality.

This '*cheri*' narrative is important as a reminder of common exclusion, but also because the relative social homogeneity of such areas in caste terms means that they can be cast as havens of security in a caste-dominated society. The *cheri*, in effect, operates as an extension of the domicile in a politicised distinction between the home and the world. As Vera-Sanso (in this volume) argues, clear topographical boundaries are insufficient markers of a settlement. Across Tamilnadu, therefore, Dalit movements have sought to establish or redefine territories precisely through a process of boundary marking. Despite the rhetorical assertion that '*cheris* do not change', the dynamic nature of social space is evident in the way that Dalit movements have succeeded in refashioning settlements and housing blocks. The open assertion of allegiance to a movement and the aggressive imagery of the movement's murals have served to re-cast *cheris* as centres of resistance and social change. Of course, it is not just Dalit movements that are attempting to transform *cheris* and their inhabitants. The democratic state, in its avowed commitment to eradicate caste discrimination, is also concerned with projects of social reform. However, the organic nature of social movement constructions – where *cheri*-dwellers alter their identity and the space in which they live over a period of time and in association with a wider project – contrasts dramatically with state-led projects.

State government programmes for social reform in the late 1990s largely concentrated on the construction of residential buildings to house members of differing castes and communities. It is clear, however, that the construction of space must be *social* as well as material, must be lived as well as planned. In this chapter, it is not the conditions of life that I want to focus on so much as the means by which the social space of Melavassel is contested, constructed and endowed with political significance. Architecturally the estate is similar to countless others in urban India, but its social composition has rendered it an important site for the work of Dalit movements. While the locality in itself fosters interaction among the residents, the movements have dominated the public perception of Melavassel by those outside. Events – such as that which brought Palani Kumar to public notice – have, in effect, redefined the boundaries, and the socio-political significance, of the estate. In this paper, I wish to explore the processes by which these redefinitions of social space were and are accomplished.

Caste into outer space

Exclusion from society and exclusion from material space are mutually rein-forcing; without connections and influence it is hard to get things done, and without land or money it is hard to gain these links. To understand the significance of Dalit movements and the symbolic and spatial importance of the emblems of assertion, therefore, the social roots of protest must first be examined. 'The Untouchables, as very impure servants', Dumont pointed out, 'are segregated outside the villages proper' (1980: 47). Dalits currently living in villages within a 20-mile radius of Madurai city cannot use the same wells or the same temples, nor can they enter the main village without permission. Even when summoned to the houses of their upper-caste patrons, they are obliged to make their way to the back of the house and then call out to make their presence known. 'Untouchables enter the system', as Deliège puts it, 'in order to accomplish their ritual and economic obligations . . . they leave it again to go back to their colonies' (1997: 119). Any unwarranted incursion into the village resulted, and still often results, in verbal or physical abuse. Even where there is no distinct *cheri*, the divisions between the Dalit residences and those of the other castes remain quite apparent and are usually rigidly enforced. As these divisions have been subjected to challenge by Dalits who are no longer willing to accept the status quo, a pattern has emerged in which an assertion of equality and consciousness by Dalits is met by fierce repression and social ostracism. During the course of my fieldwork in 1999, this was made explicit on a number of occasions (cf. Vincentnathan 1996; Chowdhry 1998; Mendelsohn and Vicziany 1998; Jeffrey 2000).

Vadianpatti is a village about 17 miles to the south-west of Madurai. It is served by city buses and is not particularly remote. This proximity to Madurai and larger satellite villages meant that Dalit movement activists visited Vadianpatti and villagers were not insulated from political change. The median position of the village was highlighted when Dalit villagers affil-iated themselves to the DPI and built a 'hall' with the images of the movement in it. They were not close enough, however, for their assertion of defiance to be acceptable. Dominant castes responded by preventing Dalits from using the common space around the bus stop, denying them work and serving them in separate glasses at the tea stall. It takes a couple of hours and a change of buses to get to the village, which partly explains why the DPI did little to alleviate the situation in which its affiliates found them-selves. There were no protests in the village, no show of force or expression of solidarity and only a few mentions in speeches at other demonstrations. The Dalits here said that the movement existed only in name and that they lacked the support networks to escalate their own protests.

Three miles along the road from this village lies the settlement of Kodankipatti. In March 1999, Dalits here insisted that they lived in fear and felt insecure each time they left the *cheri*, which was on the periphery of the *oor*. Owing to the Dalits' rejection of caste tasks, they had been subjected to social boycott. The difference between the two villages lay in the fact that, while Vadianpatti was close to a local DPI stronghold, Kodankipatti was more isolated and Dalits here could not openly align themselves to the DPI. When a rudimentary flagpole was erected, it was uprooted and cast into a nearby well. Although their defiance was less overt three months after my visit, as we shall see, the Dalits were forced to flee their homes. In both these villages, the Dalits were dependent on the dominant castes for work, resources and security. In both cases, it is worth noting that there were some Dalit families who were not subject to boycott and who did not live in the *cheris* but in separate houses nearer to the caste-Hindu area. These families were usually from different Dalit castes from the majority and my respondents referred to them in derogatory terms as 'lickspittles'. Such internal politics highlight the divisions among Dalits but also point to a sense of solidarity within the *cheri*.

Cities, slums and citizenship

The issues of social exclusion faced by rural Dalits are perpetuated today in the residential patterns of urban Tamilnadu. While issues of dependency and access to resources are not as important in cities because of the availability of caste-neutral jobs, urban localities still tend to be segregated on the basis of caste. Cities are also increasingly divided in class terms and caste-based separation is predominantly a feature of the poor, but Dalits are preponderant in urban slums, squatter settlements, and housing estates. The recurrent complaint of residents in such areas is poverty and lack of resources.[2] Dependency, in this context, means that residents may be beholden to a patron or broker for amenities and to avoid relocation or police harassment. Such (lesser) forms of dependency apply equally to an established estate such as Melavassel as to other settlements. Bensman and Vidich (1995: 197) contrasted urban and rural areas and suggested that urban communities are voluntary in nature and based on choice of dwelling. In Madurai, however, there are powerful incentives and sanctions that perpetuate caste-based segregation. Two significant reasons for this are the continuing, albeit weakening, link between caste and employment, and the sense of security in numbers and vulnerability in isolation. Many Dalits only feel comfortable living among other castes by shrouding their origins.[3]

Near one of the main cinemas in central Madurai, for example, Vincent and Rosy lived with their three children. Vincent is an artist who worked in a nearby workshop and the children went to school locally. There was nothing to suggest that they were any different from their neighbours. While this family were Dalit Christians, however, the posters of the Thevar *Peravai* (Thevar Front)[4] in the surrounding streets identified the predominant caste constituency of the locality. 'We cannot say who we are', the family insisted, 'or we would not be able to live here' (interview 20 August 1999). Dalits migrating to the city gravitate towards those areas where their relatives live, and are put off by displays of casteist political posters or similar symbols in other areas. They may also experience difficulty in renting rooms from non-Dalit landlords who are often wary of the reaction of others in the neighbourhood and ask for recommendation letters as a means of screening residents. The family had, therefore, intimated that they were Nadars and kept to themselves, but they subsequently moved out of the area.

Urban neighbourhoods can act as areas of intimate interaction that can limit contact with outsiders. Such localities serve, Escobar (2001) notes, as a means of establishing a sense of certainty and belonging. The relationship between the neighbourhood and the space around it, therefore, is perhaps best captured by the idiom of the inside versus the outside. Within the locality, neighbours form bonds based on real or fictive kinship. They exchange goods, information, services and gossip on a daily basis – borrowing rice or small amounts of money, looking after children, fetching water and so on. Where such relationships are absent, as in the earlier example, the neighbourhood can become an oppressive place to be. In what follows, the processes of locality formation and creation of an inside / outside dichotomy will be examined with reference to one particular neighbourhood.

The locality

In central Madurai, adjacent to the bus-stand, there is a housing estate for municipal employees known as Melavassel.[5] Although the inhabitants are government workers, their occupations – cleaning, sweeping, rubbish collection – mean that they are drawn from Dalit castes. The estate consists mainly of crumbling three-storey buildings clustered around paved open spaces. The buildings are commonplace and, while many of them are in a state of acute dilapidation, Melavassel is not dissimilar to other cheap housing developments in this respect. It is bounded by three walls, abutting onto the main road into town, the former Thiruvalur coach stand (now being re-developed) and a rough area of open land. Along the remaining boundary of the estate runs a thick, black and stinking open sewer. Makeshift cattle byres, and mud and coconut matting houses line its banks and the stench and mosquitoes are intolerable to most visitors. The flats abutting the sewer are in the worst condition, with rising damp making the electrical connections highly dangerous, and with shelves and balcony walls in a state of disintegration. When one person died after a balcony wall collapsed, there was talk of re-housing the occupants. As is often the case, however, the relocation plans proposed moving the inhabitants outside the city and further away from shops and jobs, and so people defied the proposals and remained in situ. The central location of the estate renders it highly desirable both in real estate terms, but also in terms of convenience and access for the residents.

All the inhabitants of Melavassel are Dalits, but most of them derive more narrowly from the Arundadhiar (Chakkiliyar) or Paraiyar communities because few castes are prepared to engage in municipal cleaning work. Although most government jobs are in high demand because of the conditions and pay, Dalits still constitute the vast majority of those at this bottom end of the employment scale. Workers and activists argue that the nature of this work accounts for the high incidence of alcoholism among Dalit men, but simultaneously concede that it provides a regular income and housing. To reside in the 'quarters', one member of the resident's family must work for the corporation. People are supposed to leave after retirement unless a member of their family succeeds them in corporation employment. Two hundred rupees are subtracted from the worker's salary in lieu of rent.[6] In theory, therefore, the inhabitants of Melavassel are either lowly government workers or related to them. From this perspective, Melavassel appears to be the equivalent of the workers' lines, or a community of employees, but within the compound it is clear that many people sub-let flats or parts of their flats in order to raise extra income. The requirement for one member of the family to work for the corporation also permits others to perform various jobs. Despite this, the link between the estate and the lowest forms of government work reinforces the traditional association of 'Untouchables' and 'dirty work'. Consequently, the DPI argument that this locality is a modern day *cheri* is attractive.

Melavassel and its occupants

Melavassel seems like a 'bounded community' fenced off from other neighbourhoods. Due to the caste constituency of its residents, it is known as a Dalit 'colony' and it reproduces, in some ways, the traditional seclusion of the (ex)Untouchable community. The flats that constitute the housing estate were built in 1955 as accommodation for municipal workers but the locality has expanded since then. In 1984, small houses were constructed on the approaches to the estate and they have been walled off from the road. Residents tend to have come from surrounding villages between 30 to 50 years ago and settled down. Younger people like Palani Kumar have lived here all their lives and do not envisage moving unless forced to leave. This is not, however, to say that the population is static. Several people moved into Melavassel during my fieldwork, either due to marriage or to stay with relatives while they established themselves and sought other accommodation. Such in-migration is facilitated both by the willingness of many residents to sub-let, and by ties of kinship.

There is now a broad generational divide between the older (45 or over) inhabitants who have close links to family and villages in rural Tamilnadu, and a younger, urbanised group for whom Madurai is home. While the younger generation may maintain ties to relatives in rural areas, they are more likely to forge bonds of friendship with residents of other *cheris* in the city or with workmates. City-wide protests and meetings mean that movement members in particular have links with groups throughout Madurai. Melavassel is affiliated to two such political Dalit movements – one is largely Paraiyar one mostly Chakkiliyar – but despite this relations between the two castes are amicable and inter-marriages were reported to occur from time to time. As Chakrabarti (in this volume) points out, high population density invariably puts a strain on resources and may lead to disputes, but it takes extraordinary events to bring people together or openly set them apart. There was only a palpable sense of 'community' during events such as the riot in 1995, and to a lesser extent in street festivals. Conversely, during elections, the estate was decked out in the banners of all the main parties, each of which had competing booths set up outside the main entrance to canvass for votes.

This brief description goes to show that, although all the inhabitants are Dalit, Melavassel is far from homogeneous, and that a common caste background does not necessarily foster unity. People have differing levels of education, careers and incomes. The majority are municipal employees who receive reasonable pay. A significant number of inhabitants are self-employed but perform similar tasks; rag and bone merchants, paper pickers and cleaners or scavengers are preponderant in the houses leading into the estate, and tricycles piled high with recycled waste often block the main approach. The houses nearest the entrance have back yards that are used to house livestock, or store the gathered materials. In the multi-storey buildings, occupations vary. There are teachers, sales representatives, auto-drivers and shop assistants. As a result of this diversity, some of the flats are well furnished and have modern conveniences like fridges and televisions, but others are more or less bare.

The open spaces planned by the architects for the heart of the building complex have become the site of rubbish heaps, flea markets, public toilets and livestock. Cattle and goats foul the streets and can be found in some of the blocks of flats, and anyone with anything to sell sets up a stall. The area is, in every sense, a contradiction of the 'bourgeois sense of what it means for a space to be a modern city'. The governing conventions and paternalistic state regulations have been inverted to create the 'loose disorder' of a village (Kaviraj 1997: 84). This inversion is functional, however, in the sense that it provides a sense of community, cheap food, affordable commodities and, in the case of livestock or home industries, added income for the inhabitants. People gather in this area to talk, children run about and play in the space, and a crèche has been established. While the buildings have contributed to and enabled this inner society to develop, it would be misleading to read Melavassel as a planning success. Outsiders, and better-off residents, see the crowding of the open spaces as unhygienic and undesirable, and many expressed hesitancy about inviting people back to their homes. The disregard with which non-residents view this area elides the functional nature of the disorder. The overcrowding and dirt are tolerated because they serve the purposes mentioned earlier. Furthermore, the hawkers within Melavassel are more inclined to offer credit than the stores outside because they deal with known customers. The antipathy of the outside world thus provides a sense of unity in adversity that can, in moments of crisis, override internal disputes and quarrels to provide a sense of community.

Melavassel, therefore, is not just delineated by the walls surrounding it, but also by the stigma attached to its inhabitants. This is not completely a result of 'traditional' antipathies, because Melavassel residents have an unsavoury reputation in the present day. When I first began my fieldwork, I was attracted to the obvious indications of Dalit movement activity in the estate but was warned against entering the locality by friends. Clashes such as the riot in 1995 and drunken brawls have given the area a reputation for violence, and many are put off by the squalor of parts of the estate. The common depictions of lower-class Dalits cast them as idle, dirty, ignorant and violent. Certainly, the locality *is* poorly maintained and unhygienic, and at first sight confirms the accusations of reproving reformers that the 'Dalits do not help themselves'. Such discourses are commonly applied to poverty-stricken communities around the world, but here they are supported by the idiom of caste.

The discursive constructions of Melavassel serve both to deter outsiders from entering, and to create a sense of unity.[7] Inhabitants were conscious of the dominant perspective and all my respondents positioned themselves in the debate. Many insisted that the corporation should come in and clean up the place, but others (especially those who profited most from the current set-up) took pains to articulate counter narratives of resistance, pride and cohesion. They insisted that Melavassel had cleaned up its image and that people had altered their behaviour. In many ways, therefore, the surrounding walls are merely the concrete representations of social narratives that present Melavassel as either an unsavoury locality or a Dalit stronghold. Despite the differentiation within the estate and the multiple narratives that could have been used to describe Melavassel (in terms of class, gender, employment, etc.) there was a remarkable convergence in all discourses that conceived of the locality as a unitary entity in terms of caste.[8] These social discourses are often based more on prejudice than knowledge, because outsiders rarely enter the estate. As in rural areas, however, such discourses establish a clear dichotomy between insiders and outsiders, and present the locality of Melavassel as a private neighbourhood sequestered off from the public spaces of the city.

Public world and private homes

In 'Filth and the public sphere', Kaviraj (1997) challenges the applicability of the dichotomy between the public and private to India. He notes that the idea of universal access was not present in traditional India, where one's social attributes served to determine one's level of access to 'hierarchical space'. Drawing upon Tagore, Kaviraj suggests that a more apt differentiation is between 'Home and the World', the inside and the outside. His contention is that the collective nature of Indian households renders them very much the reverse of 'private', because they are not driven by the desire of individuals to be accorded their own space.[9] While accepting this argument in part, it is important to be aware of the divided nature of individual houses and the gendered nature of space.[10]

For me, the significance of substituting the word 'home' for the word 'private' with regard to Dalit settlements is more apparent when it is conceived of as the interface between individual houses and public space. The *cheri* or urban locality thus may be understood to function as a partial extension of the domicile. If we define the term 'home' primarily as 'a realm of security', such an interpretation is certainly justified in a way that the term 'private' is not. The Dalit women in Melavassel draw strength, friendship and solidarity from their neighbours, but they can be systematically subjected to violence within their own houses (Ravindran 1999; Subadra 1999). In Melavassel, neighbourhood links are reinforced by caste and kinship, and the ties internal to the locality are evinced not only by the sense that everyone knows everyone else (at least by sight or by association) but also in different codes of dress and other conventions of self-presentation. Dalit movement activists wear *lungis* (informal waist-cloths) and T-shirts within the locality, but insist upon smarter attire before they enter public space and so don white *veshtis* (formal waist-cloths) or trousers. The *cheri* (both urban and rural) may thus be conceived as a 'home'. This is further emphasised as the petty vending and livestock that occupy the inner spaces of Melavassel would be less tenable – and more vulnerable to police harassment – in public space.

The 'home' (*cheri*), therefore, could be said to constitute the semi-public space between the private lives of individuals / families and the public life of the street – which, as the incidents in 1995 suggest, is much less secure. Such an approach enables us to introduce the notion of 'privacy' into Kaviraj's schema. Melavassel, thus, may be seen as a form of 'private' space in the sense that it is sequestered off from the public, but it also encompasses spaces for privacy. Family dwellings were not entirely open to all, but were divided into different areas (Sharma 1980; Donner in this volume). The porch constituted an interim zone that marked the passage from inside to outside. Friends, acquaintances and passers-by could, and did, enter this space unbidden and with freedom. Beyond this zone, however, there was always a further space that was reserved for close friends and family and could be shut off. People spoke about the importance of having space for themselves and of being able to restrict access. There were also frequent complaints about poor soundproofing and how people listening through walls spread rumours. An illustration of this division of space was offered as I made friends in Melavassel. Initially, I was seated in the porch areas of various houses and usually became the centre of small gatherings. The semi-public nature of these spaces was evinced by the reaction of passers-by. Those within the estate would stop, hang around and interject questions and comments, whereas those on the main road who looked in would merely point and stare before moving on. Movement activists gathering in Melavassel would congregate in porches, seated on beds or chairs, while women served tea and sometimes food, and other residents were free to join the discussants. Residents in Melavassel thus regarded such areas as part of their home space.

As I came to know people better, and especially when I made friends with one of the women on the estate, the setting changed. On later visits, I would be ushered into sitting-rooms away from 'prying eyes' and 'nosey parkers'. My admission to the inner sanctum of people's houses was not simply an issue of gender – although my new friend Dhanam could speak more freely behind walls – because others were always present and close friends or important guests were also entertained inside. It was by no means public, however, and for Dhanam to be alone with an unrelated man in this setting would have transcended bounds of propriety. Privacy, here, is not an individual concern – none of the flats or houses had separate rooms for each occupant, but it was familial. A further differentiation of space occurred in that the kitchen was the preserve of the women in the household. The separation of the kitchen was not physical – one had to walk through it to get to the inner room and the door to the room was never closed – but it was tangible. Any attempt to help out, clean plates or chop vegetables was rigorously repulsed. Even close friends who were allowed to help were barred from the kitchen and chopped vegetables in the main room.[11] Although the term 'private' is wholly inadequate to capture the multiple interactions within family homes, merely replacing it with a looser term such as the 'home' or the 'inside' seems to flatten out the complexity of these social relations. The distinction between the 'home and the world', therefore, seems to reproduce a slightly muted version of the opposition between public and private. Rather than replacing one dichotomy with another, I suggest the notion of a home space adding a further dimension that mediates between the two spheres.

Despite their separation in analytical terms, the three spheres are interlinked. Movements often coalesce around immediate issues to do with living conditions: the request for more land or permanent housing, or demands for the provision of certain amenities, greater security for women and legal recognition (Escobar 2001: 147).[12] Such protest is, perforce, directed at – and highlights the role of – the government in the construction and mediation of public space. The paradox of such protest is that it is both directed against the government, which is cast as unrepresentative, and at the government to whom demands are addressed. The role of the state in this context is most visible in the construction of housing for the Scheduled Castes. The sites selected for such housing are frequently undesirable, or outside the city and the main areas of employment. The housing boards in the heart of the city tend to be reserved for those engaged in 'municipal work' (cleaning, sweeping and scavenging). As such, the housing blocks constitute both an opportunity and a limitation, and serve as a material manifestation of the discursive links between employment and caste.

Movements in space

'Spatiality', according to Soja, situates life in an active arena: 'To be alive is to participate in the social production of space, to shape and be shaped by a constantly evolving spatiality which constitutes and concretizes social action and relationships' (1985: 90). This is particularly relevant in the context of caste. Thus when shoe-clad members of the Ambedkar People's Movement walked down high caste streets in rural Tamilnadu in the 1970s, they were not only challenging the dominance of caste landlords, they were establishing a claim to physical space and their rights as members of a democratic polity. Lefebvre distinguished between *representational* spaces (social, lived space, space in use) and *representations* of space (planned, imposed, controlled space) (1991: 45). Public space in urban areas often starts as the latter, such as the innumerable housing blocks constructed for Dalits by the state government, and becomes the former as people move in, add makeshift extensions and inhabit the place. This transition from spaces into places, as Appadurai notes, usually 'requires a conscious moment' – such as a house-warming ceremony or the inauguration of a project – 'which may subsequently be remembered as relatively routine' (1995: 209). The production of locality, however, is not a 'once-and-for-all' process, but must be constantly renewed and revised to match the changing nature of its constituency. Rituals that contribute to a sense of community are especially salient in this process: 'Insofar as neighbourhoods are imagined, produced and maintained against some sort of ground (social, material, environmental) they also require and produce contexts, against which their own intelligibility takes shape' (ibid. 209).

This process is most obviously apparent in times of change or challenge to the established order, when it is especially important to restore some predictability to one's environment. 'Establishing the territory' – through wall posters, graffiti and sporadic harassment of outsiders – 'generates security' (Ley and Cybriwsky 1974: 505). In Ley and Cybriwsky's (1974) study of urban gangs in Philadelphia, predominantly white suburbs were trying to maintain their 'integrity' in the face of an increasing black presence. In this sort of situation, 'graffiti are commonly boundary markers; they delineate an interface, the edge of socially claimed space' (ibid. 501).[13] Such visual markers have historically been redundant in village India, where the limits of each territory have been fairly distinct, but Bensman and Vidich (1995) suggest that urban associations, at least initially, are voluntary rather than given at birth and hence need to be constructed and reinforced. In contemporary Tamilnadu, however, such inscriptions and emblems of 'defended neighbourhoods' are common in both rural and urban areas, and flagpoles and walls become the barometers of local political opinion (see Simpson in this volume). Social movements and political parties are critically involved in the construction, or at least the identification, of such communities. But where graffiti, according to Ley and Cybriwsky, constitute 'part of a "twilight zone of communication", an outlet for often deeply felt but rarely articulated sentiments and attitudes' (1974: 492), the flagpoles, colours, posters and murals in Tamilnadu are public assertions of political identity.

Bounded spaces, territory and movement markers

There are three entrances to Melavassel off the main road that all the corporation buses travel along to reach the Central Bus Stand. In 1999, the furthest entrance from the city centre was fairly nondescript. The second had an archway painted with the emblems and name of the *Tamizhaga Arundhadiar* Youth Front (TAYF).[14] This board was getting old and the paint was somewhat faded. Further along the road, there were murals on the walls for various established parties. Standing out from the compound wall on the verge of the road was a tall flagpole embedded in a concrete plinth. The red, white and blue markings of the pole indicated that it did not belong to any of these organisations, even though it could be said to have been encroaching on their space.

The third and main entrance to the Melavassel Housing Unit had been turned into an archway and similar light blue, red and white poles supported a large board emblazoned with the striking images of a roaring leopard and the face of a man cross cut by bolts of lightning. In between the two figures, bold lettering indicated that this was a stronghold of the DPI, or Liberation Panthers. The face, staring insolently out at the Tourist Office's Hotel Tamil Nadu, was that of Thirumavalavan, the leader of the movement. On either side of the gateway, the compound wall had been turned into a series of political meeting points. The slogans and images of Dravidian Parties, the Communists and the Liberation Panthers vied with Hindu shrines for wall space.

Several parties had constructed ramshackle shelters in front of murals depicting their leaders and symbols. These 'halls' (*manram*), as they were grandiosely referred to, served little material function and adherents of the organisations tended to congregate elsewhere. The booths only came into their own during moments of political import such as elections, when the canvassers gathered with their supporters. Mostly they stood deserted save for a few stray chickens or pigs rooting around for rubbish. The bright colours and vivid portraits of the parties and movements competed for attention with the ever-present film posters, but these murals pointed to the presence of particular organisations in the area and thus served to establish a claim to the locality. While the presence of insignia and movement markers over the other gateways clearly bears testimony to the contested nature of the claim for space, the size, boldness and lustre of the DPI symbols underlined the fact that this movement was predominant.

The significance of these symbols of affiliation became apparent when I was visiting the house nearest the colony entrance. Two Dalit men approached Melavassel and addressed themselves to Palani Kumar. The manager in the hotel where they were working had abused them in caste terms and was making life unbearable. They had recently arrived from the countryside and had no relatives or friends to turn to. Having noticed the board above the entrance, they had resolved to approach the DPI. In Melavassel, they met activists who gave them advice and then sent a group of movement members to tell (i.e. threaten) the hotel owner that the two waiters were not as isolated as they appeared.

Movement markers and defended neighbourhoods

In the functioning of a movement or a party, symbols play an important role in marking off a defended neighbourhood. Dalits in and around Madurai cited deterrence as one of the primary reasons for joining an aggressive movement. Time and again, they would point to the flag of their movement as the object that stood between them and violent retaliation on the part of aggressors. This function is only possible because movement emblems are widely recognised and identify outposts of much larger, socially imagined communities that could intervene on behalf of their members. The induction of a locality into a movement is symbolised by the flag-raising ceremony. A general meeting is advertised among members and the public announcing the occasion and, on the given day, a series of speeches culminates in the leader unveiling the colours, or raising the flag, of the movement. The Melavassel flag-raising ceremony took place in 1997, but movement members still speak about the sense of empowerment they felt. Hundreds of people, from Melavassel and other parts of Madurai, blocked the main road as people crowded round to listen to speeches and watch Thirumavalavan welcome the locality into the movement. A stage was constructed and loud music and political speeches blared out of sound systems. The atmosphere was a mixture of celebration, defiance and loyalty. Thirumavalavan's decision to visit houses in the estate and eat with people was recalled by several people as highlighting his commitment to the *cheri* people.

In emphasising the boundaries of the estate, Melavassel has become a distinct locality but it is far from being cut off. The flags, statues and posters of the DPI both set it apart and linked it to other localities. 'There are 40 *cheris* in Madurai depending on SMP colony [a similar locality in the suburbs of Madurai]', as one DPI activist put it, 'and SMP colony is dependent on 40 *cheris*' (interview 23 March 1999). The presence of a movement implies the existence of informed cadres who know the legal ropes and have the resources to bring cases to court or to raise the public profile of an incident. Each branch of the movement in Madurai is perceived as part of this wider network of people who are linked by shared ideals, common fears and ties of friendship and solidarity cemented at each successive meeting. The flag-raising ceremony thus lays claim to an area, but it is also a performance that brings people together in a common project. The party lights, loudspeakers, convoys of followers, and emblems are designed not only to cement the adherence of a locality to the movement, but also to broadcast this fact to others (see Simpson in this volume). The identity of a *cheri* that has affiliated itself to a Dalit movement, therefore, is qualitatively different from one that remains unmoved by the struggle. Erecting the emblem of a movement marks the end of obedience (though not necessarily the end of fear) and the beginning of an organised struggle against inequality.

That these processes are not confined to established and legitimate settlements is exemplified by the inhabitants of 'Jansi Rani Complex' – a street village in the heart of Madurai. Makeshift tents on the pavement provide shelter, the river is their bathroom and the concourse of a Hindu shrine provides their meeting space. Working as rag and bone merchants, or as self-employed cleaners of drains and sewers, they eke out a living on the road. The walls of the shrine concourse where they gather, however, have been painted with the images of the DPI: images of Ambedkar, Thirumavalavan and a panther overlook the site. 'They are there as a security measure', Alagar, a middle-aged man slightly the worse for drink, insisted, 'to guard against people or against police raids who come at night to drag us away' (interview 22 March 1999). The residents did not attribute special powers to the mural, but they emphasised the power behind the painting. As Sekhar, a good-looking lad in his early 20s who had lived in Jansi Rani Complex all his life, said, 'It is only after joining this movement that we can be here undisturbed. Before, there were countless caste clashes and continuous police harassment, but now if he (Thirumavalavan) raises his hand Madurai District will be destroyed' (ibid.).

Movement branches thus constitute 'pockets of solidarity' and resistance, but 'assertive or aggressive graffiti', as Ley and Cybriwsky observe, 'represent more than attitudes. They are dispositions to behaviour, and as such impress a bolder outline on the fuzzy transition between perception and action' (1974: 505).[15] The domination of a neighbourhood by one organisation can inspire a sense of security as in the earlier examples, but it can also result in the creation of a counter-community and may lead to violence. The relational and political nature of movement activity is illustrated by the very symbols that mark its presence because they mimic the standards of existing institutions. The multiple flags, posters and billboards of various social or political organisations thus serve to 'map' political affiliation. Following established repertoires of action enables recognition and asserts that Dalits have autonomous organisations, but it also sets them in competition with others.

The multiple markers of political association highlight the contested nature of public space. Dalit movement claims to territory are not passively accepted. They are questioned, contested, endorsed or ignored by residents and outsiders, and must be constantly renewed and re-asserted. Even the 'bounded space' of Melavassel has boards and posters demonstrating allegiance to different organisations. This competition for space occasionally leads to conflict but, where organisations co-exist, they seek to establish a greater claim to the territory. In this context, the prominence accorded to various emblems and their relative ability to maintain or enhance their visibility assumes great importance. The significance of aesthetics cannot be ignored. Hence, the faded paint of the TAYF board indicated its decline, whereas the glossier images of the DPI suggested its ascendance. Similarly, the taller the flagpole and the better maintained it is, the stronger an organisation is, and conversely the flagpoles of discredited parties may be uprooted in the symbolic rejection of their ideals.

In 1999, movement activists claimed that the political parties were only in Melavassel 'for show', and that party loyalty derived more from patronage than from political conviction. The secrecy of the ballot renders such claims hard to verify, but informal conversations with people from different organisations in the estate served to confirm the primacy of the DPI. An accident in 2002 afforded an opportunity to tentatively assess the validity of this impression. A lorry crashed through the boundary wall by the main entrance destroying the 'halls' of the AIADMK (Akila India Anna Dravida Munnetra Kazhagam [All India Anna Dravidian Progressive Federation]), the DMK, the Communists and the DPI – all of whom had a presence within Melavassel – as well as knocking down the DPI board. This gave the differing parties a chance to renegotiate the division of space and stake out their claims to dominance in the locality. In the event, the entire section of reconstructed wall was daubed in the colours of the DPI and proclaimed the area's allegiance to Thirumavalavan. I do not wish to suggest that the political opinions of a locality can be so obviously read off its graffiti, but such markers are significant, as Bourdieu states, 'the concessions of *politeness* always contain *political* concessions' (1977: 95).

Political spaces

Social relations, as Massey (1994: 168) observes, 'always have a spatial form'. This space is not merely passive, it '*is both constructed by and the medium of social relations and processes*' (Cope 1996: 185, emphasis in original). The spaces occupied by Dalit estates are more than just homes and neighbourhoods: they constitute places in which the Dalits can be seen and represented, controlled and contained. As we have seen, however, they are increasingly places within which activism can arise and expand outward. This recognition of space as *political* serves to highlight the interconnectedness of spaces, and the 'topography of power' that links them together (Gupta and Ferguson 1999: 8). It also highlights the fact that space cannot be conceptualised independently of time and must be conceived as dynamic and constructed.

Regulations over who is allowed in, who is excluded, and the roles that both insiders and outsiders play in a social space help to shape a community's perception of itself. Space is thus critical to the production of group identity – the self-image and self-esteem of a community. In like manner, representations of space are central to the process of 'other-ing' (Ruddick 1996: 146). 'Locally constructed identities', in other words, do not emerge in a vacuum; they are 'constructed in relation to processes of classification or categorisation by the state and other social groups' (Aitken 1999: 19). The construction of locality, therefore, cannot be viewed in isolation from other, parallel, social processes. The constitutional creation of a 'Scheduled Caste' (SC) category, for example, enables solidarity between Dalits of differing regions, languages and cultures. But the government programmes for SCs – which are designed to alleviate Dalit poverty and provide better conditions for them – have often culminated in the reproduction of marginality.[16] The rows of small, single-room, concrete constructions, for example, are as sure a sign of a Dalit settlement in Tamilnadu as any that existed previously. The communities derived from such 'colonies', in Appadurai's terms, are 'context-produced' as much as they are 'context-generative' (1995: 217).

Unsurprisingly, DPI orators frequently turn their critical gaze on government housing. If such developments were really intended to advance the uplift of the Dalits, they argue, they would not be built with sloped roofs that prevent the addition of another storey. The typical 'Dalit house' has one room constructed from concrete with a little toilet at the back. The door was usually cast iron making the houses unbearably hot in the daytime, but relatively cool at night. There were no open windows, only patterned grids looking out onto similar constructions. Movement activists insisted that the quality and style of the houses could be better, and argued that the government was persisting in the construction of 'colonies' – residential areas that are identifiable in terms of caste and that are self-contained and separated from, rather than integrated into (or at least indistinguishable from), the surrounding communities. Events such as the 1995 riot, or a flag-raising ceremony, however, may serve to transform the passive space of a housing block into a meaningful place for community action. It is certainly true that Melavassel residents welcome the sense of security that is generated by living among other Dalits and would be reluctant to lose the sense of community. The problem thus appears to be not the segregation of society itself so much as the manner in which this separation is effected.

Controlled space

The rhetoric employed by Dalit movements and activists frequently draws parallels between rural and urban *cheris*. The interchangeable way in which terms such as colony, slum and *cheri* are used raises questions about the processes involved in the construction and control of the two settings, and the continuities and differences between rural and urban Dalit settlements. On the face of it, the comparison is entirely political. Rural *cheris* are usually physically removed from other habitations and lie on the peripheries of the *oor*. In villages like Kodankipatti, the *cheri* is marked out in negative terms rather than by walls or fences: thus, it is just off the main road but is not served by it and a mud track leads off to the *cheri*. There are no bus-stops here, no shops or other amenities. The school, temple, shops, Panchayat office, weekly market and health centre are all in the *oor*. Furthermore, the 'common' lands of the village are not under Dalit control. Thus, when relations between Dalits and the dominant castes were tense, Dalits were denied access to the lake (*kanmai*) that they used for washing. The boundaries in such contexts are maintained by the ever-present threat of violence and Dalit women complained of being too scared to use the open fields to relieve themselves during times of conflict.

There are few opportunities for political mobilisation and expression in such areas. Deliège (1997) found little or no evidence of Dalit assertion in his fieldwork, and in the remoter villages the recurrent complaint was dependency and powerlessness. Where landholdings and employment opportunities are monopolised by dominant castes, action is certainly beset by difficulties, but this is precisely why such villages are the sites of the most meaningful protests. It is in rural areas that Dalits are required to do 'caste-work' (beating drums at temple festivals or funerals, removing carcasses and so on) in return for normal relations, but increasingly such tasks are either being refused, or only performed in exchange for competitive rates of pay. This has often placed Dalits in conflict with locally dominant castes and led to the imposition of social boycotts. When Dalit villagers in Kodankipatti refused to perform the caste tasks assigned to them in 1990, they were refused work in the area and violently expelled from the village. After government intervention, a fragile peace prevailed until 1999 when Dalits attempted to assert their rights to use the village square (*podhu mandai*). Scuffles broke out and the police chastised the Dalits for not seeking permission to use the 'public' space. Even where boundaries are not visible, they are known – here Dalits could not sit at the bus-stop, they were served tea in separate glasses and those dependent on the local landlords for work had to display exaggerated forms of respect.[17] The earlier example, however, shows that boundaries are constantly contested and sometimes openly challenged.

In villages, social boundaries persist in large part because people and their caste backgrounds are known and whole communities can be effectively ostracised. In contrast, my respondents pointed to the relative dilution of caste sentiment in cities due to the anonymity of urban life. There is no dominant caste group in Madurai (though some groups are more powerful and 'connected' than others), and there are no specific tasks that Dalits are expected to perform in exchange for goodwill. While private firms and small businesses tend to employ staff whom they feel they can trust (often along networks of caste and kinship), there are usually jobs available. In practical terms, therefore, the dependency that characterises rural Untouchability is absent in the city. Urban residents also have easier access to support networks in the form of other estates, educated and wealthy Dalits, lawyers, police and the press. The threats, violence and debt that serve to maintain boundaries in rural areas do not apply so readily. Despite these differences, movement activists describe Melavassel as a contemporary *cheri*, and the estate is delineated both by walls and social stigma. The residents are all Dalit and, like their rural counterparts, inhabitants view their locality as a home space, and draw support from each other in the face of external hostility.

In both rural and urban settings, in other words, Dalit identities are contained and shaped by the particular form that their residential space takes. This location is not simply material but is subject to multiple discourses. Social narratives, as Vera-Sanso (in this volume) notes, both highlight social inequalities but also enable residents to redefine the character of their neighbourhood. Outsiders depict Dalit communities as idle, dirty and ignorant and they are set apart from other houses and groups,[18] which helps foster a sense of mutual disadvantage and discrimination. In Melavassel, there is a fear that the site will be relocated; in SMP colony there is a perception that the nearby hospital discriminates against Dalits; in Jansi Rani Complex people are united against police harassment. In all inner city *cheris*, people are concerned about education with many voicing concerns about the quality and cost (in terms of extras – pens, notebooks, uniforms, etc.) of state schooling, about politicians who only visit during election time and about poverty (Dickey 1993; De Wit 1996). Although the scale and intensity of exclusion in rural and urban areas differ, the continuing segregation of Dalit communities into distinct estates is arguably a means of social control. 'Visibility', as Foucault puts it, 'is a trap' (1977: 200). Thus, housing as a means of controlling and co-ordinating Dalit life offers what Foucault (1980: 72) terms a micro-physical power which works in part by reordering material space.

The mode of Dalit resistance, however, is also consistent in rural and urban settings and defies attempts to re-order Dalit space through the public assertion of political allegiance to various movements. In some ways, this is problematic: the assertive identification of a given locality with one particular movement arguably creates an enclave cut off from the rest of society. Dalit movement activity thus seems to re-emphasise the caste constituency of localities and to mark them as distinct neighbourhoods. Social and political action, however:

> militates in the long run against separatism because it assumes an orientation that is *publicist*. In so far as these arenas are *publics* they are by definition not enclaves – which is not to say that they are not often involuntarily enclaved.
>
> (Mitchell 1995: 124)

Far from cutting themselves off, when Dalit movements raise their flags, or unveil a painted board, they are raising fundamental questions about the nature of public space and social interaction. By struggling over and within the social spaces (voting booths, courts and commissioner's offices) to which their access is still restricted, Dalit movements are engaged in a negotiation of both their own identity and the limits and possibilities of civil society. Dalit movements both contest and constitute relations of power and solidarity that serve simultaneously to establish the boundaries of an urban area and transcend them. They flourish in localities where they can draw upon pre-existing networks of affiliation, but, while they emerge out of local issues and problems, the conditions they are fighting against are familiar across India: landlessness, poverty, low social status, poor working conditions, lack of amenities and facilities, and poor housing conditions.[19] Despite the constitutional guarantees of equality, caste continues to inform daily life and interaction, and Dalits continue to be regarded as lesser citizens.

Concluding remarks: power, place and protest

Space, as Massey puts it, is socially constructed, but 'the social is spatially constructed too' (1994: 254). The spatial organisation of a given society, in other words, influences the way it works. The caste-based segregation of Indian cities and villages continues to inform political and social activity in the 'modern' world. Dalits often speak of being 'imprisoned within *cheris*'. '*Cheris* do not change' was a common rhetorical flourish designed to highlight their continuing subordination and poverty. As the foregoing discussion illustrates, however, the assertion of immutability is in itself a means of 'speaking a group into being' and an exhortation to continue the work of political and social movements that have effected such significant changes already. 'The ability of people to confound the established spatial orders, either through physical movement or through their own conceptual and political acts of re-imagination', as Gupta and Ferguson put it, 'means that space and place can never be "given", and that the process of their socio-political construction must always be considered' (1999: 17).

'Public space', as Mitchell notes, 'is always and inescapably a product of social negotiation and contest' (1996a: 131). The process of negotiation, however, does not occur between equals. While 'tight and reasonable boundaries have to be drawn around public space to retain it as a place open for public political activity' (Mitchell: 1996b: 153), Dalit movements seek to create defended neighbourhoods or 'homes' within which they can mobilise and campaign for change without fear of social ostracism or retaliatory violence. The basic issues involved in both processes relate to control over space, and the power to determine access and usage of that space. 'The exercise and maintenance of these sets of power relations', as Cope observes, 'occur across space, through space, and require the use of space as an element of control, opportunity and regulation' (1996: 187). In establishing localities, Dalit movements are confounding the limitations of, and expectations attached to, marginalised *cheri* spaces and seeking to reconfigure the spatial order of Tamil society.

Acknowledgements

I would like to thank Roger Jeffery and Mai Gorringe for comments and suggestions on earlier drafts of this paper, and Iona Gorringe who provided the more recent details. I am also indebted to Chris Fuller and other members of the Localities Workshop in Sussex where this paper was originally presented. Special thanks must go to Henrike Donner and Geert De Neve for their detailed and insightful editorial comments. Any shortcomings in the paper are obviously my own and cannot be laid at the door of those who have been so helpful.

Notes

1 'Dalit', the Marathi word meaning 'downtrodden', has been adopted by politically active ex-Untouchables in Tamil Nadu. Dalits in Tamil Nadu are marginalised in socio-political terms and face discrimination in many ways; they cannot pass freely through villages, are sometimes served using separate glasses, and have unequal access to 'common resources' such as mango groves. This partly explains the pan-Indian popularity of the label 'Dalit', often supplemented in Tamil Nadu with the direct Tamil translation: *thazhtapathoor*. While many Scheduled Caste (SC) members avoid the term, I use 'Dalit' throughout because activists see other terms as demeaning (Charsley 1996).

2 Dalits are not the only Indians living in squatter settlements. Many higher- and middle-caste people subsist in similar conditions, but the 'overwhelming majority' of residents in such housing are ex-Untouchable (Shiri 1998: 11). In 1987–8, 33.4% of the total population were below the poverty line whereas the

percentage of SCs under the poverty line was 44.7%. (Source: 8th Five Year Plan 1992–7 cited in: Ponnudurai 1999: 4, Nov-Dec).

3 On ethnic / caste segregation, see Chakrabarti in this volume.

4 The Thevars are one of the most dominant Backward Castes (BCs) in TN.

5 Thideer Nagar is the official name of the housing site, but Melavassel (meaning West Gate) is the most common term and refers to its location in the city.

6 Those living outside are given Rs 200 in their salary, but, because of the cost of commercial rents, this is far from adequate. Rents for similar dwellings in the commercial sector could range from Rs 500 up to Rs 1,500 depending on the location.

7 I was more readily accepted, therefore, when I pointed out that my friend's grandparents lived in the estate and, afterwards, when I made friends with residents.

8 See Leela Fernandes' *Producing Workers* (1997) for an extended discussion of the rhetorical production of communities.

9 There is, however, a gendered differentiation of space within the home. It is often argued that Dalit women experience greater autonomy than their higher caste counterparts due to their earning potential. The segregation of women in the home, as Kaviraj notes, is a middle-class and middle-caste practice. Dalit women suffer less from such social restrictions, but this does not exempt them from the general notions of propriety and good conduct. It is, Sharma notes, 'difficult for a woman to engage in public, political or economic processes which involve contact with unrelated men since it is her business to withdraw from such situations' (1980: 213). Dalit women may work, shop and collect fuel and water, but they are not permitted to linger unnecessarily in public streets. As Mitchell (1988: 50) observes, space is polarised between the female domestic realm and the public, male world of the market-place.

10 See Gorringe (2005) for more on the gendered nature of space.

11 The gendered nature of this division was apparent as my wife was permitted into the kitchen in a show of intimacy that could not be extended to me.

12 According to MIDS (Madras Institute for Development Studies) Working Paper 134, 30.9% of SC households in Tamil Nadu have electricity, as opposed to 61.3% of non-SC households; 26.8% of non-SC households have sanitation, whereas only 9.8% of SC houses do. (Thamukku Nov.-Dec. 1999: 2).

13 There are interesting parallels here to boundary marking in contemporary Northern Ireland.

14 Arundhadiar is a more honorific term for Chakkiliyars. Tamizhaga Arundhadiar Youth Front (TAYF) is one of a handful of movements who work with and for the most deprived of the three main Dalit caste categories in Tamil Nadu.

15 Assertive slogans resound through the assertions of many Dalit movements exhorting their followers to 'return a blow for a blow'. 'Spring into action, make your enemies tremble', is one Dalit Panther Iyyakkam (Movement) (DPI) slogan; another is 'Plan for the morrow and arise with courage. Escape your fears and set out with resolve (repeated), fall upon your foes like a bolt of thunder (repeated)'. Such slogans reflect the attitudes of a younger more radical generation but also constitute an inducement to action. In 1993, caste riots in Western Tamil Nadu (Alm 1996: 116) were partly instigated because BC groups felt threatened by Dalit slogans.

16 SC settlements are not the only means by which Dalits are unintentionally marginalised. A pervasive rhetoric of 'meritocracy' also denies due recognition to the academic and employment achievements of Dalit youth.

17 Where Dalits own land or are sufficiently numerous to assert themselves, the 'cheri' is not clearly demarcated. Instead, villages tend to be bisected. In Muduvarpatti

and Kosuvangundu – both with 15 miles of Madurai – Dalit houses lie on one side of the road and higher caste houses on the other. In these examples, caste divisions were more permeable but there were still shops and tea stalls that had caste-based clientele.

18 Following Fernandes (1997: 16), such stereotyping – especially when reiterated by poor members of the BCs – highlights how the boundaries of class politics in India can only be fully understood in conjunction with questions of caste and gender.

19 Even local grievances relating to specific incidents are conceived in terms of the 'universality' of cheri / Dalit conditions: 'A huge number of hospitals, schools, colleges, co-operative banks and other "modern" institutions are controlled by thinly veiled caste institutions' (Fernandes and Bhatkal 1999: 5). Dalits feel excluded by this network of caste interests, and bemoan their own lack of organisation.

References

Aitken, R. (1999) 'Localising politics', unpublished PhD thesis, University of Leiden

Alm, B. (1996) 'The state and caste conflicts', in Jeyaram, N. and Saberwal, S. (eds) *Social Conflict*, Oxford: Oxford University Press 113–29

Appadurai, A. (1995) 'The production of locality', in Fardon, R. (ed.), *Counterworks*, London: Routledge

Bensman, J. and Vidich, A. (1995) 'Race, ethnicity and new forms of urban community', in Kasinitz, P. (ed.), *Metropolis: Center and Symbol of Our Times*, New York: New York University Press

Bourdieu, P. (1977) *Outline of a Theory of Practice*, trans. R. Nice, Cambridge: Cambridge University Press

Charsley, S. (1996) '"Untouchable": what's in a name?' 2(1) *Journal of the Royal Anthropological Institute* (N.S.) 1–23

Chowdhry, P. (1998) 'Enforcing cultural codes: gender and violence in northern India', in John, M. and Nair, J. (eds), *A Question of Silence?* London: Zed Books 332–67

Cope, M. (1996) 'Weaving the everyday: identity, space and power in Lawrence, Massachusetts', in 17(2) *Urban Geography* 179–204

Delièrge, R. (1997) *The World of the Untouchables: The Paraiyars of Tamilnadu*, trans. D. Philips, Oxford: Oxford University Press

De Wit, J.W. (1996) *Poverty, Policy and Politics in Madras Slums*, London: Sage Publications

Dickey, S. (1993) *Cinema and the Urban Poor in South India*, Cambridge: Cambridge University Press

Dumont, L. (1980) *Homo Hierarchicus*, second edition, trans. L. Dumont, B. Gulati and M. Sainsbury, Chicago, IL: University of Chicago Press

Escobar, A. (2001) 'Culture sits in places: reflections on globalisation and subaltern strategies of localisation' 20(2) *Political Geography* 139–74

Fernandes, L. (1997) *Producing Workers: The Politics of Gender, Class, and Culture in the Calcutta Jute Mills*, New York: Oxford University Press

Fernandes, L. and Bhatkal, S. (1999) *The Fractured Civilisation*, Mumbai: Bharatiya Janwadi Aghadi

Foucault, M. (1977) *Discipline and Punish*, trans. A. Sheridan, Harmondsworth: Penguin

——(1980) 'Two lectures' in Gordon, C. (ed.), *Power / Knowledge*, London: Harvester Wheatsheaf

Gorringe, H. (2005) *Untouchable Citizens*, New Delhi: Sage Publications

Gupta, A. and Ferguson, J. (1999) 'Beyond "culture": space, identity, and the politics of difference' 7(1) *Cultural Anthropology* 6–23

Jeffrey, C. (2000) 'Democratisation without representation' 19(8) *Political Geography* 1013–36

Kaviraj, S. (1997) 'Filth and the public sphere' 10(1) *Public Culture* 83–113

Lefebvre, H. (1991) *The Production of Space*, Oxford: Blackwell

Ley, D. and Cybriwsky, R. (1974) 'Urban graffiti as territorial markers' 64(4) *Annals of the Association of American Geographers* 491–505

Massey, D. (1994) *Space, Place and Gender*, Cambridge: Polity

Mendelsohn, O. and Vicziany, M. (1998) *The Untouchables*, Cambridge: Cambridge University Press

Mitchell, D. (1995) 'The end of public space? People's park, definitions of the public, and democracy' 85(1) *Annals of the Association of American Geographers* 108–33

——(1996a) 'Introduction: public space and the city' 17(2) *Urban Geography* 127–31

——(1996b) 'Political violence, order and the legal construction of public space' 17(2) *Urban Geography* 152–78

Mitchell, T. (1988) *Colonising Egypt*, Berkeley: University of California Press

Ponnudurai, V. Abraham (1999) 1(1,2) *Thamukku*, The Newsletter of the Dalit Resource Centre Sept-Oct, Nov-Dec, Madurai: TTS

Ravindran, T.K.S. (1999) 'Female autonomy in Tamil Nadu' 34(16,17) *Economic and Political Weekly* 34–44

Ruddick, S. (1996) 'Constructing difference in public spaces' 17(2) *Urban Geography* 132–51

Sharma, U. (1980) 'Purdah and public space', in de Souza, A. (ed.), *Women in Contemporary India and South Asia*, Delhi: Manohar 213–39

Shiri, G. (1998) 'Urban slums: the tragedy of those who sought escape from rural caste-class oppression' 45(1) *Religion and Society* 11–36

Soja, E. (1985) 'The spatiality of social life', in Gregory, D. and Urry, J. (eds), *Social Relations and Spatial Structures*, New York: St. Martin's Press

Subadra (1999) 'Violence against women: wife battering in Chennai' 34(16,17) *Economic and Political Weekly* 28–33

Vincentnathan, S. (1998) 'Caste, politics and the Panchayat' 38(3) *Comparative Studies in Society and History* 484–502

4

LOCAL GOVERNANCE

Politics and neighbourhood activism in Calcutta

Indranil Chakrabarti

This chapter analyses the critical role of neighbourhood organisations in improving the performance of local officials and ensuring better access to basic services in two Calcutta localities. It examines the reasons why in one neighbourhood groups were active in monitoring and supervising the role of local health care officials, whereas in another locality residents remained passive in view of unresponsive local health care officials and poor services, and it highlights the role of historical and political factors in helping to explain this.

Calcutta: a premature metropolis?

Contemporary commentators on Calcutta tend to argue that its diversity, and in particular the heterogeneity of its neighbourhoods, has prevented local inhabitants from acting collectively over issues of local concern, thereby echoing the notion, elucidated by the anthropologist Nirmal Kumar Bose more than 35 years ago, that Calcutta is a 'premature metropolis' (Bose 1965). For Bose, Calcutta did not resemble a melting pot like some other metropolitan areas found around the world, but was strictly residentially segregated along ethnic, linguistic and kin lines. In his view, ethnic groups tended to cluster together in their own quarters and it was assumed that migrants used these affinities to get their first toehold in the local labour market. Crucially, Bose argued that this ethnic exclusiveness prevented people from different ethnic groups from uniting and tackling problems of common concern collectively. Over the years, other social scientists have promoted this view of the city's neighbourhoods and their inhabitants, as reflected in the words of a social historian:

> The labour force, drawn from different provinces, castes and communities, continued to live in the city . . . as isolated social groups with no widespread communication among themselves [. . .] The predominantly rural and migratory character of labour, and

the survival of traditional identities among them, hindered the *growth* of proletarian political consciousness and class solidarity.

(Ray 1979: 51)

Decentralisation and community participation

This view of the urban poor in Calcutta as unable to join together and engage in collective action due to ethnic differences, class and caste divisions is enduring, yet it undermines many of the arguments behind the current enthusiasm for decentralisation. Most notably, it challenges the assumption that residential communities represent consensual and harmonious units, who are ready and willing to act together to exert pressure on local politicians and ensure the accountability of local officials, which has been a key tenet for encouraging greater political and administrative decentralisation in developing countries.

Decentralisation, which is seen by its proponents as a way of reforming the bureaucratic, centralised state to make it more responsive and attuned to local people's needs, has been introduced in a number of developing countries as a way to institutionalise the participation of the poor as a counter to the traditional dominance of elites in policy making. A key assumption is that it will necessarily result in the greater participation of the local 'community' in policy making. Enhanced community participation in decision making and service delivery has been a normative goal of development agencies in the last decade as a way of improving the design and implementation of development programmes. It is also seen by its advocates as a means to empower local people, and thus as an end in itself in the development process (Marsden and Oakley 1990).

The notion of 'community' participation is integral to the success of decentralisation, yet it carries connotations of consensus and homogeneity which in reality communities of residence seldom display. The consensual view hides the actual divisions, differences, inequalities and sectionalism of most such communities. As Wood and Salway have noted with reference to slums in the capital of Bangladesh, Dhaka: 'The poor are not necessarily a "group", nor therefore a unit of social action' (Wood and Salway 2000: 675).

Collective action among working-class communities: a historical perspective

Social historians, such as Hobsbawn and Chandavarkar, have shown that, while divisions and differences were commonplace among the working-class communities and in their neighbourhoods, these were not insuperable to the emergence of collective action. Indeed, both have usefully highlighted the key role that politics and political parties have had in helping to orchestrate this.

Hobsbawn, for instance, argues that workers in Europe in the nineteenth century were not homogeneous and therefore did not represent a coherent social group; he highlights how:

> The unity of all who worked and were poor was brought into the remotest corners of their countries by the agitators and the propagandists ... they also brought organisation, the structured collective action without which the working classes could not exist as a class, and through organisation they acquired that cadre of spokesmen who could articulate the feelings and hopes of men and women who were unable to do so themselves.
>
> (Hobsbawn 1987: 125)

With reference to the working-class mill districts in Bombay, Chandavarkar has shown that, in spite of the cleavages which divided these neighbourhoods along so-called 'primordial ties', it was precisely in these communities that the solidarities of the working classes were also forged:

> It was customarily supposed that it was the caste, kinship and religious loyalties of workers which constituted an insuperable obstacle to the growth of class consciousness [. . .] yet it was precisely within the social organisation of the neighbourhood that the solidarities of collective action were forged and their informing ideologies shaped.
>
> (Chandavarkar 1998: 8)

And he adds that 'Their solidarities were not the natural outcome of popular culture or a reflex of the specific character of production relations, but rather they were politically constituted.' (ibid. 9)

Dover Terrace and Swinhoe Lane: a comparison

The following sections provide an analysis of demographic characteristics and social relations in two Calcutta *bustees* (slums): Swinhoe Lane (SL) *bustee* situated in an area known as Kasba is part of ward 67 of the Calcutta Municipal Corporation (CMC), and Dover Terrace (DT) *bustee* situated in an area known as Garcha, is part of ward 85 of the CMC. Both *bustees* were located in South Calcutta and stood barely three miles apart.

Before proceeding, it should be pointed out that there were remarkable differences in performance of CMC health care officials working in these two neighbourhoods. Whereas in Kasba local health care officials were punctual, attended regularly and appeared motivated, in Garcha local health care officials consistently neglected their duties and absenteeism was pervasive. Over time, evidence emerged of careful monitoring and supervision of local health care officials and targeted popular mobilisation by the residents in Kasba, especially around health 'crises'. By contrast apathy and disinterest towards such matters loomed large among the residents of Garcha.

Local experts such as politicians, social scientists and journalists explained the vigorous activism witnessed in Kasba, and the relative indifference of the inhabitants of Garcha, with reference to the homogeneous nature of Kasba, contrasting this with the heterogeneity of Garcha. Kasba, it was stated, was predominantly inhabited by Bengali-speaking migrants from other parts of West Bengal, most commonly from South 24 Parganas and the erstwhile East Bengal (now Bangladesh), which shared a common language, religion and culture.[1] They would also emphasise the predominance of *bustees* in Kasba as a sign of its distinct working-class identity.

In contrast, they highlighted Garcha's heterogeneity, both in terms of ethnicity and class. 'Hindustanis' – Hindi-speakers from the states Uttar Pradesh and Bihar, Oriya-speakers from Orissa, as well as Bengalis – live in the *bustees* of Garcha, which are surrounded by a significant number of middle-class Bengali residents living in spacious houses or apartments. According to one eminent economist, 'Garcha is a fragmented society [. . .] people are still rooted to their *desh* (home), often outside of Bengal, and associate along lines of ethnicity, rather than in mass-based organisations which cut across social and cultural cleavages.'[2] In the words of a newspaper editor and local resident, Garcha represented 'islands of filth, poverty and degradation surrounded by relative wealth'.

The results of a household survey presented in Table 4.1 conducted in each of the *bustees* suggest that the differences attributed to these two areas were overstated

In both Swinhoe Lane (SL) and Dover Terrace (DT), most respondents gave their place of origin as Bengal, which included those born in Calcutta, although in SL 81% and thus a higher proportion of respondents hailed from the state than in DT, where 63% reported this. DT had a higher proportion of inhabitants claiming non-Bengali origin (34%) than SL (14%).

Table 4.1 Percentage Distribution of Households by Place of Origin

Place of Origin	SL (n = 98)	DT (n = 91)
Calcutta	44%	42%
Rest of West Bengal	37%	21%
Bihar	13%	27%
Orissa	0%	6%
Bangladesh	4%	3%
Other parts of India	1%	0%
Other parts of subcontinent	0%	1%
Don't know	1%	1%

In DT, over one-quarter of respondents stated that they originated from Bihar, twice as many as in SL.

While the figures clearly show that both *bustees* had sizeable Bengali populations and that DT had a higher number of non-Bengalis than SL, they also demonstrate, contrary to the perception of local experts, the relative ethnic heterogeneity of both slums.

Residential patterns

While the survey illustrated that the *bustees* were relatively mixed in terms of their ethnic composition, this section explores residential segregation, which was found to be usually along lines of ethnicity and kin.

DT was divided between a predominantly Hindi-speaking segment, a Bengali-speaking segment and a small Oriya-speaking enclave located in the latter segment. The compounds 11 and 12 DT were almost exclusively Bengali-speaking, with a couple of Hindi-speaking families. The Bengali inhabitants of compounds 11 and 12 hailed from the districts of the centre-south of West Bengal, mainly from South 24 Parganas, with a few originating from what was earlier East Bengal. And in this part of the *bustee* a small number of Christian families lived among the majority of Hindu families. Compound 14 in DT was a self-contained enclave consisting of 15 households occupied exclusively by Oriyas, mainly from Cuttack District. The rooms they occupied were linked together by a narrow passageway that led to a door, which served as both entrance and exit to this residential unit. They lived isolated from the rest of the *bustee* and separated from it by a wall. Compound 14 was male dominated, because the wives and children of its inhabitants stayed in Orissa while the men migrated to Calcutta for work. The inhabitants of this part of the *bustee* did not mix with the rest of the *bustee* and showed no interest or awareness of local issues.

Most of the Hindi-speaking inhabitants of compound 13 came from Dharbangar and Bagalpur, with one household from Madhumani District, also from Bihar. They spoke mainly Magahi, except for those from Dharbangar who spoke pure Maithili. Oral accounts suggest that compound 13 is approximately 80 years old and that the first migrants were mainly *mistris* (masons), who later adopted the surname 'Mistri' in addition to their surname Gupta. A few were weavers, although they used the surname Gupta as well. In fact, apart from three units, every Hindi-speaking household in compound 13 had the surname Gupta. Just as compounds 11 and 12 were predominantly though not exclusively Bengali, so compound 13 was predominantly inhabited by Hindi-speakers.

Settlement patterns along kin ties reinforced the separation between the different ethnic groups. Tenants, who had titles (*thikka*) began by renting ghor (rooms) to kinfolk.[3] Usually, married sons settled in rooms adjacent to their father's household and rooms in the same hutment were rented to their wives' relatives. In this way, all the rooms were occupied by kin. The pattern was broken most often if the landlord had only daughters, in which case custom held that after marriage the daughter should move to live with her in-laws. In this case, although kin were preferred, necessity meant that friends, acquaintances and even those recommended by others were usually renting rooms.

The following is an account of how compound 13 in the DT *bustee* was occupied. It is fairly typical of other accounts of how this slum came to have its current residential characteristics. Bithun Mistri, Mahabir Mistri and Kaila Mistri were three brothers who worked as masons and arrived from Bihar more than 70 years ago. They rented some land and built hutments, which they divided into *ghor*. Kaila married and occupied one such room, where he brought up his four sons and three daughters. After his death, his three unmarried sons lived with their widowed mother in the same room. Two of his daughters, one separated and one unmarried, also shared this room with their mother and their brothers. Next door lived his brother, Mahabir, who had three daughters and one son. Mahabir's son and second daughter each had their own room adjacent to one another, while after he had died Radha, his widow, lived in a converted cattle pen which the three brothers once owned. The other tenants in this hutment appeared to have no kin ties within the *bustee*, most likely because they belonged to different castes; one was a Brahmin, one a Kayasth and one a Kurmi or were Maithili-speakers, who had arrived from different parts of the city after hearing from friends that there were rooms available.

The survey data shows that SL had a predominantly Bengali population, but also consisted of a significant number of Hindi-speaking residents. As with DT, this minority lived in enclaves within the *bustee*, as the following section shows.

SL *bustee* was divided as follows: compounds 51 and 52 were mainly inhabited by Bengalis who had migrated from South 24 Parganas and consisted also of two families from Murshidabad in North Bengal, while compound 53 was predominantly occupied by Hindi-speaking migrants from Bihar and Uttar Pradesh, with a small number of Bengali-speaking tenants.

As in DT, most hutments in SL were occupied by a mixture of kin and unrelated tenants. Kin ties seemed to cut across hutment boundaries, except in the case of compound 52, which was dominated by one family with the surname Sardar, who claimed to be descents of the first settlers in this *bustee*. According to local accounts, the great-grandmother of the present landlord, a woman called Haridasi Sardar, was the first person to settle in this area. Haridasi migrated to SL from the Sunderban area in South Bengal and married a man called Moti Singh, who settled in SL, took on her surname and began to sell the tortoise – a luxury item – in the affluent Gariahat market nearby.

Their daughter, Kalaburi, continued the uxorilocal tradition as her husband also joined her in SL and adopted her surname. Kalaburi had three sons and three daughters all of whom settled in SL after marriage. According to her descendants, Kalaburi's property passed to both her sons and her daughters, which is unusual in mainstream Bengali Hindu society which is strongly patrilineal and patrilocal.

The already significant Sardar clan further consolidated its influence through affinal ties, since many Sardar men – for instance, Kalaburi's grandsons – married girls from the neighbourhood, although residents emphasised that such close marriages were frowned upon. Kin ties thus extended beyond compound 52, enhancing the Sardars' prominent social position in SL. This strategy was grudgingly acknowledged by one resident, who said about the Sardars:

> They're uneducated, and you know I don't think any of them have been to school. And they've married all the girls in the vicinity and had loads of kids. That's all they know, marry the local girls and have lots of children. That's how they've become so powerful.

Social life and worship

While residential segregation along ethnic lines was a prominent feature of these *bustees*, other divisions within as well as between the different ethnic groups also became manifest during my time researching these neighbourhoods.

In DT, the main community spaces were street corners, and it was here that the children played and adults congregated. However, the three main ethnic groups living here did not mix in these public spaces. Even within the homogeneous enclaves, divisions appeared and distrust was common. For example, Hindi-speakers from compound 13 socialised with one another in a public space, but would rarely venture into one another's lanes within the same hutment. Local clubs and societies, which often took the leading role in organising sporting and cultural events, perpetuated this ethnic exclusivity. Hence, whereas compounds 11 and 12 had a youth club close by, this was used *only* by the Bengali male youths, and not by the Hindi-speaking youths from the *bustee*.

Differences among ethnic groups crystallised during times of religious festivals. The Hindi-speaking and Bengali inhabitants of the DT *bustee* organised and celebrated their own religious festivals, in which members of the other communities did not participate. For example, during *Durga Puja*, the most popular Bengali festival, the Bengali residents of the *bustee* erected a *pandal* (tent) and installed an image of the deity in it, for which they had collected donations, but the event was largely ignored by the Hindi-speaking residents of compound 13, who did not perceive this to be 'their' festival despite many having lived in Calcutta for over three generations. On the other hand, during *Chat Puja*, a festival in honour of the Sun popular among communities from Bihar and Uttar Pradesh, which represented the most important festival of the year for the Hindi-speaking residents, the inhabitants of compound 13 were busy preparing themselves weeks in advance, while the inhabitants of the mostly Bengali-speaking compounds did not participate in the activities.

In DT, the different ethnic groups lived, socialised and worshipped separately and there was a palpable animosity between them. Residents of each cluster were suspicious of one another although this rarely descended into open conflict during the period that I spent there. The reason for this enmity was unclear, although it was suggested by older middle-class Bengali residents that it stemmed from the Bengali-speaking groups' sense of superiority over non-Bengali-speaking migrants from Bihar and Orissa, whom they tended to marginalise and look down upon (see also Donner in this volume).

As in DT, communication and interaction between inhabitants of different hutments was rare except in public spaces such as the thoroughfare, and between Hindi-speakers and Bengalis it was almost non-existent. During all the time spent studying the *bustee*, I did not witness a single conversation between the Hindi-speaking women of compound 53 and the Bengali-speaking women from the other parts of the *bustee*.

The divisions between Hindi-speakers and Bengalis first became conspicuous during the construction of a social map, about one month after my arrival in SL. The children of compound 53 were asked to draw a map of their *para* (neighbourhood). The result was a detailed map of their hutment with all the main points of reference – the temple, the tree, the water tap – clearly marked. When asked to describe the picture, the children described it as a map of their *para*, while it was clearly a map of their *bari* (hutment). I tried again, by asking them why certain features were not included. The children replied quite unequivocally that the points of reference that I had mentioned belonged to another *para*, a neighbourhood which was not their own.

Cleavages within the *bustee* were further reinforced during the celebration of religious festivals. While *Durga Puja* was carefully organised and enthusiastically celebrated by the Bengali residents, their Hindi-speaking neighbours, who resided less than ten metres away, ignored the preparations and did not participate. Perhaps most revealing was the fact that Hindi-speaking residents would dampen any enthusiasm their children may have had for participating in the *Durga Puja* festivities by reminding them that this was not 'their *puja*'.

Socio-economic differences

At least equally important were the socio-economic differences between the inhabitants of the *bustees*. These included differences between those with more assets and those with fewer assets, between those with formal education and those without, and the sometimes strained relationships between landlords and tenants. Such differences divided the residents and represented a source of conflict that cut across other important ties.

The predominantly Hindi-speaking young male inhabitants of compound 13 split into groups on the basis of education and occupation. For example, one group consisted of those who had completed secondary education; the other group consisted of those who had completed primary school or had not studied at all.

Whereas members of the first group aspired to clerical or skilled employment – for instance, one of the members of the group was a computer operator and another was a clerk – the members of the second group could at best find a regular job as a driver, but would have settled for manual jobs as masons and mechanics if nothing else was available. Members of this second group, while occasionally successful in securing temporary employment, tended to spend most of their time sitting around and playing cards, or running errands and, eventually, drinking home-made liquor. While the members of the first group were largely unsuccessful in fulfilling their aspirations, they made it a point to criticise the way of life of their less educated neighbours, keeping themselves separate from the rest.

A third group consisted of those who were barely literate but through contacts had acquired secure employment in manual occupations. This small group was keen to disassociate itself from the lifestyle of those of comparable educational status, but who were unemployed. But equally, members of this group chose not to associate with the educated but partially employed. A fourth group consisted of moderately educated men, some of whom had reached class eight, with secure jobs as chauffeurs. Members of this group chose not to associate themselves with any of the other three groups. In view of their higher educational status and regular employment, they had little in common with the second group of unemployed and illiterate men. Driving a car gave them a status, which set them apart from regularly employed manual labourers of the third group. And finally, the fact that they settled for jobs such as driving, rather than waiting for a slightly more lucrative and undeniably higher status clerical job, set them apart from the first group of educated but mostly unemployed men.

Another source of division within the bustee was the pervasive mistrust that existed between landlords and tenants. Landlords would complain that their tenants paid too little rent too infrequently, and this was used as a pretext for not carrying out necessary repairs or improvements for their tenants. Tenants were in turn asked to pay more rent and made responsible for the costs of upkeep and renovation. Landlords would be accused of avarice at the expense of the living conditions of their tenants, and tenants constantly feared that landlords would collude with real estate developers to have them evicted. Although, as registered bustee dwellers, the inhabitants of DT knew they were protected by the law, they feared that at some stage they would be offered money to give up their rights, which if refused would result in forced evictions.[4] Moreover, they suspected that the landlords would receive the lion's share of whatever deal would be made and would therefore gain from any cash inducement that may be offered to lure tenants away.

According to an anthropologist who had worked in the area in the 1970s, these tensions between landlords and tenants were not new.[5] By the time I had come to research this bustee, these tensions had given rise to a considerable level of distrust between the landlords and tenants which, when added to the residential and social segregation of the bustee described earlier, severely undermined any attempts to organise group activities in DT.

In SL, there were noticeable disparities of wealth between inhabitants of different hutments as well as between those living in adjacent rooms in the same hutment. The former caused resentment among the inhabitants of the *bustee*, whereas the latter did not.

Disparities of income and assets were most discernible between two hutments in the *bustee* – between compound 52, which stood out primarily because its inhabitants were more prosperous and could afford to furnish their rooms better, and compound 53 whose households had fewer assets and in some cases did not even have basic amenities such as electricity.

Different levels of affluence could also be seen within hutments; thus, in compound 53, two households were exceptional in terms of their assets and the space they occupied. The first of these belonged to the landlady, and the second to a Bihari Brahmin who was a member of the ruling Communist Party and a representative on the *Bustee* Federation. His place of residence showed clear signs of relative prosperity, including a telephone, its own separate water tap, a kitchen and two bedrooms.

In compound 52, some households were considerably more prosperous than others. The most prosperous households were those which belonged to the landlord and his kin, all of whom used the same surname, Sardar. The men all worked selling fish in local markets, and most ran their own stalls. The few non-kin were visibly less affluent. These included a friend who was invited to live here by the landlord, given a room to occupy and provided with a job selling fish, for which he had been deeply grateful for ever since. In the case of the second non-kin household in compound 52, the landlord employed the youngest son of the family in his fish stall.

There were a number of reasons why these disparities of wealth between households in the same hutment did not cause open resentment between the inhabitants. In compound 52, one reason was the predominance of the landlord's kin group. Kin loyalties proved a powerful bond between the inhabitants of compound 52. Even those inhabitants who were not related to the landlord's family benefited from the livelihood opportunities that he provided, and this resulted in a profound loyalty to him and his kin, which prevailed over material differences that could have been a source of conflict. For the Hindi-speakers of compound 53, the sharing of a common culture, language and ethnicity seemed to provide security which outweighed the potential divisions that differing levels of affluence could have produced. Moreover, the fact that one of their prosperous neighbours was a prominent figure in the local party in power meant that loyalty and allegiance to him carried benefits (access to social goods, security, employment), which almost certainly would not have arrived if antagonisms had been allowed to flourish.

On the other hand, it was precisely the strong local kin ties and privileged access to lucrative employment opportunities which were the source of considerable resentment towards the inhabitants of compound 52 from the rest of the inhabitants of the *bustee*. The inhabitants of compound 52 were the landlord's kin and therefore belonged to the oldest and numerically dominant family in the *bustee*. The male heads of household, and most of their male offspring, worked in the same trade selling fish from their own stalls. Selling fish does not carry a particularly high ritual status in Bengal, but it meant the owners of fish stalls were economically superior to their neighbours.

In addition to their affluence, their monopolisation of ritual life had a divisive impact on the bustee. They controlled the main place of worship in the bustee and organised the most important religious festival, which gave them a heightened social status that was resented by other inhabitants of the neighbourhood. Like anywhere else in the city, the bustee contained a temple dedicated to the goddess of smallpox, Shitala, which occupied a whole room in compound 52, a part of the bustee closely associated with the landlord's family.[6] Consequently, they controlled access to the temple and shared it with those regarded as friends, whereas those regarded as enemies were not allowed to worship there. Allies were given the keys to the *mandir* (temple) and allowed to clean and give offerings (*prasad*), whereas others less favoured had to worship the deity from a distance and were not allowed to leave *prasad*.

This attachment to the Shitala temple provided a platform from which the landlord's family branched out to take the lead in other religious festivals, most notably *Durga Puja*. For the previous seven years, they had collected the 'donations' from the other *bustee* inhabitants, hired the artisans to provide the statues of the goddess and arranged for a *pandal*. Their dominance of ritual life in the *bustee* was a potent symbol of their local power and influence, although it was entirely incongruous with their ritual status, which as fish sellers was low.

Many residents resented how this family co-ordinated the collection of donations, and allegations about the money's eventual destination were rife. Some residents alleged that most of it was channeled into the upkeep of the temple and used for personal consumption, rather than spent on the celebration of the festival. Although donations were meant to be voluntary, non-payment was said to result in quite severe social sanctions, and inhabitants of other parts of the *bustee* stated that those who did not pay were intimidated by the landlord's kin.

While donations were collected from all the inhabitants, the organisation of *Durga Puja* centred around the entrance to compound 52. Rows of chairs were set up but only members of the landlord's kin could be found occupying these. Women members of the landlord's family distributed the food, while the men looked after the technical aspects. *Durga Puja* celebrations resembled a family affair, exclusively for the enjoyment of the landlord and his kin living in compound 52 rather than for the *bustee* as a whole, which reinforced the divisions between the inhabitants of that hutment and the rest of the *bustee*.

Social divisions, along variables like ethnicity, kin ties, prominence in ritual affairs and manifest economic affluence, became apparent at various times during fieldwork. These divisions cut across important social categories such as ethnicity. Therefore, although the *bustee* was relatively homogenous, jealousies, mistrust and resentment over a whole range of issues served to divide the local 'community'. Yet in spite of their differences, local inhabitants were able to act collectively over issues of local concern. As the following episode illustrates, collective action was made possible because solidarities cut across different types of social groups.

At the time of fieldwork, one tube well, a single tap and a pond were the only water sources for the whole *bustee*. But the local population grew and access to water became a real problem for the *bustee* dwellers in the area. After complaints were made to the local councillor by the party member and Bustee Federation representative from compound 53, a water van was sent to the *bustee*. However, a few women managed to control distribution of this water and exclude most of the others, who instead had to walk long distances to fetch water. Eventually, a petition was signed and most of the local women, Bengali- as well as Hindi-speakers, began to lobby the local councillor over several months until another tube well was installed. However, conflicts arose over the exact location of this tube well. The original request was registered in the name of Madan Majumdar, the eldest son of Kalaburi's eldest daughter, that the tube well should be situated in front of his house. Those women who opposed him proposed that it should be placed at a neutral spot at the end of the lane. Eventually, municipal engineers decided that it was best to install it in another corner of the *bustee*, at the end of Swinhoe Lane.

Neighbourhood organisations in Kasba and Garcha

The demographic as well as the ethnographic data from representative *bustees* in each area challenge the widely held perception that Kasba somehow represented more of a 'community' than Garcha. Although apparent that SL was ethnically and linguistically more homogenous than DT, the survey results show that both SL and DT were ethnically quite diverse, and the ethnography of social relations in each of these *bustees* demonstrates that there were social cleavages in SL, just as there were divisions in DT. These were most obvious in the residential clustering of Bengalis and Hindi-speakers into ethnically homogeneous enclaves, but divisions also became apparent throughout social and ritual events. What emerges, therefore, is a much more complex comparative picture of social relations which serves to challenge one of decentralisation theory's key assumptions – namely, that residential communities, or neighbourhoods, represent consensual and harmonious units for collective action. At the same time, the data also questions the opposite view – namely, that the heterogeneity of Calcutta's neighbourhoods prevents their inhabitants from acting collectively over issues of local concern. Cleavages, conflict, divisions and differences between inhabitants characterised social relations in each of the research areas, yet these did not prevent the proliferation of neighbourhood organisations in Kasba, comprising local residents, that applied pressure on officials to perform their roles adequately. In spite of this, political pressure by residents on local officials was a feature of public life in Kasba but not in Garcha. This section of the chapter describes the activities of the neighbourhood organisations in Kasba and suggests some reasons why they were a feature of local governance there and not in Garcha.

Kasba was characterised by having a very vibrant and diverse set of neighbourhood organisations that took an active role in local politics and had a positive influence on the work of local CMC officials; in contrast, Garcha was thought to be a more marginalised place. Although neighbourhood groups did exist in Garcha, their role was more limited and not comparable to those in Kasba. This final section discusses the historical and political factors that contributed to the emergence of these organisations.

There were a number of neighbourhood organisations active in Kasba. Every lane had a party-affiliated neighbourhood committee, which reported to the party's committees at ward level such as the *Nagorik Samiti* (Citizens' Committee), the *Mahila Samiti* (Women's Committee) or the *Jonosastho Samiti* (Health Committee). Representatives of these committees played an active role in monitoring local officials. For instance, the secretary of the Citizens' Committee would accompany the councillor during the regular weekly surgeries. At other times, members of the Citizens' Committee or the Health Committee would come to talk to the doctor in charge of the CMC's health facility. These meetings were impromptu and informal, more resembling an *adda* (chat) than a formal political event, although their purpose was to advise the health officials of emerging risks to public health in the area – for example, a blocked sewage drain or the accumulation of stagnant water with mosquito larvae. With malaria a serious risk in an area like Kasba, the various committees played a crucial role in its prevention through planning adequate measures many months before the monsoon had started. In many instances, they insisted on sanctions against those persistently creating threats to public health. Other local organisations, such as the

Women's Committee, were seen encouraging mothers with young children to participate in vaccination campaigns, and supervising the vaccination camps, and many members were well known for their proactive role in protecting female residents from domestic violence.

This active part of local committees appeared to galvanise local health care officials and had a positive impact on their work. For instance, at the behest of the Health Committee, local health care officials organised a campaign to raise public awareness about malaria, culminating in a conference on malaria prevention and control held in Kasba and attended by local people. Health care officials meticulously noted down their daily activities in a movement register, they maintained a repair book and on some occasions were even seen to work on Sundays. According to the officials, this was done to protect them against accusations of negligence from these neighbourhood organisations. As one of them pointed out, 'This (repair book) is for us to hold up when they come to organise a demonstration against us [. . .] our protection against a *gherao* (mob attack).'

To understand why these neighbourhood organisations were so influential in Kasba, it is important to appreciate the political and historical context within which they emerged. The *Nagorik Samiti*, (Citizens' Committee), in Kasba was established following the visit of a senior Left Front (LF) minister to the area in the wake of a spate of murders and gang warfare.[7] According to newspaper reports, the *Nagorik Samiti* was set up by the parties united in the Left Front, mainly the Communist Party of India (Marxist) (CPI [M]), in response to the situation of lawlessness which presided in Kasba in the late 1970s. During fieldwork, prominent local CPI (M) members reported that, after the Left Front came to power in 1977, the party felt that it needed to be vigilant to the possibility of threats in the local area.

Clearly, the committees remained closely allied with the CPI (M), although their leaders claimed that these organisations were 'independent, autonomous and open to all with no political allegiances'. The organisational structure, norms and ideology of these neighbourhood organisations closely mirrored the wider CPI (M) ideologies, representing a party organised under a system of democratic centralism which expects its cadres to maintain discipline and accept a strict internal hierarchy. The leaders of the different local committees were members of the CPI (M) and saw themselves as responsible to the 'Party' – for instance, they would insist on consulting the local party committee secretary before allowing me to interview them. Similarly, they would never share information about any aspect of their neighbourhood organisation without permission to do so. Regardless of their leaders' claims to the contrary, these neighbourhood committees were part of the front organisations of the Communist Party of India (Marxist).

The fostering of such organisations is widely recognised as the cornerstone of the CPI (M)'s organisational strategy in West Bengal, and their strength and effectiveness in guaranteeing election victories for the CPI (M) in the state have been noted by many political scientists (see Chatterjee 1997). But another important role for these organisations was spelt out by one of the first CPI (M) Members of the Legislative Assembly, who stated: 'We are proposing the setting up of committees everywhere, to observe how officials, including the police are working, and to suggest how they should.'[8]

While ostensibly committed to improving the living conditions of local people, particularly in terms of access to basic services, infrastructure and security, these organisations also provided a link between the party and the people at the grassroots. Kasba's volatile political history meant that the monitoring role of such committees has been crucial, and they were well placed to provide advance warning of potential threats, dissent and opposition to the party's hegemony; in fact, they acted as the CPI (M)'s proverbial finger on the local pulse. Underlying all this was the clear practical need for these mass organisations to generate political support for the CPI (M). If there was a problem at the local level – for instance, a blocked drain or a broken sewage pipe – the network of committees at the grassroots level ensured that these problems were reported to the local councillor and assembly member.

Officials in Kasba complied with the request made by these local organisations and by the local councillor, even though statutorily they were under no obligation to do so, because of their connections with the CPI (M), which nominated the councillor, who was therefore likely to be a powerful political figure. Pressure from these committees was successful because, through their links to the higher echelons of the party, they had the support of the state's political leadership. It was to this political leadership that bureaucratic line managers were ultimately accountable. If local officials did not respond to pressure from below, it could be combined with pressure from the top. Ultimately, it was the former combined with the risk of the latter that proved decisive in influencing the performance of bureaucrats for the better.

Furthermore, the local committees negotiated access to the distribution of social goods that the state controlled for the area as a whole and its inhabitants. The living conditions in Kasba underwent a significant improvement over a period of 15 years during which the area benefited enormously from development-related funding. It was estimated by the local secretary of the Nagorik Samiti that close to Rs 10 crore had been spent in Kasba in that period, mainly on slum improvement, and investment in the area was continuing.[9] For instance, there were plans to build a new sewage and drainage system for an estimated Rs 60 lakh to prevent flooding, which is a perennial problem in this low-lying area.

But access to such 'privileges' came at a price: staunch loyalty and a willingness to dedicate time and resources to the party were expected in return. Those who did not, for whatever reason, place themselves at the disposal of the party leaders, had access only to the most basic of services. A case in point was a neighbouring *bustee* to Swinhoe Lane, where residents reported limited participation in neighbourhood organisations and committees because of a lack of time, and where local services were inadequately provided relative to neighbouring *bustees*; the clearance of rubbish was arbitrary, and during six months health care officials were seen only once.

It has been argued that local organisations in Kasba, like the Citizens' Committee, emerged and gained influence as a result of the 'political opportunity structure' provided by the CPI (M).[10] The CPI (M) helped by ensuring that money for development was spent on the area, which in turn allowed local inhabitants to be rewarded for their loyalty and activism in the form of better living conditions and local public services like health care. In this way, local organisations provided their members with a return on their investment of time and resources by giving them privileged access to the social goods distributed by the state, which in turn fuelled people's willingness to participate in such organisations, a fact that ensured their continued vibrancy.[11] At the same time, sanctions for those who wanted a free ride resulted in parts of Kasba having poor local services.

Whereas in Kasba local officials performed their duties well, in Garcha services were poor and local health care officials performed below par: there were no movement registers or repair book for local inhabitants to inspect, and absenteeism was rife.[12] At the same time, local residents were never seen to mobilise in reaction to this, and in Garcha as a whole there was nothing resembling the activism of neighbourhood organisations seen in Kasba. Garcha had large numbers of *bustee* dwellers living in poor conditions for which access to well-provided local services was vital, and the area was peppered with clubs and associations of different kinds; yet local associations and clubs could not be compared with the network of politically organised and affiliated local organisations in Kasba. It has been argued that the reason for this was that the political and historical factors, which contributed to the emergence of such neighbourhood organisations in Kasba, did not exist in Garcha.

Unlike Kasba, Garcha is a Congress Party bastion, where the Left parties were unable to gain a foothold. Its large non-Bengali population had probably been instrumental in ensuring Congress dominance and, as in other parts of the city, this political alliance has been a phenomenon which the Left has been unable to challenge.[13] Since Independence, the Congress Party has pursued a different strategy at the local level in West Bengal than the Left Front. Rather than operate through broad-based mass organisations belonging to the sphere of 'civil society', the type seen in Kasba, Congress's preferred approach was to build a 'political machine' around a posse of key leaders who were career-orientated rather than driven by ideological principles.[14] The machine provided an efficient system of spoils directed towards the rural gentry and urban business communities, who were permitted to evade government laws and restrictions so as to pursue their own interests in return for financial support. It also gave rise to an extensive system of patronage to the poor and the promotion of avenues for social mobility for local leaders.[15]

Essentially conservative and conflict-averse, the Congress machine avoided bringing about any far-reaching social change through social upheaval. Instead, it worked through men who were 'influential in the social structure of their localities and can sway a needed portion of the electorate by particularistic appeals' (Franda 1971a: 99). This became the *modus operandi* of Congress in the state, justified by the need to prevent 'the rule of the mob', which they believed would ensue if the Communists came to power.

Although later attempts were made to pursue a wider support base through mass organisations like the *Chattro Parishad* (Youth Wing) or the *Mahila Mandals* (Women's Sections), factionalism and poor leadership depleted their strength. Whatever mass organisations may have existed in Garcha had disappeared in a maelstrom of allegations about corruption and malpractices, and local leaders showed no interest in replacing them. Instead, the peddling of patronage and perks by the candidates through a handful of locally influential *mastaans* (leaders) remained the cornerstone of Congress organisation in Garcha. This strategy was apparent in the CMC elections in 2000, when a prominent Congress assembly member admitted 'Congress is not strong in mass organisations, it is not in the ethos [. . .] Congress organisation depends on individual councilors – we believe that you can't beat the personal touch, the CPI(M) organisation is too mechanical and it lacks the personal touch.'[16]

Unsurprisingly, given the missing organisational strength of the Congress Party in West Bengal as a whole, Garcha lacked grassroots organisations that monitored local issues or represented local people's needs, and linked slum dwellers with the locally dominant political party. Instead, local politics in the *bustees* of Garcha was organised around prominent local leaders, referred to as *dadas* (elder brothers) or *mastaans*, and a pervasive system of patronage thrived. In Dover Terrace *bustee*, the *mastaan* was both respected and feared, and therein lay his power and influence. He was respected due to his role as guardian and benefactor who would, for example, provide income-earning opportunities for local youth through his illegal activities and shady connections. He was also considered to 'protect' the *bustee* from the unwanted attention of others, both criminals and police, and residents trusted his ability to protect them because of his past as a violent and ruthless *dacoit* (bandit). But this reputation invoked, paradoxically, both a sense of fear and of security. He was feared by his neighbours, although they were also reassured by the fact that his very reputation would prevent outsiders from 'messing with' anyone in their neighbourhood, and his clients assumed he never mistreated 'his own'.

This *mastaan* was not the typical patron in a traditional dyadic patron-client relationship. He needed the protection of the local councillor and the police to continue unperturbed with his illegal business. In return for this, he was expected to provide money and, perhaps just as importantly, guarantee the loyalty and passivity of *bustee* dwellers, who had to provide their votes. In this locality, a classic triadic relationship existed, in which the patron became a broker, an intermediary between client and higher official. In triadic patron-client networks, each person is only directly related to the one above them, and has no linkage with those above his superior. A patron must be able to interact with followers, which thus limits the number of followers that he has. Clients may often have to compete with one another for resources controlled by the party.

Except for the very top and the very bottom, the relationship is wracked with competition. Peers compete with one another for the allegiance of followers, and for the limited resources of superiors (Grindle 1977).

In Garcha as elsewhere, the patron was under pressure to gain rewards for his clients or risk their transferring their loyalties elsewhere, and the clients were constrained in their capacity to seek redress, protest or complain to ensure better service from higher officials. Clients could break out of this constraint by leaving the relationship, but by doing so risked threatening what little access they had to goods and services. Unsurprisingly, alliance was the favoured path, a phenomenon that has been described as 'inverse incorporation', defined as 'incorporation into vertical patron-client relations for the purposes of having basic needs addressed' (Wood 1998: 19). Wood has argued that the urban poor will often engage in such structures because they help them to satisfy their immediate needs, even though it means fore-going their rights as citizens of a modern liberal democracy (ibid.). In practical terms, it means that the urban poor will tend to attach themselves to a patron, and will not, for example, attempt to hold bureaucrats and politicians directly accountable.

Conclusion

The chapter began with the view popular among many who have written and commented on Calcutta's political and social development, that the city's heterogeneity – particularly the ethnic and linguistic differences among inhabitants of the same neighbourhoods, led to a form of social, labour and residential segregation, which prevents collective action. I then proceeded to contrast this with the approach that favours decentralisation as a means to incorporate into the development process the 'lower strata' or the urban poor, who are assumed to be represented by consensual and harmonious residential groups, which are in turn able to bond and exert pressure on local government.

Based on evidence from fieldwork in two Calcutta *bustees*, the chapter has argued that neither of these assumptions sheds any light on how pressure by representatives of neighbourhood organisations in one locality helped to ensure that local officials were responsive and performed their duties relatively well. A detailed description of social relations in the two *bustees* showed that the inhabitants were far from representing units of social action. Neither consensual nor harmonious, the *bustees* were characterised by divisions: residential segregation on account of ethnicity and language as well as jealousy and rivalry on account of economic differences and kin loyalties. Conflict-inducing fault lines emerged which cut across some of these categories, and solidarities which bridged these boundaries emerged where issues of common concern were at stake.

What the chapter has tried to show is that collective action was a feature in one of the research sites because of a configuration of historical and political factors, and because of the decisive role played by a political party that has dominated the state government since 1977 (see also Gorringe in this volume). The CPI (M) for practical and ideological reasons encouraged the proliferation of mass front organisations in Kasba and these were successful in mobilising the residents to exert pressure on local municipality officials to perform their roles appropriately so that local services were provided. By contrast, Garcha was dominated by a political party that had eschewed the creation of an organisational network at the grassroots, preferring instead to rely on local thugs and those who were socially influential to secure support and contain dissent in a triadic system of patron-client relationships. There were no active neighbourhood organisations, basic services were poor and the performance of local officials was indifferent. The critical variable, therefore, to explain the proliferation of neighbourhood organisations that represented the needs of local residents and took an active role in local governance was neither ethnicity nor class, nor on account of decentralised local government, but politics. Echoing the findings of social historians such as Hobsbawn (1987) and Chandavarkar (1981, 1998), I have argued in this chapter that a left-wing political party, the CPI (M), had a decisive role in encouraging the disparate inhabitants of a poor Calcutta neighbourhood to participate in local organisations and to demand better services and more responsive local officials.

Acknowledgements

Fieldwork was carried out as part of my PhD thesis at the London School of Economics (LSE) between September 1999 and October 2000; I am grateful to the Department for International Development (DFID) for their financial support. I would like to express my special thanks to Henrike Donner and Geert De Neve for their constant encouragement and helpful comments, which have helped me to complete this chapter. Thanks also for the input by participants at the workshop, 'The meaning of the local: revisiting the urban neighbourhood in India', held at the LSE in May 2001, where an earlier version of this chapter was first presented. The usual disclaimers apply with regard to all errors and omissions.

Notes

1 South 24 Parganas is a rural district south of Calcutta.
2 Interview with Professor Biplab Dasgupta MP, 30 June 2000.
3 Calcutta *bustees* have traditionally been organised on a three-tier tenancy system, known as *thikka* tenancy. Originally, Zamindars rented their land to *thikka* tenants who built hutments on the land and subdivided them into rooms. The *thikka* tenants have since become the de facto landlords (*bariwalla*), though not owners of the land, and rent out to tenants.
4 The law referred to here is the *Thikka* Tenancy Act (1981), which was an attempt by the state to gain control of land to be able more effectively to upgrade *bustees*. Landlords were permitted to convert their properties into multi-storey buildings to accommodate more tenants, and landowners were compensated for the loss of their income. It is beyond the scope of this chapter to discuss the impact of these changes, but see Ghosh (1992).
5 Dixit Sinha, personal communication, March 2000. Further evidence of this is provided in Sinha (1972).
6 It is traditional among farming castes in southern Bengal to worship Shitala, the goddess of smallpox, as a way to ward off illnesses. Many of the present-day inhabitants of Swinhoe Lane had surnames like Halder, Mondal and Das, which suggested they belonged to these castes. This may explain why the Shitala temple was an important place of worship for the residents of this *bustee*.
7 The Statesman, 24 November 1977. The Left Front (LF) is the name assumed by the Left-wing coalition of parties that have governed West Bengal since 1977. The largest party in the LF is the Communist Party of India (Marxist), or CPI (M).
8 Prabir Kumar Sengupta, Member of the Legislative Assembly for Bansberia in Hoogly District in Sengupta (Sengupta 1979: 28)
9 1 crore equals 10 million Rupies; 1 lakh equals 100,000 Rupies.
10 According to Brockett, who coined this term, political opportunity structure represents 'the configuration of political forces in a group's political environment that influences that group's assertion of its political aims' (Brockett 1991: 254).
11 Baiocchi reported that in Porto Alegre the poor participated in associations if they saw returns on their investment of time and resources (Baiocchi 2000).
12 The contrast in the performance of local health care officials in the two areas was illustrated by the fact that Garcha was a focal point for the malignant malaria 'epidemic' in the last months of 1999, but in Kasba, a low-lying flood-prone area, infection rates were much lower.
13 This allegiance was discussed by Ashraf (Ashraf 1970: 60) and reaffirmed in personal communication with Professor Saugata Roy, a Congress Member of the Legislative Assembly.
14 Franda (1971b: 89–108) has applied Banfield's definition of a 'political machine' as 'a party organisation held together and motivated by desire for personal gain rather than political principle or ideology' (Banfield 1961: 132) to the Congress Party in West Bengal.
15 See Franda (Franda 1971a) and Chatterji (Chatterji 1985: 31–61)
16 Interview with Professor Saugata Roy, a Congress Member of the Legislative Assembly, 30 September 2000.

References

Ashraf, A. (1970) 'Politics of urban Development: the Case of Calcutta', Unpublished PhD thesis, Ithaca, NY: Cornell University

Baiochhi, G. (2000) 'Transforming the city: political practices, civil society and participatory governance in Porto Alegre, Brazil', Mimeograph. Madison: Department of Sociology, University of Wisconsin-Madison.

Banfield, E. (1961) *Political Influence*, New York: Free Press

Bose, N.K. (1965) 'Calcutta: a premature Metropolis' 213(3) *Scientific American*, Special Issue 'Cities', September, 90–105

Brockett, C.D. (1991) 'The Structure of political Opportunities and Peasant Mobilisation in Central America' 23(1) *Comparative Politics* 24–46

Chatterjee, P. (1997) *The Present History of West Bengal*, Delhi: Oxford University Press

Chatterji, R. (ed) (1985) *Politics in West Bengal: Institutions, Processes and Problems*, Calcutta: The World Press Private Limited

Chandavarkar, R. (1981) 'Workers Politics in the Mill-Districts of Bombay between the Wars' 15(3) *Modern Asian Studies* 603–7

——(1998) *Imperial Power and Popular Politics: Class, Resistance and the State in India c. 1850-1950*, Cambridge: Cambridge University Press

——(1999) 'Questions of class: the general strikes in Bombay', in Parry, J.P, Breman, J. and Kapadia, K. (eds) *The Worlds of Indian Industrial Labour*, London: Sage Publications 205–39

Franda, M.F. (1971a) *Radical Politics in West Bengal*, Cambridge: MIT Press

——(1971b) *Political Development and Political Decay in Bengal*, Calcutta: Firma K.L. Mukhopadhay

Ghosh, B. (2000) 'Panchayati Raj: Evolution of the Concept' 25 *ISS Occasional Paper Series*, New Delhi: Institute of Social Sciences

Ghosh, S. (1992) *Thikka Tenancy in Bustees of Calcutta*, Calcutta: Centre for Urban Economic Studies

Grindle, M.S. (1977) *Bureaucrats, Peasants and Politics in Mexico: A Case Study in Public Policy*, Berkeley, CA: University of California Press

Hobsbawn, E. (1987) *The Age of Empire*, London: Weidenfeld and Nicolson

Marsden, D. and Oakley, P. (1990) *Evaluating Social Development Projects*, Oxford: Oxfam.

Ray, R. (1979) *Urban Roots of Indian Nationalism: Pressure Groups and Conflicts of Interest in Calcutta City Politics, 1875-1939*, New Delhi: Vikas

Sinha, D. (1972) 'Life in a Calcutta Slum', in Sinha, S. (ed) *Cultural Profile of Calcutta*, Calcutta: Indian Anthropological Society

Sengupta, B. (1979) *CPI (M): Promises, Prospects and Problems*, New Delhi: Young Asia Publications

Wood, G.D. (1998) 'Investing in Networks: Livelihoods and social Capital in Dhaka Slums' Mimeograph. Bath: Centre for Development Studies, University of Bath

Wood, G.D. and Salway, S. (2000) 'Policy arena introduction: securing livelihoods in Dhaka slums' 12(5) *Journal of International Development* 669–88

Wright, S. and Nelson, N. (eds) (1995) *Power and Participatory Development: Theory and Practice*, London: Intermediate Technology Publications

5

TEMPLES AND CHARITY

The neighbourhood styles of the Komati and
Beeri Chettiar merchants of Madras City

Mattison Mines

This chapter examines how the great merchant traders of Madras City have contributed to the form and manner in which the City has developed, describing this development as changing arguments that remain expressed in the built landscape. By 'argument', I mean a public presentation that is made to others with an aim to convince and to persuade, and which may lead to conflict on occasion. My interest is to demonstrate how the present-day urban landscape continues to express tracings of these past arguments of its earlier inhabitants, just as present-day residents are re-inscribing their meanings, purposes and debates on the spatial face of the City today. The City, then, can be read as a palimpsest. I take as my principle subjects two wealthy and influential merchant castes whose members played important economic and social roles in the City from its inception, the Beeri Chettiars and the Komatis, the latter a caste closely allied to the Balija Naidus, also a merchant caste. My aim is to demonstrate how and why these two communities, together with their allies, constructed their neighbourhoods in quite different manners, expressing their contrasting integration into south Indian society and the changing authority of British rule. Prior to Independence, these two systems of meaning – social integration and British authority – framed public understanding of urban spaces and standards of estimation of public presentations of identity and esteem. Since Independence, the political economy of the City has changed dramatically as have also uses of urban space. Yet the legacy of earlier times continues to underlie the developing urban landscape and to influence social relationships.

The English East India Company established itself at Madraspatnam[1] (Madras Place) as a favourable location for trade in 1639. The presence of the English traders quickly attracted Beeri Chettiars, the pre-eminent trading caste of the Tamil north, who were members of the left-hand section of south Indian castes, and Komatis, a premier Telugu-speaking trading caste, who were members of the right-hand section of castes.[2] This right-hand / left-hand divide was a central feature of caste organisation in south India and of the developing Black Town, or 'Petta', and rivalry between the two principal merchant castes left an imprint on the landscape of the old Town that persists to this day. Over time, these two premier trading castes appear to have been more-or-less equal competitors in trade, but the two communities had different public styles and were differently integrated into the broader society of the Coromandel Coast and of the Indian states that surrounded Madraspatnam. Both castes also played roles in the governance of Madras, but did so differently, reflecting their contrasting organisational styles and locations in society. In the City, the Beeri Chettiars portrayed themselves as a kingly caste; the Komatis, by contrast, affected the style of *karmayoga*, correct action expressed as piety and charity.

In addition to the right-hand / left-hand caste distinction, underlying the evolving social morphology of early Madras are three discernible interrelated social configurations that framed the polity of Madras during the seventeenth and eighteenth centuries and helped define social meanings. First is the nature of the English East India Company itself, that its primary purpose in Madras was to trade, not to administer, and that Indian trade always depended on Indian brokers or *dubashes* (lit. two-languages, a person who knew English and Indian languages). Second is the participation of castes in Madras civil governance and the use of caste-controlled kingly temples as political institutions. And, third, are the English and Indian customs of using processions to express publicly the rank and authority of individuals. Each of these configurations influenced the manner in which early Madras took shape.

During the first two centuries of Company administration, the actual number of covenanted servants of the East India Company resident in Madras remained small. In 1652, they numbered 10; in 1654, 7; in 1699, 30 (Love 1913, vol. I: 106–7, 117; Wheeler 1990, vol. I: 268). Even as late as 1800, there were no more than a few hundred persons, British and Indian, 'of the better sort' resident in Madras (Dodwell 1926: 125). There are two obvious consequences of these numbers. First, to engage in trade the Company depended on Indian systems of production and trade, which the Company servants accessed through Indian *dubashes* whom they appointed to represent the Company's interests and their own private interests. This system of brokered trade entwined the lives and interests of Indians and English alike. Second, the Company government was too small and too weak to govern the Town directly, and, consequently, the Company depended on the co-operation of Indians to govern themselves, holding caste leaders directly responsible for the behaviour of their caste fellows. A corollary to this was that the Company recognised caste leaders as having the authority to settle affairs among their caste fellows, and it was Company policy to allow them to do so until the end of the eighteenth century. Not surprisingly, there was considerable overlap between Company government, brokered trade and caste governance, and it was common for important caste leaders to serve as *dubashes* to the Company and to individual Company servants as well.

Caste leaders met in councils when administration of caste affairs was the concern. They typically held their meetings at a community *mandabam* or covered platform, commonly associated with a kingly temple or caste monastery that had been endowed by the pre-eminent headmen of the caste, who served as temple trustees, or managers. Temples, then, doubled as political institutions for the caste leadership and the governing councils that endowed and controlled them. But not every caste built or endowed such temples. As we shall see, each of the important left-hand castes does appear to have built or endowed temples associated with the exclusive administration of its own affairs. But the temples of the right-hand castes appear to have been built primarily by high-ranking Balija Naidus, who were powerful brokers, and by agrarian-based landowning castes, initially for the joint use of all castes, right-hand and left-hand, reflecting the political hegemony of the right-hand castes in the petty principalities surrounding Madras. Tapping into this political reality, the Company initially drew its Indian brokers from among these politically powerful castes. Thus the first Town Pagoda was endowed in 1640 by the Chief Merchant of the Company, Thimmappa, a Balija Naidu, who in his role as broker to the Company founded the original Black Town and invited caste communities to settle there (see Map 5.1). Town meetings involving leaders from both sections were held at this temple (see Muthiah 1999: 318–19). The many grand kingly temples that exist in present-day George Town, the old central core of Madras, are a legacy of this past governance, as is also the fact that the majority of these temples are almost forgotten: little used today because they no longer serve political functions and because residents have moved away.

Public processions, the third characteristic of the social configuration of the early city, were important ways in which the eminence and authority of individual leaders were expressed and argued publicly. There were two broad kinds of processions: one secular, the other ritual. Secular processions were those that publicly presented the wealth and political eminence of an individual and which sometimes involved signs of office. During the early centuries, when a man of importance went out, he would proceed with a considerable train of retainers, making an eminent figure hard to miss. The English followed this practice, too. Thomas Salmon (1744: 232), who lived in Madras between 1699 and 1704, describes how when the Governor would go out, he would be carried in a palanquin shielded from the sun by umbrellas borne by retainers walking alongside and preceded by singing girls, country music, drummers and armed guards (Mines 2001: 37n). Indian processions were also quite elaborate, specifying distinct flags for different castes, lighted torches and other signs of rank in addition to the country music and female 'choristers'.

Ritual processions were and are of two types: temple processions, which were a kind of royal procession similar to secular processions, and pilgrimage

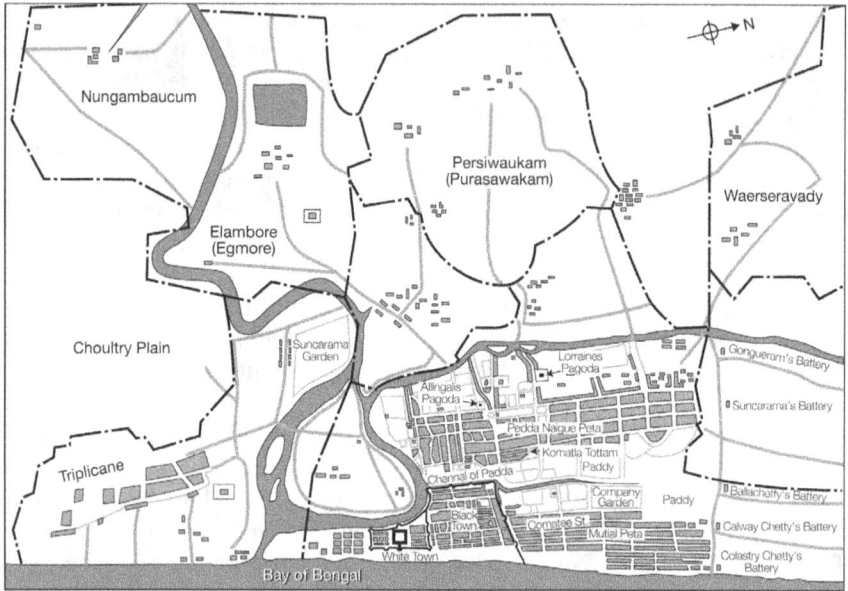

Map 5.1 Madras in 1733 (based on Subrahmanya Aiyar's 1902 enlargement of Talboys Wheeler's map)

processions. Temple processions, which occurred during temple festivals, were used to circumscribe the core area of a temple's territory, often the core area of a caste neighbourhood that included the residential streets of the most important families, who were singled out with ritual honours during the procession. Some temples also had special processional routes that linked the temple's god and the sponsors of the procession to more distant ritual locations, a kind of temple pilgrimage procession. During processions, the managing trustee of a temple occupied a place close to the icon where he enacted a kingly role, including distributing ritual honours to others along the processional route and receiving the respect and regard of those who observed him. Like secular processions, temple processions were important public presentations of eminence and authority, as they are today (Mines 1994: 69–71).

To these three social configurations that defined the political economy of Madras social practices, we add the right-hand / left-hand caste distinction. If one considers the British as a primary factor framing the organisation, uses and meanings of Madras social topography, then the left-hand / right-hand caste division is another key factor framing social meanings that historically was inscribed within this British urban mapping. Let me first describe how this moiety opposition of castes expressed itself in the process of City development. I shall then describe the caste morphology of the two divisions and sketch the roles the castes of the two divisions played in the governance of

George Town sociality. I shall then show how the neighbourhood topography of the great trading castes belonging to these moieties today still expresses their former roles and quite different positions in this urban sociality.

George Town, 1652–1800: Phase 1

Today, as a twenty-first century observer, if one walks the streets of George Town, the Petta, what one sees is the physical imprint of what historically were the social dynamics of the right-hand / left-hand distinction. The locations of temples, the layout of streets, of residential patterns, of formal and colloquial street names, all are the remnants of long-past arguments. And arguments they were indeed! Almost from the Town's inception, the peace of the Petta was disrupted by periodic riots between the two moieties. The first riots occurred in 1652, just ten years after the inauguration of Fort St. George, and resulted in the original Black Town (Map 5.1) being segregated into two residential zones, one the locality and streets of the right-hand castes, Pedda Naickenpet, and one the domain of the left-hand castes, Muthialpet. The underlying cause of this early riot had to do with struggles for control of trade with the British (Mines 1992, 1994; Brimnes 1999). But this and later riots also had to do with the authority these castes claimed to govern their members and to regulate social space in the Town and in the surrounding polities.

In 1652, as the then Agent of the English Company was embarking to return to England for a spell, he inadvertently triggered the first riots when he publicly expressed his favour of the left-hand traders by stating promises of future preference and by giving symbolic gifts of honour to leading members of the Beeri Chettiars, even while he refused to accept the gifts of the right-hand castes, who until then had held hegemonic control of trade with the Company. Standing ignored on the beach, the right-hand traders, led by the Balijas, were enraged. Running back to the Town, they raised members of the right-hand to attack their competitors of the left-hand section. In the riots that followed, ears were cut off and property was plundered and destroyed. The Balijas instigated the riots in order to disrupt commerce, hoping to bring Company disapproval upon the departing Agent and his Beeri Chettiar allies. In this manner, the right-hand castes designed to re-establish their own hegemonic control of trade and relations of production, and to reassert their right to ritual precedence that marked their claim to pre-eminence and authority within the Town.

After 1652, major riots again broke out in 1707, for similar reasons of control and precedence, this time with Sunca Rama, the young headman of the Komati caste, playing a prominent role. Riots between the two moieties occurred frequently throughout the rest of the eighteenth century. But the 1707 riots were a major disruption, lasting well into 1708. To invoke a settlement, the Company again separated the Town, which had again become mixed, into two residential divisions. This new segregation largely recognised the principal localities in which the members of the two caste sections resided and had built their institutions, and key determinants of this division were temples and the temple processional streets controlled by the two moieties.

The 1707–8 settlement remains the organisational foundation of George Town to this day (see Map 5.3). The informal dividing line shown in the 1733 and 1755 maps (Maps 5.1 and 5.2) is a water channel that runs north-south (right-left on these eighteenth-century maps) between the two moieties, and was covered by a broad road at the end of the century named Popham's Broadway. The principal locality of the left-hand castes is Muthialpet, the area east of this north-south divide, and Pedda Naickenpet to its west remains the chief area of the right-hand castes. The 1733 map also shows that the Komatis occupied the western-most street of Muthialpet, described as 'Comatee Street'. Today, what likely is a portion of this street still bears the name Sunkurama Street after the Komati, Sunca Rama, who was headman at the time of the 1707–08 riots. With this exception, following the settlement, the Balijas Naidus and the Komati Chettiars lived predominantly in Pedda Naickenpet with their right-hand associates to the west, while the Beeri Chettiars lived to the east with other left-hand castes in Muthialpet. In Conradi's 1755 map of Madras, one sees two large temple complexes symmetrically mirroring one another, one located in the heart of Muthialpet, the other in Pedda Naickenpet.

The main left-hand castes of Madras City were three: the Beeri Chettiars, the Panchalars or Acharis, a fivefold caste of artisans (the goldsmiths, blacksmiths, braziers, carpenters and stone carvers), and the Tamil weavers, the Kaikkoolars. Of these, the Beeri Chettiars were the wealthiest and most

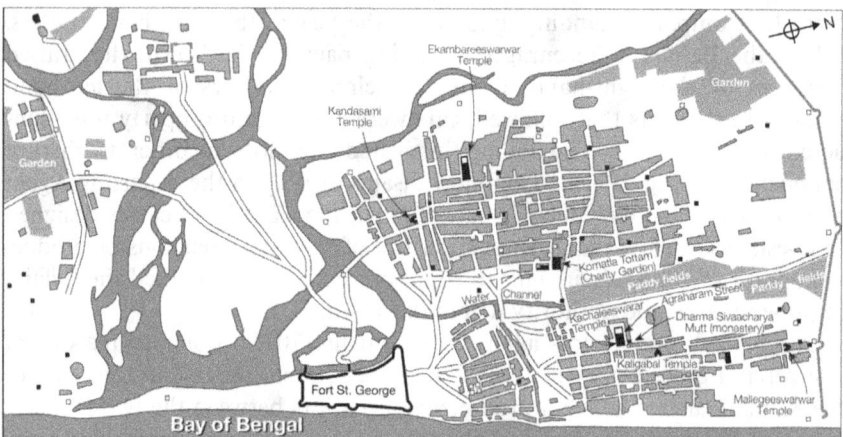

Map 5.2 Madras in 1755 (based on *A Plan of Fort St. George and The Bounds of Madraspatnam* by F.L. Conradi)

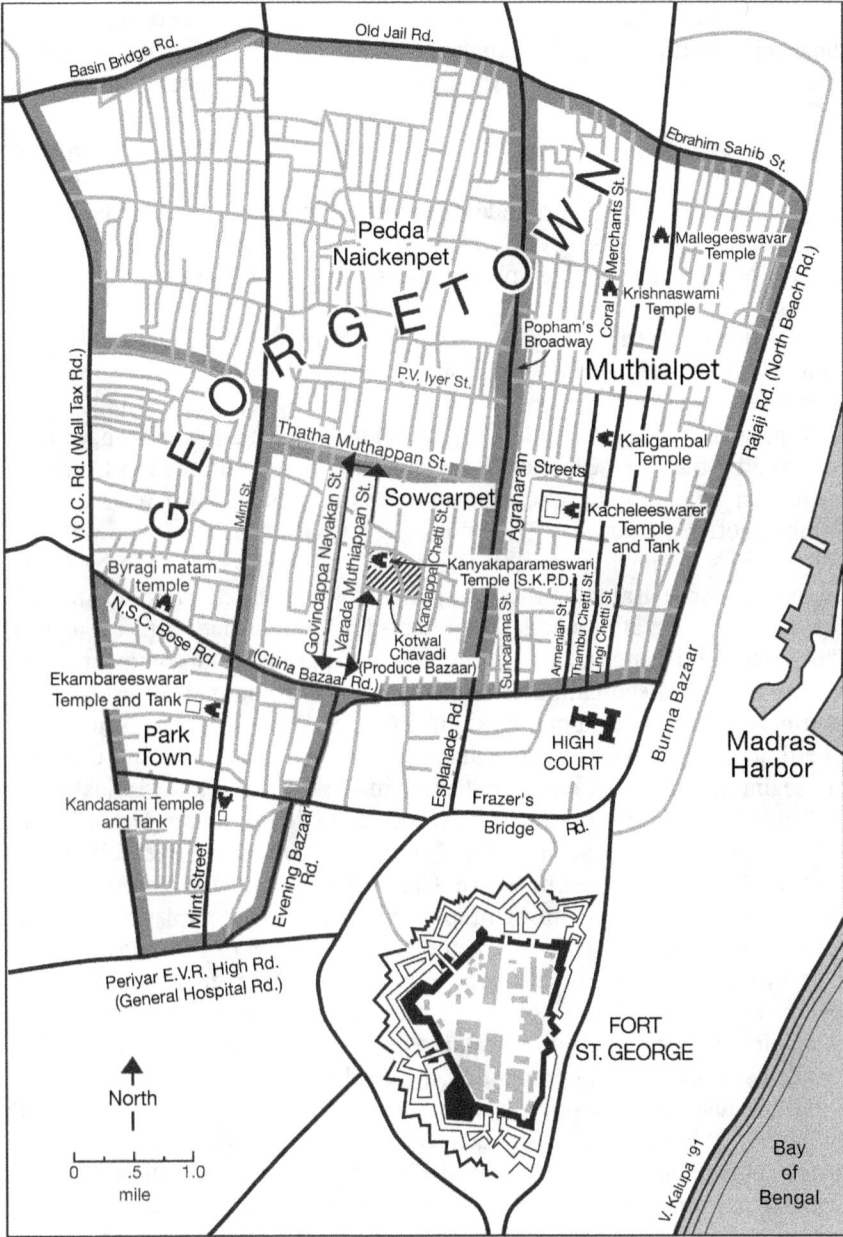

Map 5.3 George Town and Fort St. George, Madras City, c. 2000

powerful. The Acharis also lived in Muthialpet, but they were poorer than the Beeri Chettiars and the daughters of some Achari families worked as servants in Beeri Chettiar homes, a mark of subordinate status. The Kaikkoolar weavers resided largely outside Black Town because weaving required open space for them to stretch warps. One of the things apparent about this list of left-hand castes is that it does not represent an integrated caste hierarchy, and, indeed, relationships among these castes were attenuated while each styled itself as a dominant caste and claimed control of its own kingly temples as a feature of its management of its own affairs.

The Beeri Chettiars began endowing temples and serving as trustees almost from the Town's inception. They built their first temple, the Kalahasteswarar temple on Coral Merchant Street in the 1640s. The Mallegeswarar temple ('Mally Carjun's Old Pagoda') appears to have been endowed by the Beeri Chettiars a bit later; it is first mentioned in Company records in 1652. In the mid-eighteenth century, the British refer to it as Tambi Chetti's pagoda, after a famous Beeri Chetti headman, who was then the temple's managing trustee (Love 1913, vol. II: 41). Tambi Chetti succeeded Sunca Rama as the Company's sole merchant in 1731, and it is probably this man after whom the present-day Tambi Chetti Street is named. This street and Lingi Chetti Street, running parallel and commemorating another famous headman, are residential streets in the main Beeri Chettiar Muthialpet neighbourhood. Next, in 1673, a Beeri Chettiar, Velur Mari Chetti, and his Achari friend, Kandappa Achari, established and endowed the beginnings of the Kandasami temple in Park Town. This area just south of Pedda Naickenpet appears to have been a smaller outlying Beeri Chettiar neighbourhood. The Kachaleswarar temple on Armenian Street followed in 1725, built on land owned by Kalvai Chetti. Temple construction typically is an ongoing process and through the centuries all these temples have undergone renovations and additions, including the addition of *raja gopurams*, the majestic entrance towers that today grace each of these temples. In the eighteenth century, the Beeri Chettiars developed the Kachaleswarar temple and its adjoining streets as their central institutional complex in Muthialpet. The temple itself was and is bordered on three sides by *agraharam* streets, which house the residences of priestly Brahmans, and on one of these is the caste monastery, the *Abanatha Dharma Siva Acharya MaDam*, once home to the caste's celibate guru or religious head. The *MaDam* was also where the Beeri Chettiar caste headmen met to administer caste affairs as a collegial body known as the *Periyagramam*. Together these institutions, the Kachaleswarar temple complex, including MaDam and Periyagramam, and the other temples formed an institutional galactic polity of the Beeri Chettiar caste within the Town. The temple trustees and the headmen administered the main assets owned collectively by the Beeri Chettiars as a community, and the Periyagramam with the ritual blessing of the caste guru administered caste affairs according to religion and custom, although not without contest from time to time (Mines 1994).

The Acharis also early endowed and administered the Kaligambal temple, located on Tambi Chetti Street, as an institution of their caste gover-nance. Reflecting the alliance between the Beeri Chettiars and the Acharis, during the Kandasami temple Spring Festival (*Vasantha uthsavam*) the idol of Kandasami is joined by the idol of Kaligambal to float on a raft in the Kachaleswarar temple tank, there to pay their respects to the god-king Kachaleswarar (Mines 1994: 75). In this way, the Achari caste is symboli-cally linked by royal procession and ritual to the Beeri Chettiar temple polity. In contrast to these two castes, as previously noted, the Kaikkoolar weavers resided primarily outside George Town. It is unknown what their early organisation was, but by 1800 it appears the localities were interlinked by a network of councils known as *naaDu*, and each naaDu council held meetings at an associated Saivite temple. Chennapatinam (Black Town), Tiruvellikeni (Triplicane) and Elambur (Egmore) were part of this Kaikkoolar naaDu council system (fieldnotes 1984).

The archival evidence suggests that in the eighteenth century the right-hand castes and their Brahman allies were the politically and economically dominant castes in the states adjoining Madras. In the Petta, these castes were: (1) kingly Brahmans who, with ties to both Indian polities and the English, were interpreters of Hindu law, estate managers to large landowners, and *dubashes* between the British and Indian polities as well as between the networks of production and trade; (2) Vellaalas, who were the landed gentry of the district surrounding Madras and also *dubashes* to the English; (3) Balija Naidus, traders and *dubashes*, who were wealthy landowners and merchants in the surrounding countryside as well, and the (4) Komati Chettiars, also merchants and *dubashes*, who were the pre-eminent right-hand merchant community associated with the Telugu states that controlled the region from south to north when the English East India Company settled on the Coromandel Coast. This, then, was the section of castes asso-ciated with agrarian-based, stately power, and they were the benefactors and generators of agricultural and commercial wealth for these kingly states, as they were for the Honourable English East India Company (Subrahmanyam 2001: 135ff). At the bottom of this hierarchy were the Parayans, a large caste of agricultural labourers who were poor dependents of the Vellaalas. They formed the right-hand castes' informal militia during riots.

How then was this right-hand caste hierarchy personified in Madras? The *Sarva-Deva-Vilasa*, an anonymous Sanskrit text written sometime during the last decade of the eighteenth century, offers a valuable description of the courtly lifestyle of some of the leading men of these high-ranking castes, whom we know played central roles enacting the order of Madras society at the time. The text describes these men as the leading aristocrats of Madras, and in fact V. Raghavan, the modern compiler of the text, is able to correlate several with persons who appear in the Company records (Raghavan 1957–58). Prominent among these aristocrats are wealthy landowning Vellaalas and their kingly Brahman associates. All the aristocrats belonging to these two castes are portrayed as temple trustees, *dharmakarttaar*, and as wealthy patrons of the arts and religion. Each supports a personal entourage of scholars, poets, musicians and dancers, and a large garden in or near Madras where he hosts dinners at which his guests are entertained by artistic performances and scholarly presentations and debates. What is portrayed therefore is the courtly lifestyle of patrons for whom kingly temples are institutions of eminence and political authority, and gardens, temple processions and entourages are displays of princely pre-eminence.

One of the characteristics of the aristocrats described in the *Sarva-Deva-Vilasa* is that their patronage and wealth was not limited to Madras. Some among them had major landholdings outside the City, and several were trustees of temples in the surrounding countryside. The *Sarva-Deva-Vilasa* depicts these men as leisurely moving with their entourages from one locality to another in processions that regularly and publicly displayed their affluence, cultivation and fame. One recognises that these processions were themselves public presentations that located these aristocrats topographically. One can imagine the English maps of the eighteenth century with processional routes traced onto them leading into the Town and gardens from the villages and temples of the agrarian aristocracy, while within the Town temple processional routes moved along the streets where leading families lived and defined caste territories and alliances. Both forms of procession therefore represented a kind of geographical mapping of power, a form of argument about eminence and authority. It is no wonder that riots broke out when the processional route of a new temple intruded into the streets of the opposite moiety.

Interestingly, in the *Sarva-Deva-Vilasa*, there is no confirmable mention of any of the foremost members of the left-hand castes. The aristocrats principally eulogised were the aristocracy of the agrarian economy with in fact only the briefest of references to two of the magnates of business at the time, both Komatis: Collah Ravanappa and a merchant named KoTa Krsna (Raghavan 1957–58: 38).

Today nothing is known about KoTa Krsna, but Collah Ravanappa is a well-documented figure from the period and perhaps the most important Komati merchant from 1790 to his death in 1822 (Mines 2001: 55ff). Yet the *Sarva-Deva-Vilasa* merely states that Collah Ravanappa is 'the chief of the Telugu merchants of the city and an adept in negotiating with the English' (Raghavan 1957–58: 36). KoTa Krsna's description is even briefer. He, the text states, is a generous patron.

The *Sarva-Deva-Vilasa's* concision with regard to these two merchants, especially to Collah Ravanappa, puzzled Raghavan, the text's compiler, because he knew him to have been a major figure at the end of the eighteenth century. But what Raghavan missed was that what was being described was the lifestyle of the leading men of the right-hand social polity that organised much of Madras sociality and integrated it into the hegemonic caste order of the surrounding agrarian society. The focus of the *Sarva-Deva-Vilasa* is the courtly lifestyle of the landed gentry, the zamindars or agrarian princes, and the ingredients of this lifestyle are leisure associated with agrarian wealth and its associated power to command, stately processions, patronage of the arts and learning, garden dinners associated with a cultivated lifestyle and temple trusteeships. These are politically dominant men, and importantly management of temples is an instrumental feature of their princely status. By contrast, as a Komati, Collah Ravanappa is not a member of the landed gentry nor at this juncture was he the trustee of a temple. In the social hierarchy of the right-hand section, Komatis are not landed princes. They are merchants who defer to the political dominance of the landed elite.

George Town, 1800–90: Phase 2

The nineteenth century was a period of major change in Company rule. One of the most important changes from the perspective of George Town sociality was that, at the beginning of the century with the founding of the independent judiciary, the Company moved the locus of authority to decide civil matters among caste members from headmen to the courts. The consequences of this shift were profound (see Mines 2001). At the personal level, throughout the nineteenth century, access to the courts gradually changed the political economy of the family, establishing legal limits on joint family claims on individuals and giving the individual the legal tools to dispose of self-acquired property. As a consequence, individuals acquired an increased ability to make choices and to plan their own estates. Nonetheless, at the community level, during the first half of the nineteenth century, headmen still exercised a great deal of autocratic power over their neighbourhood caste fellows, especially as regarded conduct and social observances considered for the good of the community – and possibly for the regulation of its trade (with reference to the Beeri Chettiars, see ILR 1887: 150–51). But social changes were occurring that were to erode neighbourhood social cohesion. Alternative lifestyles were being made possible by western-style education, foreign travel, new civil service jobs and then new opportunities in administration and in shared governance. Christian College, which proved highly influential among Indians, was founded in George Town in 1837. Towards the end of the nineteenth century, individuals and their families began openly to rebel against the strict behavioural codes that traditional caste leadership enforced, and to challenge the authority of headmen in court. And after 1863, wealthy merchants sued to establish management boards to replace the autocratic control caste headmen and *dharmakarttaar* had over caste temples and the community resources that these institutions

controlled. By the end of the century, a new kind of court-regulated bureaucratic administration acting in the name of the community had replaced the
authority of caste leaders. These two judicially derived trends, the displacing
of caste headmen with bureaucratic community control and the establishing
of individual property rights, significantly changed neighbourhood and
family structures of authority.

Both the Beeri Chettiars and the Komatis were affected by these trends in
similar ways, but with different effects because of their contrasting organisational structures and business fortunes. The general trend was the diminishing
role of caste headmen. Among the Beeri Chettiars, the judicial system
usurped the Periyagramam's authority to adjudicate civil relations. But the
council continued to administer the caste's Muthialpet-centred temple polity
and to enforce caste behavioural codes until, in the last quarter of the century,
the council ordered several individuals and their families outcaste for
behavioural breaches. The council's actions split the community into conser-
vatives and educated progressives, and the embodiment of conservative
behaviour, the caste guru, left town, never to return. The lawsuits that followed
challenged the Periyagramam's power to outcaste and, when the council lost
in court, it became dysfunctional (Mines 1994: 101ff.). The individual headmen
faired little better, increasingly seen by caste progressives to be barriers to
social progress and irrelevant to modern life. Individuals were pursuing new
careers in government service, the professions and banking that enabled or
required them to live elsewhere and families began to move away from
George Town, selling their ancestral homes. Their power gone, the ability of
wealthy leaders to use temples as institutions of local political authority
crumbled and the Beeri Chettiars' temple polity came apart. No longer
significant institutions of neighbourhood cohesion and leadership, the individual Beeri Chettiar kingly temples began a half-century decline. By the
mid-twentieth century, most of these temples were little attended and all but
forgotten (see also Muthiah 1999). At the end of the twentieth century, only
the Kandasami temple survived under caste control, its *dharmakartta* still
bestowing courtly patronage supporting music, poetry, the arts and grand
processions in the style of the eighteenth-century magnates (Mines 1994).

The Komatis began the nineteenth century differently. In 1790, Collah
Ravanappa, of *Sarva-Deva-Vilasa* note, challenged the leadership of the
then Komati caste headman, Suncu Kistnama Chetti, and with the interested help of the covenanted servants of the East India Company financially
ruined him and his family (Mines 2001: 55ff). The Suncuvar family had held
the headmanship of the caste throughout the eighteenth century, during
which time the family had been one of the wealthiest and most powerful
merchant family networks in south India. Collah Ravanappa's challenge
split the Madras Komatis into two factions, one supporters of the Suncuvar
family, the Suncuvar *katchi* (faction), and the other allies of Collah
Ravanappa, the Collahvar *katchi*.

Whereas by the mid-eighteenth century the Beeri Chettiars had built themselves an impressive galactic temple polity as a feature of their caste governance in Muthialpet, by the beginning of the nineteenth century the Komatis controlled no caste temple. The temple polity of the right-hand castes, we have seen, were the temples built by the dominant Balija Naidu, Vellaala, and secular Brahman magnates. Their temples included the new Town Pagoda, built by a Vellaala with East India Company support, and the Ekambareswarar temple in Pedda Naickenpet, also originally endowed by a Vellaala. In addition to the first Town Pagoda, built in the 1640s, Balijas built the Bairagimadam temple, while a Brahman magnate mentioned in the *Sarva-Deva-Vilasa* built the Krishnaswami temple in 1790 (Map 5.3).

Rather than temples, the institution the Komatis did control as a whole community was a charity vegetable garden, the *Komatla Tottam*, situated on Audiappa Naick Street, which was dedicated 'to the General Body of the Vysya caste people [i.e. the Komatis] for the performance of the ceremonies, festivals and charities of the caste' (SKPD 1967: 97). The earliest reference to the garden that I have found is a record of a parchment dated 10 November 1708 that records the sale of a property, stating that the property's eastern boundary is the *Komatla Thota* (fieldnotes[3]). The garden is clearly visible in the Conradi map of 1755 and borders Elephant Street on the less accurately drawn map of 1733.

Early nineteenth-century records reveal that, prior to 1790 and his deposition by Collah Ravanappa, Suncu Kistnama had held the garden in his name as Pedda Chetti, headman, not as his personal property, but in trust on behalf of the Komati caste as a whole, and that he had superintended the charity associated with it (Madras District Records 1802). However, because the property had been held in his name, in 1790 the Company government had ordered the confiscation of the garden in lieu of payment of a fine levied against him by the Board of Revenue, the government only returning the property to the caste in 1802 after discovering its earlier error.

Then, in 1803, Collah Ravanappa's elder brother, Collah Moothoorama, did something unusual among Komatis: he collected a subscription and built a temple at the edge of the garden, the Sri Kanyakaparameswari Devasthanam, or SKPD, dedicated to the Komatis' ancestral goddess. Collah Ravanappa subsequently assumed the trusteeship of the temple upon the death of his brother in 1804. Court records suggest that Collah Ravanappa and his family, who controlled major segments of the produce trade, including trade in betel, then developed the Komati charity garden as the Town's produce market. This was the beginning of Kotwal Chavadi, Madras City's main produce market until 1996 when the market was relocated.

The SKPD was the first and only temple to be built and controlled by the Komatis in George Town. But this was a singular temple for several reasons. First, the temple was dedicated to an ancestress, a *kuladevam*, or caste goddess (lit. family god), whereas the temples previously built and controlled

101

by both the right-hand and the left-hand castes as a feature of their political authority and caste governance were kingly temples dedicated to high gods, Siva, Vishnu or Kali in one or another of their manifestations. By contrast, the SKPD was dedicated to a young woman, Vasavamba, whose story locates the origins of the Komati caste in her selfless virtue. According to the story, when a king of Kshatriya caste threatened to marry by force the beautiful Vasavamba, she saved her own virtue and the reputation of her caste by committing suttee. Upon immolation, Vasavamba was transformed into the goddess, Kanyakaparameswari, the virgin Parameswari. One hundred and two caste ancestors then followed her into the fire, and from these ancestors the present-day Komatis are said to have descended.

A second unusual feature of the SKPD is that it is a Saivite temple, whereas the majority of Komatis are Vaishnavites. This means that, while Komatis today acknowledge the Shivite goddess Kanyakaparameswari as their caste ancestress, the SKPD only serves the religious interests of a Komati minority. Even today, at the beginning of the twenty-first century, Komati Vaishnavites generally do not attend temple religious functions, although sectarian attitudes are not as strong as they once were.

Why did Collah Moothoorama and Collah Ravanappa build the temple? I believe they did so so that Collah Ravanappa could displace Suncu Kistnama as Komati headman and lay claim to the management of the Komati Charity Garden. Prior to this, the Collah family had not resided in the Petta. But building the temple located Collah Ravanappa in his role as trustee at the heart of the Komati neighbourhood. Thus, the temple's processional route taken by the goddess during Navarathri, the temple's main festival, proceeds through the wealthy core of the Komati community: from the Market, processions turn out of Audiappa Naick Street, proceeding north along Varada Muthiappan Street (also called Godown Street), then west at Thatha Muthiappan Street, then south along the length of Govindappa Nayakan Street before turning north again along Varada Muthiappan Street, returning to the temple (see Map 5.3). Govindappa Nayakan Street is colloquially known among Komatis as the 'Pedda Viithi', the 'Big Street', because it was the residential street of the wealthiest Komatis in the nineteenth and early twentieth centuries. Varada Muthiappan Street, or Godown Street, was, as it is today, the most concentrated business street in the whole of George Town. Today, every building on Godown Street houses 20 to 30 businesses, 2,000 businesses on a single street, annually conducting many crores of business (fieldnotes, 10 February 1994). In procession, proceeding with the goddess, Collah Ravanappa would have presented himself as the trustee of the caste community's founding ancestress and as a pre-eminent, commanding figure before the wealthiest families and businesses of this central Komati neighbourhood, and he the wealthiest and most powerful of them all.

Interestingly, even two hundred years later, followers of the two Komati factions still interpret Collah Ravanappa's claim differently. Supporters of the Suncuvar *katchi* say that, long before the Collahvar family arrived on the scene, the office of Pedda Chetti or caste headman belonged to the Suncuvar family as a hereditary right, and that this office had always represented the whole of the Komati caste. By contrast, they argue, the Shivite Collahvar family has had a hereditary claim only to the trusteeship of the SKPD, a temple with a minority congregation among the Komatis. Supporters of the Collahvar *katchi* counter that after Collah Ravanappa's triumph he assumed the role of Pedda Chetti. Whatever the case, the issue for followers of the Suncuvar *katchi* was that the Collahvar family conflated the temple trusteeship with the management of the Komati's Charity Garden. This also posed a dilemma for the Komati Vaishnavites: they had no special interest in the temple, but the garden (now Kotwal Chavadi) and the charities associated with it were community property in which they had great interest. And it was that interest that led in 1863 to a lawsuit and eventually in 1895 to the establishment of a committee of financial management to administer the temple and charities. The *dharmakartta* chairs meetings but has no vote except in case of a tie (Civil Suit 1896: 5).

In 1967, the income of the SKPD temple and its charities, at the time principally stall rentals in Kotwal Chavadi – the former Komatla Tottam – annually amounted to Rs 332,000, which was then a sizeable sum (see *SKPD Vysya Students' Home, Chetput, Golden Jubilee Souvenir*, 1967: 97). After taxes and expenses, this income funded:

> (1) Daily Worship ... and Festivals in the said temple of Sri Kanyaka Parameswari, (2) mass feedings during Navarathri [the temple's main festival], (3) daily feeding of about 100 students and the poor of the Arya Vysya [Komati] Community, (4) maintenance of four Schools, two for boys and two for girls, (5) maintenance of two Hostels for the benefit for the Vysya Students, (6) distribution of Maintenance Allowance to the poor and infirm of the said community, (7) scholarships, etc., to poor Vysya students, (8) maintenance of a Burning Ghat in DeMellows Road, Choolai and (9) a Ceremonial Garden in Sydenhams Road, Choolai, Madras.
>
> (SKPD 1967: 97)

The last two charities are the Vysya's cremation ground and the grounds used for death ritual ceremonies. Both are located just to the west of the Petta.

If one recognises the Charity Garden as the oldest institution held by the Komati community as a whole, one sees that the Komati's public style was not then, nor is it today, that of a kingly caste, but one of *karmayoga*, the practice of right action: of piety and charity. Comparing this style to the styles of the Beeri Chettiars and of the landed aristocrats of the *Sarva-Deva-Vilasa*, one observes that the Charity Garden was used to meet the needs of the caste as a whole, to fund education, to feed the poor, and to sponsor worship. In 1816, six years before his death, the Company government awarded Collah Ravanappa a gold medallion and chain, a palanquin and silver staffs, the latter to be carried before him when he went out in procession (Mines 2001). The government honoured him with these emblems of regard in recognition of his public benefactions, his funding in that year of four rest houses for Brahman and Komati religious pilgrims, and for entrusting the Company with a large sum of money for the everlasting maintenance of the properties. Today when the goddess is taken in procession, the staffs and palanquin are features of her retinue, perpetuating Collah Ravanappa's identity with the temple and the esteem in which the East India Company held him. *Karmayoga*, then, when expressed as great public benefaction, could be used to earn public awards from the colonial government. This pattern of recognition was formalised in the twentieth century, when the government created a ranked series of honorary titles to recognise exceptional public charity.

Opulence and charity, 1890–1960: Phase 3

At the end of the eighteenth century, British companies moved into the south-eastern portion of Muthialpet and along the Beach Road, opposite the harbour. They also opened enterprises along the new Popham's Broadway. Indian merchants formed relationships with these British companies and businessmen, serving them as employees and *dubashes*. Muthialpet was ethnically heterogeneous (Neild 1976: 173ff.). Pedda Naickenpet, however, remained a homogeneous high-caste Hindu area with the principal residential streets of the Komatis clustered west of Kotwal Chavadi (Map 5.3).

In the 1840s, the first of the great twentieth-century Komati business houses was founded and the basis of late colonial fortunes was laid. A characteristic of the Komati caste in Madras is that through the years poor Komatis have migrated from the Telugu north to Madras in hopes of making their fortunes. Many family stories begin by describing how an ancestor first came to Madras as a young child and through dint of hard work and good character became a successful merchant earning great wealth. During this period, Komatis specialised in wholesale trade in produce, particularly black pepper, grains including rice, pulses, garlic, onions and betel nut. They monopolised the gunny trade and engaged in wholesale and retail trade in cloth, holding a near monopoly in this trade until World War I. Similarly, they were pre-eminent wholesale and retail dealers in paper, cardboard and stationery items, in gold, in silver and in diamonds. Money lending was also an important business in the nineteenth and twentieth centuries. In the twentieth century, the big owners of urban land and shops also made substantial incomes from rentals. Fewer in number but also important were exporters of commodities such as jams and jellies and Indian spices, the latter sold to the Indian diaspora around the world. Prominent Komati merchants were also importers of Burmese teak and other woods, both costly and ordinary, as well as foreign luxury goods, including textiles and Scotch whiskeys.

Who were the great Komati merchant families and what were their contributions to the City? Because my space is limited, let me outline here the enterprises of just two among them, to give a sense of the scale and character of their enterprises.

My first example is the Vupputur family, which founded a stationery business in 1840, V. Perumal and Sons, which still exists in the Petta. Later in the nineteenth century, the business became the principal supplier of stationery and related products to the government. Members of the family also served as chandlers and sole agents – *dubashes* – of the Madras South Maratha Railways (MSM Railways), supplying everything from uniforms to flags. They continued in this business until 1950, when the railroads were merged to become the Southern Railways. The family were also auctioneers specialising in railroad scrap (Muthiah 1999: 260). In 1894, at the government's behest, the family opened a printing press, Hoe and Co., which became the most prestigious printing press in Madras. The press served the government as its principal printer, including all printing done for the Madras municipality and for the railways in Madras Presidency. The company printed in English and in the four major Dravidian languages. This business continued until the reorganisation of the states in 1956. Finally, in 1920–1, members of the family joined with other prominent Komati businessmen to take over a failed government pencil factory, which they then ran successfully until the factory's closing in 1996–7. At their height, these companies together employed over 1,000 workers.

Taticonda is another pre-eminent Komati family name of the late nineteenth / early twentieth century, although the family's prominence is attributable to one man, Taticonda Namberumal Chetty (b. 1856, d. 3 December 1925). Founding his business in 1880, he was a general contractor. Some of the grandest government buildings designed in Indo-Saracenic style in Madras were built by him, including the High Court, the Museum and Museum Theatre, the National Art Gallery, the GPO, the National Bank of India, the Law College, part of the General Hospital and more. These imposing landmarks are known locally as the 'red brick' buildings because brick, fired in his own kilns, was his medium. He also built many palatial garden houses for Europeans and wealthy Indians. The British recognised Namberumal for his work in 1901 with the title of 'Rao Sahib', later designating him 'Rao Bahadur', and, in 1923, 'Diwan Bahadur'. As his business prospered, he purchased land and houses, owning at one time over two thousand grounds and 99 houses (Muthiah 1993). He was not a man who shied from opulence and public display. In 1905, he purchased for himself a sprawling garden mansion, 'Crynant', in an area to the west of the Town that became known as 'Chetpet', a corruption of 'Chettiar-pet', 'Chettiar-place'. He was also the first Indian owner of an automobile, a 1901 Dideon, licence number MC-3, the third registered car in Madras. In keeping with his wealth and Komati ways, Namberumal gave charity to Brahmans in a grand and innovative manner. Thus, he 'ran a monorail service from Avadi to Thiruvallur meant only for "Iyengars" [Vaishnavite Brahmans] to reach an ancient temple there' (Muthiah 1993). And when in 1919 the ill and dying mathematical genius Srinivasa Ramanujan, an Iyengar, returned to Madras from Cambridge University, Namberumal hosted him as his guest, first at Crynant and then at Gomitra, another of his palatial garden mansions.

Many names could be added to those of these two prominent Komati merchants of the nineteenth and twentieth centuries. Men of the Mukkala family were cloth merchants and today own several kinds of businesses in George Town. They are also major urban landowners. In the 1990s, they razed their Petta residence on Kasi Chetty Street and erected a multi-storey department store. The Candagaddalas, also major urban landowners for over a century, today own a modern cinema and more than 100 commercial properties in the Petta, many of them converted residences. Ega Vencatakisnamah Chetty founded a general merchandise business in 1884, and a decade later opened a factory manufacturing 'chutney, curry spices, and preserved fruits and jellies' under the 'Temple' trademark (later P.V. Condiments). These he exported all over the world (Playne 1914–15: 657). He was also a major importer of hardware, stationery and general merchandise from the UK, Europe, and America (ibid.).

This truncated list suggests noteworthy features of the way Komatis did business during this period. First, the enterprises these families founded and managed were large, in many cases multinational, concerns involving manufacturing and agencies that controlled major continental and international distribution for a wide range of commodities. Second, the growth of these family enterprises into major businesses was dependent on the entrepreneur establishing ties with the British and sometimes with other Europeans. Notably, the flow of economic advantage was in both directions, as the case of the Indian businessmen taking over the failing pencil factory suggests. In this instance, the Indians bailed out the government. In recognition for their contributions to civic life and to the public good during the early twentieth century, the Crown government gave titles to a number of these prominent Komatis. Third, these were big-man enterprises. Stories about these most successful of entrepreneurs always reveal them to have been flamboyant individuals who combined a luxurious lifestyle with a certain religious orthodoxy, presenting themselves in public in grand and opulent fashion. Before the automobile, these men maintained stables of fine, matched horses to pull their carriages. And stories are told that in the evening when these merchants drove to their George Town clubs, the public paused to line the streets to watch the spectacle of them passing. When the automobile was introduced, they were the first Indians to own them. The Vupputur family owned a Rolls Royce, symbolising their pre-eminence. Daimlers, I was told, were almost as good.

By 1900, Black Town, or George Town, as it now was called, was crowded and some of the most affluent families, seeking a better living environment, moved west of the Petta along Poonamallee High Road. This area – roughly from Raja Annamalai Chettiar Road west to just beyond Taylor's Road – was then mango grove and open countryside. Between 1909 and 1912, prominent Komatis built houses along both sides of the road. First, the frontage to Poonamallee High Road was developed and then the backside. Informants explained to me that by 1920 wealthy Komatis occupied the whole length of the road up to Taylor's Road and a short distance beyond (Map 5.4). By the end of the twentieth century, half of the Komatis had moved out of George Town, but still maintained their businesses there.

The local organisation of the wealthy Komatis who moved to this new area preserved their close personal relationships. The four houses east of Taylor's Road were occupied by the Ega / Candagaddala family, the Calve family (major landowners and scions of a wealthy Pondicherry merchant family), the Surra family (suppliers of sleepers and other items to the railways) and the Pottur family (wholesalers and retailers of textiles and partner to T.A. Taylor). All these families were major city landowners, and each of the houses was connected by private gates to the others so that members of the families could visit without going out onto the street. Other major Komati business families also had houses in this expanded neighbourhood.

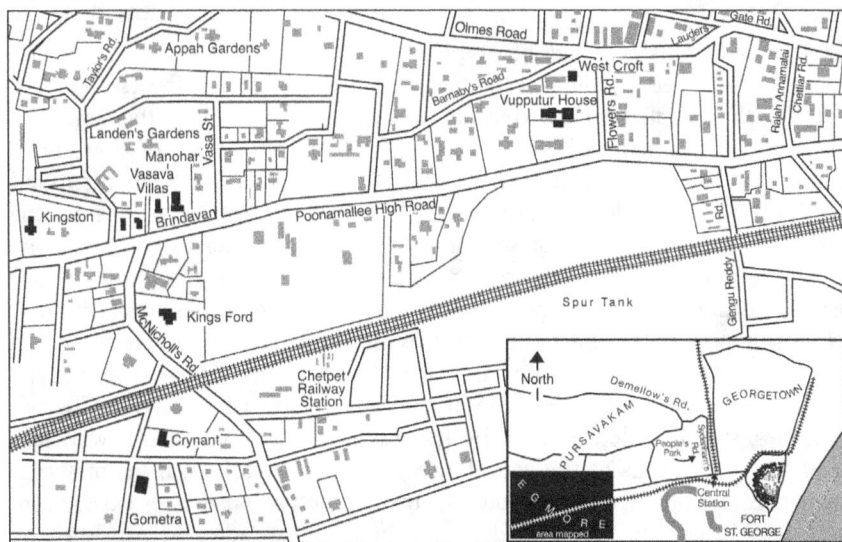

Map 5.4 Chetpet in Egmore, c. 1950

The Calavala brothers built 'Kingston House' just beyond Taylor's Road and 'Kings Ford' on McNicholl's Road a short distance from 'Crynant' and from another huge mansion built by the Chinni family also on McNicholl's Road. In 1940, the Vupputur family built 'Vupputur House' and 'West Crofts' off Flowers Road. It is no wonder the area became known as 'Chetpet'. And so, Komatis lived, repositioned, in grander houses than were possible in George Town, but now their houses were set in spacious gardens. Here these Indian magnates entertained their British and European contacts. In keeping with their orthodox ways, they entertained British and Indian guests separately on different nights so that they could administer their hospitality in keeping with the sensibilities of their guests. For Europeans, there were ballrooms and ballroom dancing; for Indians, there were gardens with Carnatic music and *bharatnatyam* dance. Here we see modern adaptations of the eighteenth-century magnate's garden entertainment style.

The Komatis' palatial garden houses were intended to match the grand houses of the British elite and to be conspicuous public displays of personal wealth. These were Indians who lent money to the British. But there was hidden in this grandeur a negative circumstance, which has left a more enduring legacy in the cityscape. A striking feature of the genealogies of prominent Komati business families is that all the genealogies include successful merchants who were childless, or, if they had daughters, were sonless. Adoption was often a solution, but in some cases the adopted son died without children. During the first half of the twentieth century, the wealthy Komati's response to these circumstances was to create a charity in his name and, almost as frequently, in the name of his wife. This Komati pattern of charity is different from the Beeri Chettiar pattern. Beeri Chettiars without descendants typically left their estates to one of the temples controlled by their caste, adding to the wealth of the temple, and enabling the temple trustees to use the accumulated wealth for the benefit of their community (Mines 1994). Occasionally, Komatis too have followed this practice and left their estates to the SKPD. But Vaishnavite Komatis found the SKPD unsuitable because it was a Saivite temple with ties to the Collahvari *katchi*. Instead, these Komatis hit upon the idea of creating charities to perpetuate their name 'not by descendants', but by schemes of public benefaction. The founding of personal posthumous charities took off from 1915 and continued until the 1940s with the exceptional charity being founded up to the 1960s. During this period, approximately two dozen charities of this sort were created. One of the first, Narayana Guruviah Chetty's Charities, was founded in 1915 by the will of a cloth merchant, who had been sent to Madras at the age of five to live and work with his maternal uncle (Mines 2002). In adulthood, Guruviah Chetty's businesses earned him considerable wealth, but he had no children and an adopted son 'died by want of divine grace' without issue (Trust Deed of Narayana Guruviah Chetty's Charities 1968: 2).

It was explained to me by an older Komati businessman that being issue-less is believed a sign of past sin, the negative affect of actions in previous lives that have not been dispersed through counter actions such as altruistic giving. The hope, my informant explained, is that through acts of selfless generosity the sin will be countered and in rebirth the benefactor will be blessed with children. In this belief, one recognises the logic of *karmayoga*. But, the purpose of creating charities goes beyond the effort to reverse the karmic effects of sin. The wills of these men make it clear that their charities were designed to be memorials to themselves in the hope of perpetuating their names and memory in the community. In this goal, the charities have been quite successful. Because they involve real property, the charities and the names of those who founded them continue today in the social geography of the City. Typically, the ancestral home of the founder serves as the management office of the charity and as a marriage hall and travellers' guesthouse. A few are student hostels. The charities generally fund three kinds of activities: religious events such as *pujas*, *utsavam* or festivals, and religious learning, including Sanskrit scholarship; education, including the funding of schools and colleges, hostels, scholarships, and student mess halls and meals; and public benefactions for the poor, including monthly distributions of stipends for the destitute, support of orphanages, the building of wells, medical dispensaries, the feeding of poor children, children's milk programmes and the support of hospitals. The private charities fund these activities from the founders' estates and in particular through rents and earnings from commercial properties developed in the charity's name by its trustees.

The following excerpt, drawn from the Centenary Celebration Souvenir (18 January 1993) Dharmamurthi Rao Bahadur Calavala Cunnan Chetty Charities Hindu Higher Secondary School, Thiruvallur, illustrates such a Trust and the style of his remembrance:

> The Vysia community, usually blessed by Dhanabhagyalakshmi [the beneficent Lakshmi] with great wealth is also noted for its charitable disposition. The two Calavala brothers have shown to the world at large that the Channel of Charity, if it is to be of lasting benefit to humanity, should be vidyadhan [the gift of knowledge] . . .
>
> The Calavala brothers were doing a profitble [*sic*] business under the name of King & Co., dealing in high class timber from Burma and costly spirits like Scotch Whiskey from Great Britain. . . . Their policy of honest, truthful and contented salesmanship increased their wealth largely and they came to be called 'Timber Kings' and Merchant Princes. They were held in high esteem and great respect. Both brothers were unassuming in manner, despite their huge wealth.
>
> The elder of the two brothers was Cunnan Cettygaru who lived mostly in 'KINGSTON' on the Poonamallee High Road in

Kilpauk, where the present Trust Board have located the 'Seetha Kingston House School'. He had a house 'Calavala Graham' in Govindappa Naicken Street [the 'Pedda Viithi'], where the Management Office of the Trust Board is located. He spent his last days in this house and died there on 5th August 1920.

The younger brother, C. Ramanujam Chetty lived in his bungalow, 'KINGSFORD' in McNicholls Road in Chetput. . . .

CALAVALA CUNNAN CHETTY had already started Charitable institutions of different kinds [during his life]. His charities were many-sided. He had been managing a Middle School at Trevellore. Several high schools in Madras and one in Tiruninravur [*sic*]. Free supply of pure milk to the poor children was another notable form of charity. Many other benefactions were listed in his will. . . .

During his lifetime, in addition to feeding daily thousands of poor people and every Sunday thousands in George Town, he paid the school fees of poor children. He established a library for the benefit of the students of Madras, built a *choultry* (rest house) near Egmore Station 'for the benefit of the passengers alighting at Egmore and struggling for want of accommodation', and founded and ran three Ayurvedic hospitals. It is said that at the end of his life Calavala Cunnan was spending Rs 50,000 per annum on charity, a small fortune in the early twentieth century.

Today, the Rao Bahadur Calavala Cunnan Chetty's Charities is the largest private Komati charity. The Trust owns and manages valuable commercial properties in the City, including the Larson and Turbo Office and the Philips Block on Mount Road. Other private Komati charities also own substantial commercial properties, including several of Madras's largest modern marriage halls. In other words, the imprint of these Komati charities on the social geography of the City extends well beyond the Petta and occupies a central place in commercial Madras.

Decline, 1960–2000: Phase 4

If the late nineteenth century and the first half of the twentieth were the heyday of Komati public prominence, the second half of the twentieth century brought a new, major period of change. After Independence, many of the businesses founded on close relationships with the British lost their connections and quickly succumbed. It will take varying periods of time for descendants to spend down the great fortunes that their forbears made or for these fortunes to dwindle through the processes of inheritance. However, there are some families whose members are holding their own and some charities that are prospering. But many of the great fortunes are well on the way to disappearing or now exist only as charities, legacies of an opulent past.

The Urban Land [Ceiling and Regulation] Act of 1976 has also had an impact. Many of the garden houses have been sold or developed for other purposes because of this Act and to facilitate inheritance. Thus the Vupputur House was sold in 1980 and in its place the purchaser has built a large luxury apartment complex. Many of the palatial garden houses of Chetpet and Poonamallee High Road have undergone this transformation, some developed by the original owners. Other owners have divided their property, selling off part of the grounds or developing them as commercial property. Even as late as the 1960s, Madras was known as 'The Garden City' because of its open spaces; now the open spaces of the City have been all but filled in. Thirty years ago, apartment buildings were almost non-existent in the City; now apartment complexes are common. In the first half of the twentieth century, the Komati style was one of luxury and grand private charity; at the end of the century, informants told me that one tried to keep a low profile to avoid unwanted attention from grasping politicians and income tax authorities: 'The days of keeping diaries are over. Now we don't write anything down, not even figures on a scrap of paper.' This same man explained that the big families are in decline. Business has changed. Real money now is in services and technology, but Komatis are still in commodities. The conditions surrounding charities have also changed. Some time ago, the private charities found it necessary to join together for protection and to preserve their private management. Interestingly, they are now all under the SKPD and charities umbrella, institutions of the community as a whole, although de facto they are still managed independently by their separate boards of trustees.

Despite the collapse of the great merchant houses, George Town remains today an important centre of business and commerce in Chennai, although one that is changing substantially. The Komati charity houses on Varada Muthiappan Street, the 'Pedda Vidi' or Great Street, are monuments to the former opulent lifestyles of the Komati merchant princes, but, victims of the twentieth-century Komati exodus, these houses now go largely unused as caste marriage halls or guesthouses. Today, wealthy Komatis prefer the cleaner surroundings and easier access of the modern marriage halls located elsewhere in the City. As for the SKPD and Kotwal Chavadi, the SKPD temple underwent a major renovation and *kumbabisheekam* (ritual renewal and purification) ceremony in 1994, and a few years later in 1999, following the shifting of the wholesale produce market from Kotwal Chavadi, the Komatla Tottam of old, the SKPD redeveloped the land as a women's college, which opened for its first classes in 2000. Responding to the high commercial value of land in George Town, some of the Komati houses also have been redeveloped as multi-storied 'department' stores, with the owner's penthouse residence occupying the top floor. These department stores lease out shop spaces to commercial enterprises, predominantly wholesalers and retailers of a wide range of commodities. And George Town continues to be an important centre of the retail jewellery trade, involving several prominent Komati families as well as members of other communities who specialise in the gold and gem trade.

The Beeri Chettiars too continue to have an important commercial presence in the Petta. The streets adjoining the Kandasami temple are an important locus of dealerships in ferrous and non-ferrous metals, hardware and other commodities, businesses that are Beeri Chettiar specialties. However, more so than the Komatis, starting in the nineteenth century, many prominent Beeri Chettiar families shifted from commerce, preferring sons to take employment in government service, banking and the professions. In the twentieth century, daughters also joined the ranks of university-educated professionals. In consequence, while a few prominent families still reside in their ancestral homes, commerce no longer compels Beeri Chettiars to reside in the Petta, and since the mid-twentieth century they have sold their houses in number to new owners who have converted these homes into commercial buildings. Komatis have been among the buyers. Nevertheless, despite diminished numbers, as the twenty-first century begins, the Beeri Chettiars continue to have a visible public presence in the Petta, largely because of the great popularity of the Kandasami temple with its spectacular festivals, and its dramatic and lengthy processional routes that draw crowds of thousands.

It is apparent, therefore, that the public styles of these two important merchant castes, the Komatis and the Beeri Chettiars, continue to contrast and to represent the different manners in which the communities position themselves in City society. Komatis portray themselves as patrons of charity and education, enacting the style of *karmayoga*. Beeri Chettiars perform a commanding, kingly style, which leaders of the caste enact as trustees and patrons of the Kandasami temple and of the Karnatic arts that form a feature of their courtly patronage.

Conclusion

Through the centuries, one discerns continuities and transformations in George Town sociality that have left their imprint on the cityscape. During the first centuries, competition between the right-hand castes and the left-hand castes led to riots that were resolved by imposing and maintaining a spatial separation of the Petta into two moieties. During this period, the East India Company depended on caste headmen to govern community civil affairs, and in response the headmen of each of the moieties developed temples as venues for caste governance, and processional streets as features of their authority. But the moieties were not symmetrical. The Beeri Chettiars developed an impressive temple galactic polity and affected a kingly style, but the Komatis, as merchants among politically powerful landed castes, built no temples.

At the end of the eighteenth century, the Company established an independent court system, and caste headmen were displaced as adjudicators of civil affairs. This new legal system gave individuals greater control over their estates and provided individuals with the means of perpetuating their names by creating charitable endowments. Collah Ravanappa was the first to create an enduring charity administered under the law and maintained by government regulation. But the real florescence of personal charities occurred after World War I, when the British began to award titles to Komatis who through their charitable benefactions made major contributions to city life. It is these charities that remain a vital part of the contemporary City because they include well-known educational institutions and commercial properties that perpetuate the names of wealthy former merchants and their wives.

If caste headmen dominated the eighteenth and early nineteenth centuries, then the latter half of the nineteenth century was a period when new commercial names emerged among the Komatis. It appears to have been a time of diversification and expansion when new fortunes were created. Then, at the start of the twentieth century, the greatest of the Komati merchants moved just west of the Petta to Poonamallee High Road, building palatial garden houses that marked a new phase in City development and in merchant style. These Indian garden houses, many with English names, were a colonial blending of the English garden house and the courtly gardens of eighteenth-century Indian magnates. The blending was predicated on a colonial collaboration that was to be short-lived.

Since Independence, their British ties gone, many of the great commercial families have seen their enterprises close. The privilege that the garden houses expressed had made sense in colonial India, but in the late 1960s and 1970s the economic decline of families, populist democracy and the urban land ceiling created a new logic. The old houses are coming down; the City is rapidly being transformed. Seeing these transformations, one realises that the effect of the Komatis and the Beeri Chettiars on the landscape of Madras City has been impermanent, altering and adapting to changing circumstances. Yet many features of the past remain: fragments of the Petta's old defensive wall, street names, temples, processional streets, Popham's Broadway, the red brick buildings, even some of the old garden houses. When one knows what to look for, one can read the streets and in them the social dynamics of the City's past.

Acknowledgements

This chapter is based on field and archival research conducted in Chennai (Madras City) and the Tamil Nadu State Archives with the support of a J. William Fulbright Senior Research Fellowship and a John Simon Guggenheim Memorial Foundation fellowship. An earlier version of this paper was presented at the University of Sussex in 2001. I especially wish to thank Geert De Neve, Jonathan Parry and Chris Fuller for their very helpful ideas.

Notes

1 'Patnam', from pattana, means 'market-centre' or 'riverine settlement'.
2 Historically, the castes of south India were divided into right-hand and left-hand sections. Brahmans were not members of either section, but priestly Brahmans typically served only members of one or the other section, and many politically influential secular Brahmans were closely tied to the landed aristocracy of the right-hand section. Taken as a body, the right-hand castes formed the familiar transactionally defined caste hierarchies associated with the agrarian-based political economy with which students of village India are familiar from the writings of Louis Dumont (1970) and McKim Marriott (1960). In Madras, included among their number were merchant castes such as the Balija Naidus and Komati Chettiars. The left-hand castes were principally artisan and merchant castes, and often economic and ritual competitors of the right-hand castes. In contrast to the right-hand castes, the left-hand castes lacked extensive ties with service castes, ties that were the sine qua non of right-hand caste dominance associated with the ability to command others.
3 In 1994, the trustees of the Sri Kanyakaparameswari temple, which administers the Garden Trust, generously allowed me to read the temple's archival register, but asked that I take no direct notes or quotes from the records. My account of the temple and Garden differs from that of S. Muthiah (1999: 305) and from that of Joanne Waghorne 1999, both of whom believe the Collahvari family owned the Garden. Collahvari family records indicate that the temple was built in 1803–4, contrary to Muthiah's account.

References

I. Secondary sources

Brimnes, Niels (1999) *Constructing the Colonial Encounter: Right and Left Hand Castes in Early Colonial South India*, Richmond, Surrey: Curzon Press
Dodwell, Henry (1926) *The Nabobs of Madras*, London: Williams and Norgate Ltd.
Dumont, Louis (1980) *Homo Hierarchicus: the Caste System and Its Implications*, Chicago, IL: The University of Chicago Press
Love, Henry Davidson (1913) *Vestiges of Old Madras* (vols. 1–4), London: John Murray for Govt of India
Marriott, McKim (1960) *Caste Ranking and Community Structure in Five Regions of India and Pakistan*, Poona: G.S. Press
Mines, Mattison (1992) 'Individuality and achievement in South Indian social history' 26(1) *Modern Asian Studies* 129–56
——(1994) *Public Faces, Private Voices: Community and Individuality in South India*, Berkeley, CA: University of California Press
——(2001) 'Courts of law and styles of self in eighteenth-century Madras: from hybrid to colonial self' 35(1) *Modern Asian Studies* 33–74
——(2002) 'Memorializing the self: the autobiographical will and testament of Narayana Guruviah Chetty, Madras City, 1915', in Mines, Diane P. and Lamb, Sarah (eds), *Everyday Life in South Asia*, Bloomington, IN: Indiana University Press

Muthiah, S. (1993) *Madras Discovered, Revised*, Madras: Affiliated East / West books Pvt. Ltd.

Muthiah, S. (1999) *Madras Rediscovered: A Historical Guide to Looking Around, Supplemented with Tales of 'Once Upon a City'*, Chennai: Eastwest Books (Madras) Pvt. Ltd.

Neild, Susan Margaret (1976) 'Madras: The Growth of a Colonial City in India, 1780–1840', unpublished PhD thesis, Department of History, University of Chicago

Playne, Somerset (1914–15) *Southern India: Its History, People, Commerce, and Industrial Resources*, London: The Foreign and Colonial Compiling and Publishing Co.

Raghavan, V. (1957–58) *The Sarva-Deva-Vilasa*, Madras: The Adyar Library and Research Centre

Salmon, Thomas (1744) *Modern History or the Present State of All Nations*, vol. 1. London: T. Longman

Subrahmanyam, Sanjay (2001) *Penumbral Visions: Making Polities in Early Modern South India*, Ann Arbor, MI: The University of Michigan Press

Waghorne, Joanne Punzo (1999) 'The diaspora of the Gods: Hindu temples in the new world system 1640–1800' 58(3) *Journal of Asian Studies* 648–86

Wheeler, J. Talboys (1990 [1861–2]) *Annals of the Madras Presidency*, vols. 1–3, Delhi: Low Price Publications

II. Primary sources

Centenary Celebration Souvenir (18 January 1993) Dharmamurthi Rao Bahadur Calavala Cunnan Chetty Charities Hindu Higher Secondary School, Thiruvallur.

SKPD *Vysya Students' Home, Chetput, Golden Jubilee Souvenir*, 1967.

Madras District Records [MDR] (1802) 986 Tamil Nadu State Archives (TNSA) 169–70, Letter: to the Board of Revenue, September.

Trust Deed of Narayana Guruviah Chetty's Charities, November 1968.

III. Law records

ILR (Indian Law Reports). 1887 Madras Series, vol. 10.

Civil Suit No. 222 of 1895. In the High Court of Judicature of Madras, 5 October 1896. Mr. Justice Boddam.

6

PARHAI KA MAHAUL?

An educational environment in Bijnor, Uttar Pradesh

Roger Jeffery, Patricia Jeffery and Craig Jeffrey

In small towns in north India, educational institutions of one kind or another are increasingly visible features, and they are central to the generation of local discourses on progress and modernity. While the content of the curriculum, the messages that are directly and indirectly communicated through textbooks, examinations, teaching styles and so on, are all important, educational institutions are also embodied in buildings that help to shape the urban environment. School campuses are not only major contributors in themselves, but they also help to give meaning to the buildings that surround the schools. These meanings are not, of course, negotiated and reproduced locally in a vacuum. School buildings copy models derived from India and elsewhere; curricula are national or state-wide; managers, teachers and principals (and sometimes pupils) are mobile. Schools also derive their strength, in part, from the possible futures that schools and colleges may provide for their students – futures that may be in other Indian urban centres or further afield.

The idea of an 'educational environment' (*parhai ka mahaul*) is a familiar one in Bijnor District, where we have carried out research intermittently since 1982.[1] Rural parents have often told us that one problem they face in getting a good education for their children is that there is no educational atmosphere or environment in the villages, which places their children at a major disadvantage compared to their peers in town. An 'educational environment' means several things including, for example, reliable electricity to let children study in the evenings, good tutors to supplement what is learnt at school, as well as the more diffuse effects produced when all the neighbours' children regularly attend school. The imagined alternative environment is, in this context, an urban one. For many villagers, a town like Bijnor presents a somewhat undifferentiated opportunity for educational advancement. Others are more aware of the diversity and differentiation that urban areas offer, and their conceptual maps of the town are divided. On the one hand are *mohallas*, primarily residential zones with distinct names and populations within a densely populated town, where residents may share caste, class and communal characteristics. Opposed to these are *colonies*,[2] newly opened suburban settlements, which are usually regarded as the more desirable places to live, especially those accessible to the 'good' secondary schools. Proximity to educational institutions thus gives some particular urban spaces social, economic and political importance. In urban Bijnor, there are several such combinations of 'good' schools and desirable colonies: in some cases, the colony came first, and the school later, but elsewhere the school came first and attracted colonies with particular characteristics to cluster around it.

In trying to understand the significance of one such 'educational-cum-residential space', we start from the work of urban geographers who have characterised how groups are 'inscribing spaces and zones with particular meanings and discursive practices' (Bridge and Watson 2000: 252–3). In a specifically north Indian context, Orsini reminds us that, for Hindi intellec-tuals in the late nineteenth and early twentieth centuries, 'a modern, centralised system of education' was important 'both as an *institutional* and a *discursive* space' (Orsini 2002: 89, her emphasis). While individual schools obviously constitute such institutional spaces, and the curriculum (formal, informal and/or hidden) provides some focus to the discursive spaces, processes of inscribing meaning and creating identities are also attempted, challenged and negotiated in the neighbourhoods in which the schools are placed, or which develop around the schools.

In this paper, we will describe and analyse one such hybrid urban space, which we call 'NW Bijnor' for the sake of simplicity, because it has few obvious boundaries and was rarely referred to as a coherent space by locals. It has a mix of residential and institutional properties, including schools and colleges. Most people approach this space either from town, where it is marked by a crossroads at the edge of the Civil Lines, or on the road from Meerut and Delhi, where another road junction marks the beginning of the built-up area of Bijnor town. In discussing this space, we focus on three dimensions of its meaning: as a space of transitions; as one locus of a post-colonial civilising mission that involves dominance and exclusion; and as a space of political contestations. First, we provide a partial account of Bijnor town and its physical characteristics.

Bijnor: a post-colonial town?

Small towns like Bijnor are not well represented in the literature on post-colonial urbanism, which is highly focused on a few agglomerations, large enough to count as 'world cities' (King 2000: 266).[3] Yet in demographic terms, the 98 towns with populations of between 50,000 and 500,000 made up about one-third of Uttar Pradesh's 'urban' population in 2001, as much as the 11 cities with populations larger than 500,000. Bijnor, as an agglomer-ation (i.e. including adjacent areas that are under different local authorities but contain built-up land contiguous to the area under the Bijnor Municipal Board) had a population of just over 90,000 in 2001 and some basic demographic characteristics similar to other towns of its size (see Table 6.1). In 1971, its population was evenly divided between Hindus and Muslims, although in the district as a whole the urban population is roughly 65% Muslim and 33% Hindu.[4]

Bijnor's urban space can be understood as a combination of pre-colonial, colonial and post-Independence spaces, although these are not neat categories. The pre-colonial core of the city is a maze of narrow shopping and residential streets centred on the retail market (selling fruit and vegetables, dry goods, etc.). The main colonial buildings are the clock tower, for many years devoid of a clock, and the main post office on the northern edge of the old town (see Map 6.1). The other large buildings are mosques and temples. These are mostly in the *mohallas*, several of which bear names suggesting caste or community origins. Like other nearby towns, in the eighteenth and nineteenth centuries Bijnor was a *qasba*, a town dominated by a Muslim service elite. In the course of the twentieth century, it has increasingly taken on the characteristics of a *ganj*, a town dominated by Hindu merchants, with close relationships to a predominantly Hindu civil service (Bayly 1983; Freitag 1989; 102–3). Beyond the post office to the north of the old town are the colonial Civil Lines, which still retain that name, with the government Inter-Colleges, the bus station, the office-cum-residence of the District Magistrate, set in its own fields and orchard, the houses and offices of other district administrators, the church and school of the Methodist Mission, the jail and the district courts. Post-Independence,

Table 6.1 Sizes and characteristics of towns in Uttar Pradesh as defined by the Census 2001 and compared with Bijnor

Town size class	No. of towns	Total Population	% literate	% male literate	% female literate	Female: male ratio	% children aged 0-6
0-49,999	595	10,191,890	53.7%	61.6%	44.8%	886	17.2%
50,000-499,999	98	11,274,998	60.1%	65.9%	53.5%	880	14.7%
500,000+	11	12,766,634	65.8%	71.5%	59.2%	872	12.5%
(Bijnor agglomeration)	*1*	*90,495*	*61.3%*	*64.7%*	*57.5%*	*897*	*15.7%*

Source: Census of India, 2001, tabulations made available in electronic format

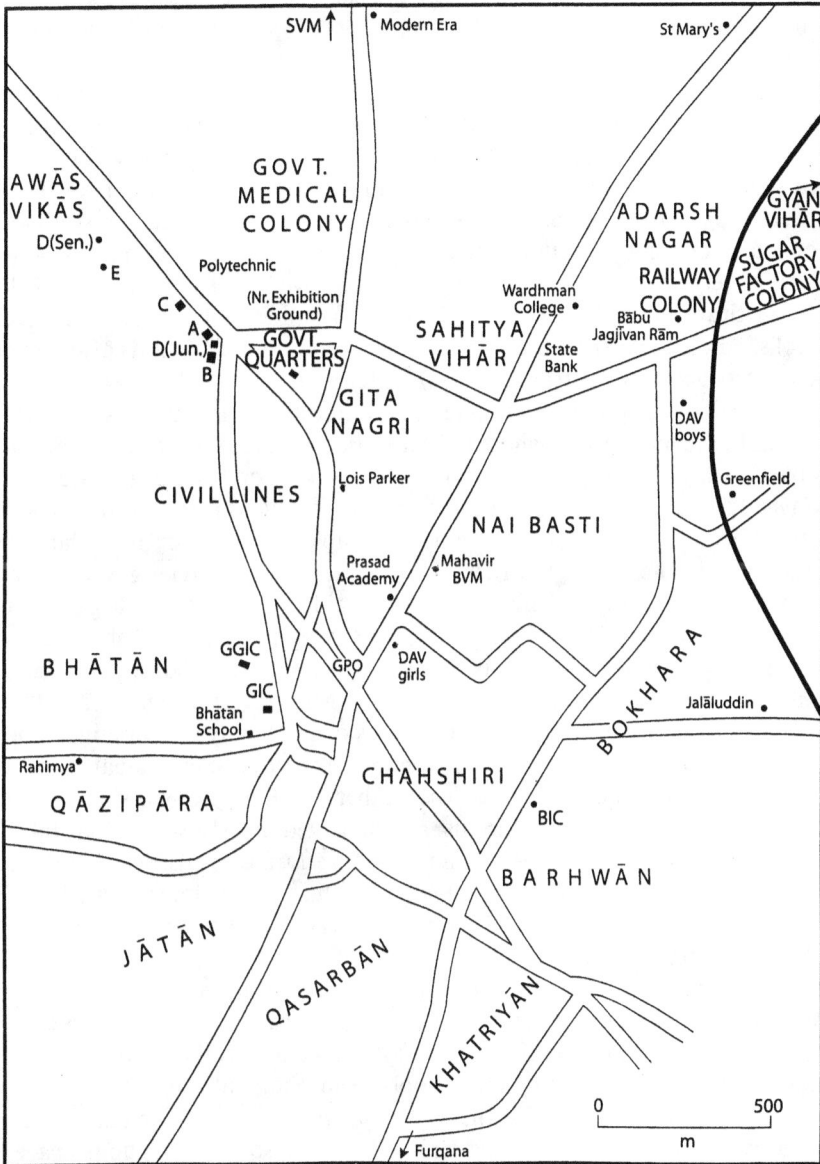

Map 6.1 Bijnor town

new housing developments included Nai Basti, a colony to the east of the old town dating from the 1950s; beyond it are the railway station and the sugar mill, still the largest local employer apart from the Government of Uttar Pradesh. Beyond the old town to the south and west, and beyond the

119

Civil Lines and Nai Basti to the north and east, are other areas of post-1950 housing and shops, with small offices and workshops, and, increasingly, non-state schools.

Government schools are mostly in the heart of the *mohallas* or in the Civil Lines. Non-state primary schools are spread through the new residential areas, often using converted houses. Non-state secondary schools are mostly in purpose-built structures on the main roads leading out of town, or on the makeshift ring road. This reflects the relatively recent growth of secondary schooling in Uttar Pradesh in general, and in Bijnor in particular: of the 32 secondary schools serving Bijnor, 23 have been founded since 1972. New institutions could not afford land in the middle of Bijnor, and were established on cheaper land on its outskirts. These vantage points also allow them to attract students from the rural hinterland.

NW Bijnor is different, because its educational institutions are not isolated but form a group, whose collective meaning is more than the sum of its parts. They line the main road that has, since the opening of the Madhya Ganga Barrage in 1985, carried the main traffic to and from Delhi. All five institutions are managed by the same charitable society, and are on land it bought in the late 1940s. In order of founding, they are (A) a government-aided boys' Inter-College; (B) a government-aided girls' Inter-College; (C) a women's Degree and Post-graduate Degree College; (D) an English-medium co-educational public school, operating on two sites in 2000–2, junior and senior; and (E) an Engineering College (see Map 6.1 and Table 6.2).[5] The first four are named after deceased members of the family who dominate the charitable society; the fifth bears the family surname. The individual schools and colleges share many features with others in Bijnor town; similarly, a further six educational institutions are managed by the same charitable society elsewhere in Bijnor District and in Muzaffarnagar District. The three schools teaching secondary-age pupils (A, B and C) contribute over 25% of the secondary school places in Bijnor town. Table 6.2 lists some basic data about these institutions.

On the opposite side of the Delhi road are the government Industrial Training Institute and three other education-related spaces: the Nehru Sports Stadium (almost entirely used by school and college children); an empty plot of land owned by the school-based National Cadet Corps; and the Indira Park, managed by the Forest Department but including children's swings and a roller-skating rink. There is also an ambiguous space, known as the exhibition ground and used to park buses and trucks on a regular basis, where an annual 'exhibition' with stalls and a circus takes place during the monsoon.[6] Lining the road are shops, some on land abutting and paying rent to the schools, a few houses and some other government offices including the Telephone Exchange, the Irrigation colony, a Public Works Department office, the Life Insurance Office and the office that manages primary schooling in the district. All these buildings

Table 6.2 Educational and related institutions on the Main NW Road

Name of Institution	Date of Founding	Number of students in 2001-02	Annual fees in 2001-02
A: Arya Boys' Inter College	1945	2,122	800
B: Girls' Inter-College	1972	1,145	1,150
C: Women's Degree College	1971	950	Varies by course
D: Public School	1990	1,246	5,500
E: Engineering College	1999	255	60,000

Source: Publicity leaflet (undated) and surveys conducted by authors, October 2001 – March 2002. Annual fees for the Inter-Colleges and the Public School are those charged in total to pupils in class 6; fees from class 9 upwards are at least 10 per cent higher.

were established over the last three decades on ground that was either used as mango orchards or for general agricultural purposes – and signs of these earlier uses remain.

The density of educational institutions makes this space unusual. Its educational nature is made clear in several ways, at least along the main Delhi road. Most of the posters on special boards or hanging from poles advertise education-related topics (usually, private computer training institutes), and, after a fatal accident involving a school child in 2000, speed-reducing bumps were put into the road surface on either side of the first and last school. Immediately north-west of the English-medium school is the Awas Vikas colony (where we lived in 2000–2). It was established from the mid-1980s and is not yet complete: new houses are still being built on some of the vacant plots. It is by far the largest residential area on this side of town. Its three qualities of housing – upper, middle and lower income – are graded by size of plot and accessibility to the main road. Many of those living in the upper income group housing are teachers, not only in the neighbouring schools and colleges but also in the government colleges. Other residents send their children to the neighbouring schools, and the proximity of these is one positive feature of this colony often mentioned by other people. But the area is not entirely educational in the activities it supports. In addition to the shops selling school books, or offering snacks or photocopying services mostly to school children, there are also car parts shops, general merchants and phone booths.

Relational webs

Manuel Castells contrasts:

> ... the cosmopolitanism of the elites, living on a daily connection to the whole world (functionally, socially, culturally), to the tribalism of local communities, retrenched in their spaces that they try to control as their last stand against the macro-forces that shape their lives out of their reach
>
> (Castells 1994: 29–30.

This dualistic approach has been challenged by others:

> The social space of what we take to be the city is thus a complex layering of time-space rhythms of multiple time-space relations, some of which are narrowly confined to a particular part of the city, others of which spread across many places near and far from the city. Interweaving with these multiple relational webs are the processes by which identities are constructed, in all their range and diversity.
>
> (Healey 2002: 1780)

Certainly, NW Bijnor is the site of particular relational webs, which operate on a series of different scales of time and distance. The continuous flow of traffic on the main road is dramatically enhanced by daily flows of school children coming from within the town and the surrounding villages. These flows are of major concern for the town authorities: flocks of children on bicycles, loaded onto rickshaws or travelling on the bicycles and scooters of parents or older siblings pose traffic hazards. Before and after the school day, older pupils on cycles and motor-scooters come and go from the residential colonies, visiting the homes of tutors, who are also often teachers. In addition, private buses transport students to a second Engineering College, located in farmland some 16 km from Bijnor town, on the far side of the River Ganga. Its 'camp office' is located in the Awas Vikas colony, and its bus collects and delivers students along the main road as well as from other parts of the new residential colonies.

These schooling-related flows are not, of course, the only ones: men and a few women leave the residential colonies for their work; other men come in to deliver newspapers, sell vegetables, press clothes, or to collect and deliver people by rickshaw. Women move in and out to cook and clean the houses, to wash clothes or to provide childcare. Trucks, tractor-trolleys and buffalo-carts on the main road transport sugar cane to the sugar factory on the other side of town, and local and long-distance buses, three-wheeler vans, rickshaws and horse-drawn buggies take people on their everyday business past the school campuses. Above and beyond these daily flows are longer-term movements – for example, of students from elsewhere in Uttar Pradesh or even abroad to attend the Engineering College at the same time as Bijnor students move elsewhere for higher studies. The schooling provided by these institutions is a stepping stone towards imagined futures, sometimes very specifically so. Thus, in 2001–2, the advertisements for computer training festooning the telephone posts along the road included some promising 'Destination USA' for successful graduates. In this way, one can see some of the 'concrete local processes through which globalisation exists' (Sassen 2000: 169).

These flows make obvious how misleading simple-minded dualisms of local-cosmopolitan or urban-rural are for understanding spaces like these. Imagined localities, imagined futures and imagined modernities are interrelated, and spaces such as NW Bijnor are central to some – but not all – of such processes. For example, the old town of Bijnor, and the villages in its hinterland, appear as relatively static spaces, compared to the new colonies and the educational institutions; yet they also play active parts in contributing flows and movements that link them to regional, national and global processes of various kinds. Migrant labourers go to Delhi, Bombay and the Gulf, and Islamic scholars from Bijnor end up in Deoband, Lucknow and the Arab world, either permanently or temporarily. We must enter one caveat here, however: focusing on flows may tend to draw attention away from the bedrocks of power and difference on which the flows them-selves are based, and which they help to reproduce. Control of the old town, the villages and the educational spaces is contested with greater or lesser success by different social groups: imagined futures for some require the exclusion of others. We now turn to these contestations of dominance and exclusion that lie behind efforts to assert the nature of this particular educa-tional space.

Difference and educational spaces

Western, formal schooling in north India, as elsewhere in South Asia, is part of a civilising mission with its roots in the colonial period when, according to Krishna Kumar, 'some of the natives had to be educated so that they could be civilized according to the master's idea' (Kumar 1991:24). For the different institutions in NW Bijnor, the 'masters' are a closely knit social group with an urbanising and gentrifying project, but the 'natives' have varied class, caste, gender and community social characteristics – which occasionally emerge into open conflict (see later).

The Bijnor charitable society's two Inter-Colleges teach in Hindi and have reputations for serving mainly rural land-holding students, reputations justi-fied in the case of the boys, 60% of whom have rural backgrounds, but not in the case of the girls, only 32% of whom have rural addresses. The urban students attending the Inter-Colleges and the English-medium school are largely from the urban middle- and upper-class populations. We were told by managers that poor children, who represent roughly 20% of the pupils, received free schooling in the boys' Inter-College, that only the very low fees permitted by the government for subsidised colleges were charged, and that these fees were also waived for pupils belonging to the officially recognised Scheduled Caste (SC) groups in the girls' Inter-College.[7] In practice, however, fees of various kinds (both legal and illegal) generate monthly charges for the families of boys starting at around Rs 70 per month in Class 6, going up to at least Rs 140 per month in Classes 11–12, with additional charges for examinations, laboratory work, etc. According to the clerks dealing with collecting these payments, not a single student was exempted from these charges. Students are also required to wear a school uniform, although some of them may receive free items of clothing from the school management (see later). Not surprisingly, then, within the villages we studied, the institutions were perceived as the preserve of the rich.

Muslim and SC children were also underrepresented. Muslims, who made up 35–40% of the surrounding population, formed 10% of the pupil body in the girls' Inter-College and the English-medium school, and 3% in the boys' Inter-College.[8] SC children, who stemmed from groups making up 20% or so of the local population, represented 12% of the girls' Inter-College pupils and 17% of the boys, but no children in the English-medium school were identified as SC.[9] About 80% of the pupils in both Inter-Colleges belonged to the officially recognised Other Backward Classes (OBC) (mainly Jats, the dominant Hindu land-owning caste) or the 'General' category, roughly twice their combined shares in the population as a whole, both in the town itself and in the district.

As a condition of receiving government aid, the Inter-College fees are limited, but the English-medium public school has no such limits and clearly serves the urban elite. Its fees place it well beyond the reach of all but the richer farmers in the nearby villages. Some of the richer farmers in one of our research villages said they had complained about the fees, but had been unable to get a reduction. But even when expressing their displeasure about the manager and his schools to us, they acknowledged the strengths of the institutions. One said:

All his schools are very expensive. .... [In the English-medium school] if a child gets a good number in their class, even then to get into the next class, they must pay Rs 1,100. They must also pay Rs 300 in fees each month and it costs Rs 2,400 to get admission. Every month it is necessary to pay fees on the 15th, but if you pay them on the 16th there is a Rs 10 fine. There are many expenses in his schools. Imagine that a child needs a pencil. The pencil may cost just Rs 2 in a shop in the bazaar, but they will say that the child must buy the pencil in the school's own shop where it costs Rs 5, and the school is very strict in this respect. . . . But he [the manager] has a sharp mind and he does all the work related to his schools himself. So the teaching in his schools is very good and the teachers are very good. . . . For these reasons, despite the high fees and expenses, we like to send our children to study at his schools.

In this quote, more general issues of quality, such as the need for owners and managers to take a personal interest in the management of the school if the institution is to flourish, and how such interest translates into 'good' schooling, are merely hinted at. Others, such as the personal characteristics and networks of the founders, managers and teachers, are also very important reasons why some schools are preferred over others. But for most local people English-medium teaching is also a necessary element in high-quality schooling. The women's Degree College, which teaches in Hindi and English, the Engineering College, which teaches mostly in English, and the English-medium public school, all attract relatively wealthy students, mostly from urban backgrounds, who are the only ones to have heard and spoken sufficient English at home to have a chance of gaining entry to and benefiting from the education offered.

The two older institutions are in cramped quarters. The three more recent institutions, those serving the urban elite, are set in extensive landscaped compounds, with lawns, flower-beds, trees and shrubs, the largest being for the English-medium school and the Engineering College. All are walled, with single points of entry. All are new, quintessentially urban buildings with few decorative flourishes. Nevertheless, they share family resemblances to schools and colleges in India's larger cities, where a 'school building was indispensable to proper education, preferably a grand edifice costing enormous sums of money, for which large-hearted donors had been mobilized by unusually enterprising spirits' (Kumar 1996: 141).

In Bijnor, the large-hearted donors are mostly the family and friends of the descendants of a man born in about 1880 whose forebears came from Mandawar, 12 km north of Bijnor town. He rose to the rank of Chief Engineer in the United Provinces and was granted substantial lands north-west of Bijnor in the 1920s. He met and became a follower of Madan Mohan Malaviya (1861–1948) a prominent member of the Congress party, but also founder of the Hindu Mahasabha and the Banaras Hindu University. He became a local president of the reformist Arya Samaj, founded a school in Meerut, and lived in Banaras for eight years, helping to build the Hindu University. He was also involved in the construction of the Birla Temple in New Delhi. He died in September 1944.

125

His eldest son became an officer in the Indian Colonial Service (ICS), and served as Nehru's Cabinet Secretary as well as Governor of Karnataka and West Bengal. The second son, a businessman, lived in Lucknow for many years (and one of his own sons, a retired senior civil servant, has houses in Delhi and outside Bijnor, and now chairs the family's charitable society). The third son, born in 1911, returned to Bijnor after university education in London before 1939, and has managed the family's lands in the district, as well as being a very prominent politician. He was a member of the Congress party until 1975, when he was jailed under the Emergency and turned to Janata, being elected to the Uttar Pradesh Assembly in 1977 and serving briefly as Minister for Technical Education. He administered the educational institutions established by the family trust until his death in 2003. He appears as 'the manager' in this chapter. He inherited his father's involvement in a small Arya Samaj school in Bijnor, turned it into a senior high school that became the boys' Inter-College, and moved it to its present site in 1952, when its foundation stone was laid by Govind Ballabh Pant, the first Chief Minister of Uttar Pradesh.

The remaining charitable society institutions were opened from the 1970s onwards. Unquestionably the 'unusually enterprising spirit' was the manager. He was a figure of some considerable respect in Bijnor town and its surroundings, but his political influence waned in the 1980s and 1990s. Nonetheless, he remained politically active until he died, using his networks within and outside the district to maintain patron-client relationships and to forge factional links in the Congress and Samajwadi parties. His extended family, part of India's cosmopolitan elite, has members serving with distinction in the Indian Administrative Service, in academia in India, the UK and the USA, and in international banking. As such, they can play only fleeting roles in Bijnor's affairs and the manager sought assistance from some local notables: landlords, lawyers and teachers, all from urban upper-caste Hindu origins. Inevitably, he also needed the support of the local administrative elite, the District Magistrate, the District Inspector of Schools and the District Sports Officer, who manages the Nehru Stadium. In 2002, recognising a potential crisis of transition, he renewed his efforts to bring some of the Delhi-based family members into more active management roles, and to widen the base of charitable society members from Bijnor, possibly even to include a representative of an elite Muslim family from the old town. The lifestyles of secularised modernity followed by the Delhi-based family have become increasingly out of kilter with the resurgent Hindu nationalism espoused by the Bharatiya Janata Party (BJP), who have provided most of the district's elected politicians since 1991.

The manager and his family and associates have used their dominance of the NW Bijnor institutions to try to inscribe them with particular meanings.

In managing the schools, they employ particular discursive practices, especially through their support for special events put on by some of these institutions. Obviously, daily routines are crucial. But social dominance is also regularly reaffirmed and assured through visible and semi-public 'events', ranging from the least public (daily assemblies, in which outsiders often play a role) to substantial advertised events based on many days' planning and involving the pupils' parents and relatives as well as local notables.[10] These events open up possibilities to subvert, spoil or disrupt what is happening. The prevailing moods may be tense and uncertain, since these events are a means of testing, reaffirming and developing a range of uncertain loyalties, for instance between parents and management, pupils and teachers, or the local administration and the management. Most of the institutions have founders' day celebrations, as well as marking national holidays – Independence Day, Republic Day, Gandhi's birthday, etc. To give a flavour of what happens at these events, we describe a Sports Day, which is common to the five institutions, two functions at the Engineering College, and a Founder's Day function at the girls' Inter-College, before drawing out some common themes from these and other events we attended.

Sports Day, November 2000

For these schools, a Sports Day is a very recent invention, although it clearly borrows from much longer traditions. According to the manager, the idea came from his third son, who had been a sportsman and had attended elite public schools, and wanted to copy their sports days for the charitable society schools.[11] The manager said, 'Before that Bijnor was very backward', suggesting that he saw the successful staging of public functions comparable to those found in the larger cities and elite schools as a crucial indicator of modernity.

In 2000, the Sports Day was held at the Nehru Stadium over three days, but the public ceremony was restricted to the morning of the first day. By 10.30 there were maybe 500 children sitting in the middle of the running track in fairly straight rows and columns. Around the running track were other groups, including young men from the Engineering College. At 11.00 prompt the District Magistrate arrived at the stand; everyone stood up, and he was shown to the seat next to the manager. Other local notables were in the front two rows. In addition, there were about 100 teachers and parents in the stand. After patriotic songs, the District Magistrate declared the proceedings open, and released two doves and a bunch of balloons. Fireworks were set off, and the District Magistrate sat down for the march-past, led by a girls' band. Each group, including a Scout troop, a group of young girls in yellow dresses, two National Cadet Corps platoons and groups representing other smaller schools, had a banner and a flag. One boy took a lit torch and ran half-way round the track, passing it on to another, who brought it back to the stand, accompanied by rhythmic clapping all the way round. Then a young woman from the Degree College led all the students in a pledge: she said a phrase and they all repeated it back to her, loudly and with enthusiasm, ending with a *'Jai Hind!'* (Long Live India).

A series of small 'skits' followed, lasting 90 minutes or so: singers, dancers, a series of body-building exercises with small dumb-bells and tambourines, human pyramids, a skit set in a classroom, where the teacher came in and started teaching the English alphabet. Three groups in the middle then went through mass exercises in turn. Each set started with the students standing to attention and shouting *'Jai Hind!'* One pupil banged out the rhythm on a drum to accompany each set of waving, standing, bending exercises, including in each case a set carried out seated. Then the first race took place, a 50-metre dash for 5–6-year-olds. The District Magistrate stood up and took the microphone for a very short speech, in which he praised the manager and the contribution he had made to the development of the district by his educational work. Then a College principal responded briefly, but no-one in the stadium seemed to take much notice of either speech. The front two rows of spectators left the stand, going to the Degree College for tea and snacks with the District Magistrate, and the sports continued in their absence.

An 'Old Boys – Young Boys' [sic] function at the Engineering College, September 2000

Each of the 100 or so new 1st year students (88 male, 7 female) introduced themselves to their peers and to the 2nd year students in a formulaic manner. Students came forward one by one and later in twos, gave their name, father's name, place of residence, the Inter-College they attended and their overall percentage in the 12th class exams, and stated their hobbies (for example, reading books, chemistry, physics and maths, cricket, chess and singing). Some students started by thanking or paying respect to the manager, teachers and/or senior students. They spoke in a mixture of English and Hindi. Students who could sing were asked to perform, and some of them performed three or four Bollywood numbers, mostly received with great enthusiasm by the other students. The manager occasionally teased or harassed nervous-looking students and the seniors sometimes openly laughed at the juniors. The audience consisted of male teachers, senior students and juniors, two members of the management committee and three social researchers. The students all wore their uniforms of grey trousers and shirt for the men, and *shalwar kamiz* (loose cotton trousers and a loose long-sleeved shirt) for the women.

The Engineering College Annual Function, December 2001

This started when three small lamps with clarified butter were lit on an ornate brass candle stand in front of a small statue of Saraswati. The function followed a printed programme and a cameraman filmed the acts and the audience's reactions. Two other men took photographs, one using a digital camera. The scheduled acts mostly involved singing and dancing, and followed a common pattern. All started with an introduction in formal Hindi or more often in English, which contextualised the act and illustrated its artistic worth, moral value or capacity to operate as social commentary. Some performers gave a *namaste* (Hindu greeting) to the Saraswati statue before they started. Fillers between the acts included impressions of Hindi film stars, jokes and small comic skits. Four of the more substantial events were as follows:

First, a mime involving five male students was performed. One stood in the centre of the stage in a position that suggested that he was at prayer as a Hindu. His body was then shifted by another student applying an imaginary hammer to his limbs, so that he took up a series of poses. The last three were: a position of Muslim prayer, with his forehead on the ground and kneeling down; the position of Christ on the cross; and finally Gandhi in a walking position, holding a staff and with back bent. A young man said, in English, that the act demonstrated how all religions are in fact just one, that India contains many religions, and that people respect others whatever their religion.

Second, a 'Choreography (Women Liberation)' [sic] was introduced (in English) with reference to social surveys in India that demonstrated the extent and nature of physical violence and psychological harassment perpetrated against women in marriage, even in Kerala where literacy rates are high. Although women have learnt to be silent in the face of this harassment and violence, the motto of this act was 'silence no more'. A woman dancer mimed breaking the chains that held her, and then three groups of three students mimed domestic scenes in which a woman was beaten or slapped by drunken men. One trio mimed burning the woman. Then the three women held up three small paper banners, with the words 'dowry', 'illiteracy' and 'physical abuse', before setting them alight. The act closed with a short speech, again in English, saying that women still experience silent bondage.

This was followed by a mime on drug abuse. A drug Mafia don tells his middleman to distribute drugs to some College students. The dealer persuades the students to take the drugs, and one dies, while another becomes critically ill and is saved by a doctor. The students realise the dangers of taking drugs, and in the final scene the actors displayed a banner with a skull and crossbones and a packet of cigarettes, a bottle of whisky, a tin of marijuana and a packet of *paan* (betel leaf mixed with tobacco, areca nut, lime, etc.). Across the top of the banner was written 'Say No To Drugs'. This was greeted with clapping and cheers.

129

And, last, a dramatisation of Prem Chand's short story, *Namak ka Daroga* (The Salt Inspector), was performed in Hindi. A man tells his son that he must take a job with a good income above his salary. The son wishes to remain honest and not take bribes. When he gets a job as a salt inspector, he captures the employees of a powerful local Brahman, who were illegally transporting salt. He refuses to release them despite being offered increasingly large sums of money by the Brahman, and eventually loses his job. But the Brahman is so impressed by the inspector's honesty that he offers him a job as manager of his own estates, and the ex-inspector inherits the Brahman's fortune.

Girls' Inter-College Founder's Day, October 2001

In 2001, this was held on the death anniversary of the manager's wife, after whom the College was named. In the morning, her statue was unveiled after a Hindu ceremony of worship conducted within the school premises. The ceremony was attended by the manager's family and their friends, with teachers from the charitable society schools making up the rest of the audience. In the evening, a full dance and song programme was put on by the students, preceded by a science exhibition located in one of the classrooms. The acts included a dance for Saraswati and a dance to the tune of '*Phir bhi ham Hindustani hai*' ('Even so we are still Indians', a famous Bollywood song). The student who introduced this act said (in Hindi) that Muslims, Hindus and Sikhs are all first of all humans: 'We all feel the same patriotism. A cultural programme would not be complete without a patriotic song.' This was followed by a folk dance. The Principal's address, from a prepared text, was in highly Sanskritised Hindi and stressed images of duty, energy, development and progress. She talked about reverence for the founder and for the manager. She mentioned computer education as a new separate subject and the buildings' construction in progress, and noted the school's successes in state-level competitions in sports, girl guides and science exhibitions. She gave credit for this to the chairman, the manager and other respected members of the district's 'glorious institution', the charitable society. She thanked the chief guest, the District Magistrate, for taking time to attend their function, and all the parents who gave ideas and money to develop the College, as a result of which they were moving further and further towards progress. Then the official cameraman photographed the manager handing out free uniforms to several needy students. The dance show then continued, with fillers of one-line jokes between the acts, for the rest of the evening.

Here we discuss three aspects of how these spaces are being inscribed with particular discursive practices: their apparent espousal of a Nehruvian vision; their obsession with discipline; and schools as a political resource. We then consider some signs of resistance to these attempts.

The Nehruvian secular project

These functions are a testament to the enduring appeal of a Nehruvian vision. Nehru was committed to science, and especially to the embodiment of science in dams, power stations and steel mills, to non-discrimination on the basis of caste or religion, and to the ending of ignorance and inequality of opportunity (see Corbridge and Harriss 2000: 24–32; Drèze and Sen 2002: 1–11). Schooling was central to that vision, and the charitable society schools (like others we visited in Bijnor), as well as most pupils, showed a public commitment to Nehruvian ideals (Jeffery *et al.* 2005). Women's empowerment, honesty in public servants, the absence of significant differences between members of different castes and religions, and the importance of science and reason were elements stressed again and again, in different ways, in all the functions we attended. In many functions, claims were made that pupils could, through hard work and ability, use the educational system to achieve goals that would take them far from their roots. In the course of his address to the pupils at their second annual day function, the chairman of the Engineering College put it like this (in English):

> The efforts of the pupils of the College are even more important than the actions of the management. You must be determined and work hard to overcome the obstacles that you will inevitably face. You can raise the reputation of the College through hard work, commitment and good conduct. I am sure that you are capable of this. The results are very good and I have been impressed by the science exhibition. Your will has also been demonstrated by the items on display in the cultural programme this evening. It is a struggle, but you can do it. The first batch of students will be passing out this year, and their names should strike awe in future generations of students. The names of the current students would live on in the institution. I will be more specific about this College. We are not satisfied. We want to continue to improve the College so that it becomes one of the best engineering colleges in [Uttar Pradesh] and then in India.

Examination results were stressed, not only in the speeches given by head teachers and the manager, but also in the Annual Review published by the boys' Inter-College. Examples of individuals who had managed to enter one of India's elite Institutes of Technology were regularly reported to us, as were the successes in Uttar Pradesh-wide examinations – for example, for entry into medical and engineering colleges.[12]

These commitments to secular ideals were, however, often subtly undermined. The most obvious were the ways in which religion entered into aspects of apparently secular ceremonies. Some ceremonies, such as the

131

unveiling of the statue at the girls' Inter-College, were entirely Hindu in their orientation, and non-Hindus were almost entirely absent. But others with no apparent 'religious' purpose were imbued with 'banal Hinduism', such as the lighting of lamps and the presence of a Saraswati statue at the Engineering College's annual function, or the use of Hindu imagery in the Sanskritised Hindi routinely used in the speeches.[13] The Colleges are also connected to more overtly Hindu institutions. The principal of the boys' Inter-College was the chief guest at the Independence Day celebrations organised by Seva Bharti (a BJP organisation), and another Hindu nationalist group organised competitions at the girls' Inter-College, handing out shields and prizes at their Republic Day function. Thus we can see how Nehru's vision is being subverted from within. Commitment to some of his ideals (science, progress) is increasingly being framed within a specifically Hindu modernity, one that increasingly excludes Bijnor's non-Hindus. Our 24-year-old Muslim research assistant could see the changes made to the daily morning assemblies at the girls' Inter-College: since she had left, for example, *Vande Mataram* (Hail to the Motherland!), an anthem with distinctly Hindu imagery, had been introduced as 'the national song'.

Disciplined bodies, docile behaviour

Krishna Kumar has suggested that the main contribution of schooling in independent India is 'the maintenance of law and order' (Kumar 1991: 19), and we would argue that school functions such as those we have described here contribute to this in several ways. First, and most obviously, many parts of the Sports Day function were based on the idea of disciplined bodies, marching in time, standing and sitting in straight rows, exercising together, wearing uniforms and speaking with one voice.[14] Similar but less public and elaborate routines were followed in daily assemblies and other events.[15] The girls' Inter-College had a half-time male member of staff, whose main role seemed to be to lead the mass exercises. At the Republic Day ceremony, he was responsible for the 15 minutes of standing to attention, saluting and shouting '*Jai Hind*' with clenched fists raised into the air that preceded the flag-raising.

Discipline was a particular issue at the boys' Inter-College. Physical threats and beatings are a routine part of everyday life within the Inter-College. Two or three watchmen and messengers, armed with staves, control the entrance to the school. A newly appointed teacher reported that the school was somewhat unusual in its focus on this kind of discipline:

> In our school you will find all the teachers have sticks, it is the uniform of the teachers. And this is the uniform only of our school, not of any other school. When I first came here I didn't have the habit of taking a stick in my hand. I used to go with an empty hand

into the class to teach. So other teachers told me to certainly take a stick with me because here it is the uniform of the teacher. So having come here, slowly I adopted this habit.

The Principal wrote in the annual school magazine that discipline was what made a school good or bad: 'Discipline is the breath of life to a student. He is today's, tomorrow's citizen. Without discipline a student cannot be made a citizen. And nor can he succeed in his individual life' (Tyagi 2001).[16] He regularly threatens to hit pupils himself. Newspaper reports (*Amar Ujala* 2001; *Bijnor Times* 2001) refer to students beating teachers and teachers fighting back. It seems that some teachers see beating as a necessity, not just to maintain order within the school but also in its relations with the outside world. One said:

> We don't often raise our hand against children. But if I give one or two people a sound beating, the others all understand that if I beat someone they MUST have been doing something wrong. The parents of children who come here also understand that I don't beat someone without good reason. It is sometimes the case that boys at the school *challenge* me. They say: 'Come outside the College and THEN let's see what happens.' Sometimes I accept this *challenge*. I have even sorted out a few boys outside the College! There are some old students who try and corrupt the children here. Some ex-students – rotten types – keep on hanging around in the College interfering. I sort them out. I only raise my hand once or twice a year. But that is quite enough to fill the year. You will have seen even now that the principal *sahib* called me to see what was going on outside the gate. I am notorious among the teachers for beating!

The current principals of the boys' Inter-College and the government Inter-College were both reputed to have brought discipline to these institutions, and this received considerable support from newspapers and from the educated middle classes. One innovation is that the boys' Inter-College gates are now locked for a substantial part of the day, to prevent pupils congregating outside and making a nuisance of themselves to passing pedestrians, including the young women going to the women's Degree College.[17] The Colleges also insist on uniforms for their pupils, in part so that they can be identified outside the institution if they are misbehaving.

Schools as a political resource

The manager played an active part in local politics for over 50 years, and the schools have been a central part of his political resource. Through his control over discretionary admissions, his dominance over staff recruitment and the opportunities his schools offer for contracts of various kinds, he was able to build a network of supporters under an obligation to help him in politics. Others also see the schools as politically valuable. Thus, in the run-up to the 2002 Uttar Pradesh Assembly elections, the manager was told that he would get official permission for extending his schools only if he joined the BJP – which he refused to do. He also claimed that a dispute in one of the rural schools run by the charitable society reflected an attempt by the BJP to take the school over, believing that it provided a platform for political advance in the region.

During the horse-trading before the 2002 Assembly elections, the manager's son, already a member of the District Board for the constituency that included the Awas Vikas colony, was refused a party ticket, and stood as an independent candidate. The charitable society headquarters in NW Bijnor were turned into his election campaign office, and school resources were commandeered for the three weeks of the campaign. As a teacher in the boys' Inter-College put it, 'The management were involved in the elections, so we had to co-operate'. A major plank of the campaign was inter-religious harmony; another was the manager's promise to build a medical college in the town. But the manager's political procession through the town consisted largely of charitable society employees, and the manager's son received only 3.3% of the votes, losing his deposit and humiliating the manager. There were, in other words, limits to the extent to which the manager could impose his preferred meanings of the schools in general, and the work of the charitable society in particular, on the local populace. *Noblesse oblige* is an increasingly inadequate means of mobilising support. The chairman of the Engineering College, for instance, was forced to acknowledge in his speech (in English) at the Annual Function in 2002 that improving the College would require the help of Bijnor's citizens:

> There is a mentality in India that things should be provided without the people's direct involvement, but they must learn that, if they want an institution like the College in Bijnor, then they need to contribute to it in some way: in cash, in kind, or through some other sort of help, such as assisting at events such as these.

In these ways, the manager was portrayed by those around him as the town's supreme benefactor. This image was reinforced by his ability to persuade the senior government officials in Bijnor, the District Magistrate and the Superintendent of Police, to attend some of his school functions. But the middle classes of Bijnor are showing up the hollowness of these claims, not just by staying away from the manager's political bandwagons, but in more direct ways as well.

Contesting meanings

The locations of buildings, their naming practices, their design and arrangement 'have been manipulated so as to present the current social hierarchy as
natural and permanent' and what we have here is an 'urban form as an ideological project' (Philo and Kearns 1993: 13). To what extent is this project of
displaying 'what constitutes a "good" or "proper" way of living' (Kearns
and Philo 1993: ix) being challenged?

Most subversions were indirect. The speeches of the District Magistrate
and the headmaster of the boys' Inter-College at the Sports Days were
simply ignored. Collecting so many young people together is always a risk to
public order, and the following year students of the boys' Inter-College
fought those of the Engineering College, after some Inter-College boys
jeered the Engineering College girls' folk dance. The police broke up the
fight, but one boy had a cut on his head. There is also contestation over
what should be presented on these occasions, with the more cosmopolitan
managers objecting to the reliance on recorded 'Bollywood' rather than live
music and the practice of including a dance by a cross-dressed boy instead
of more traditional 'high culture' dancing.[18]

There were also some apparently spontaneous refusals to engage with
aspects of the public events. For example, at the end of the first Engineering
College function, the final item was a speech by a senior male student. The
student began to complain about standards of teaching and teachers at the
College, about the accommodation and about the College's refusal to allow
the student to rag the 1st year students.[19] He became angry when the College
proctor interrupted him and told him to go no further. He eventually apolo-
gised and finished with a simple 'I wish you all well'. Immediately after this
half-hearted apology, most of the male students rushed away from the
floodlit function area towards the exit from the College grounds, explicitly
rejecting the snacks that had been laid out for them and embarrassing the
principal, teachers and the manager. A small group of students talked to the
principal and the manager, but the principal told them that because they
agreed with the protestors they should also leave, and they did so. After the
function, the proctor resigned.

More generalised opposition to the whole project was provided by those
who criticised the manager for naming the schools and colleges after
members of his own family. No other Bijnor schools were named after
family members, although some were named after prominent outsiders –
for instance, Jagjivan Ram, the SC former Union Minister. Some people
disputed the benefits of the Engineering College, because there were no
reservations for local residents and the fees were far too expensive for people
from Bijnor. The manager's desire to open a medical college in the town, as
the culmination of his lifetime achievements, had widespread support, but
some argued that it would bring glory only to the family charitable society

because, again, no students from Bijnor would be able to afford to study there.

Tuition outside school is also a morally ambiguous arena, and one of increasing conflict between teachers, management and pupils (Jeffery *et al.* 2006). These contests over educational meanings are especially visible in NW Bijnor, because much tuition is offered in residential colonies like Awas Vikas. The rising significance of tuition reflects the 'curricularisation' of children's everyday lives (Ennew 1994: 127), but it is also a sign of a withdrawal of legitimacy from the schools, by teachers and pupils and/or their parents. Parents complain that teachers do not teach properly in schools, or threaten pupils with failure in internal examinations, in order to pressurise pupils to take private tuition with them. Most people seem to believe that there is a law against tuition, although the official in charge of secondary schooling in the district explained that teachers must get permission from the management or the principal to take on one or two tuition classes. He said that this rule was not being followed, and some teachers took many classes. If the government wanted to stop tuition it could do so, he said, but he himself was ambivalent about the practice, noting that there is considerable demand from parents and pupils, the same people expected to complain when the rules were broken. No-one supports teachers who 'compel' pupils to take tuition, either by outright demands, by failing students who do not take tuition, or by failing to teach properly in school. Many teachers object to the attempts to impose discipline on them, and argue that there is no reason why they should not be allowed to do tuition, given that pupils request it and it is hard to give pupils individual attention when class sizes are so high. But even they criticise teachers who seem to be motivated solely by commercial factors, as one teacher explained:

> Teachers are being defamed because people are saying that they are forcing children to take *tuition*, but children and their parents want *tuition* to be arranged. Every child is taking *tuition*, whether they are *Science Side* or *Arts Side*. Without *tuition* the children themselves don't progress. It is not at all unusual for children to take four, five or six *tuitions*, but no child takes less than four. That makes Rs 1,000 at the end of the month, for sure. Why will teachers oppose this? But I have seen teachers who are willing to be beaten [by a student] in order to teach in *tuitions*. They accept a beating if it means that they will get tuition work, because their *aim* is to make money.

And another one suggested: 'Their aim isn't to teach; their aim is to make money. There is a Sanskrit saying: "by hook or by crook they have to seek wealth". Now they have to bear so much shame, but they certainly give tuitions.'

The charitable society management felt, not surprisingly, that teachers should teach properly within the school, but also felt hamstrung by their lack of control over those teachers whose salaries were paid by the government. The manager was unable to sack a teacher who gave higher marks to pupils who took tuition from him. He told us (in English) that he had stopped the teacher's increment because 'He had done such a wrong thing, it was immoral. What distinction would there be between a foolish and an intelligent boy? It was very bad.' Although the charitable society tried to ban tuition by the teachers it paid, it was unsuccessful, as the chairman of one college pointed out (in English):

> We have banned tuition. . . . we have put out a directive that tuition is banned and if anyone is caught doing it there will be serious consequences and they could maybe be dismissed. . . . But having said that, we are not pro-actively going round trying to catch them. Mostly we find that it is other teachers jealously complaining about someone, or some parents complain.

Tuitions certainly provide opportunities for very different, less hierarchical and less formal relationships to develop between teachers and pupils, which some teachers and managers see as a threat to discipline within the school. Others, especially boys, see tuition as an opportunity to escape the home for a while, and to tour around the town on their bicycles, whereas girls are more likely to go and come back directly. Our evidence suggests that more boys than girls take tuition classes but, nonetheless, tuitions are social spaces where unrelated boys and girls can occasionally meet on neutral territory. Tuition, of course, also tends to exclude: tutors are often selected from family, caste and religious networks and, given the costs involved, tuition systematically tends to reduce the chances of poor children – even those from SC backgrounds who have scholarships to help keep them in school – from being able to use education to gain social mobility.

Conclusion

This paper has documented the rising importance of a class of 'educational mediators' in the production of urban space in India (see Lynch, 1990, for a comparable account in Ireland). The manager and other members of his charitable society have tried to orchestrate the cultural resources represented by the schools they manage to create particular kinds of young adults, as well as to bolster their own social, political and economic positions in the region. They use their own cultural and social capital to project particular visions of modernity, progress and success, ones that are seamlessly linked with their own life-worlds, highly westernised, international in orientation and secular. In some measure, these meanings mesh well with those being chosen by teachers, students and other members of the urban elite, as can be seen from the explicit messages communicated in the skits put on at the functions organised at the Engineering College and at the girls' Inter-College. But increasingly, such meanings are being contested and undermined, as 'Hindutva' (a Hindu way of life) models of modernity and Hindu symbols and iconography become integral to the everyday practices of these institutions. Bijnor's new Hindu middle class dominates the colonies, the Civil Lines and most of the wealthier parts of the old town, commerce and government service, as well as the teaching profession and Bijnor's student body. Muslim and SC children are being pushed to the margins of this modernity. These moves are consonant with developments at the level of Uttar Pradesh, which had a BJP-led government until the 2002 elections, and that of India as a whole, which had a BJP-led coalition from 1999 to 2004. These years saw a major push by the BJP to claim the academic worlds of historical research and teaching for a revised, Hindutva model, a push which was accepted if not actively welcomed by teachers in Bijnor. The charitable society is also facing competition from expensive, English-medium schools and colleges and from explicitly religious foundations, Hindu and Muslim alike. What is clear, however, is that all these changes tend to undermine the Nehruvian models that underpinned the charitable society schools from their inception. The imagined futures that gave these models meaning have turned out to be illusory: if the new visions of the future also turn out to be unreal, we expect the scapegoats – the excluded Muslims and Scheduled Castes – to suffer the consequences.

Notes

1   We are grateful to the Economic and Social Research Council (grant R00238495), the Ford Foundation, and the Royal Geographical Society for funding the research in Bijnor District (Uttar Pradesh) on which this paper is based, and to the Institute of Economic Growth, New Delhi, for our attachment there in 2000–2. Earlier research in the district was funded by the (then) Social Science Research Council and the Overseas Development Administration. None bears any responsibility for what we have written here. We also thank our research assistants, Swaleha Begum, Shaila Rais, Chhaya Sharma and Manjula Sharma, the people of Qaziwala and Nangal Jat, the school staff and the many others who so readily answered our questions. We are also grateful to Hugo Gorringe, Martha Caddell, Nick Prior, Geert De Neve, Henrike Donner and participants in the SAAG conference for comments on early drafts of this paper.
2   The English word is used. In the rest of this chapter, extracts from our fieldnotes have been translated from the Hindi (unless we specify that the original was in English) and words in English in the original will appear in italics.
3   For an insightful journalistic account of how India's small towns are changing, see Mishra (1995).
4   As far as we are aware, population data by religion by urban area have not been published since 1971. In the Bijnor urban agglomeration, Hindus probably now outnumber Muslims, because Hindus predominate in the new colonies, although Muslims probably predominate in the area under the Bijnor Municipal Board.
5   In Uttar Pradesh, secondary schools that teach Classes 6–12 are usually known as Intermediate or Inter-Colleges.

6 The exhibition ground and Indira Park are also noted for assignations between young men and women.

7 Brighter urban children try to get admission to the government's own boys' and girls' Inter-Colleges, which have lower fees but higher academic reputations.

8 In addition to *madrasahs*, the Muslim elite manage the Bijnor Inter-College, the Muslim Girls Middle School, the Rahimya Public School and Jalaluddin High School. All these are, by contrast, dominated by Muslims although the Bijnor Inter-College and Jalaluddin have substantial numbers of Scheduled Caste pupils.

9 Scheduled Caste children were well represented in the government schools, reflecting the reservation of places for them there.

10 Although there were no formal checks on who attended these functions, informal social controls ensured that the audiences were restricted in practice to men and women from the middle and upper sections of Bijnor society.

11 This is only one among many examples of how these schools are connected to educational practices elsewhere in India and further afield. For example, the chairman of the Engineering College is also a vice-chairman of Delhi Public Schools; the nephew of the manager, who is taking over some of his functions, is also on the board of the United World College in Pune. Family links to the Doon School, India's nearest equivalent to Eton or Harrow, are also exceptionally strong.

12 Each of these successes, of course, takes the successful student away from Bijnor, not only for higher study but for careers that Bijnor town cannot offer.

13 The idea of 'banal Hinduism' is derived from Michael Billig's discussion in *Banal Nationalism* (1995) and elaborated further in Chapter 3 of Jeffery and Jeffery (2006)

14 The issue of time-keeping was important the following year, when the District Superintendent of Police was the chief guest: he arrived late, when the organisers were debating whether to start the proceedings without him because the children were all sitting ready.

15 At the Sports Day, the two Hindi-medium Inter-Colleges were far more successful at keeping time in the group aerobics than was the public school, whose Principal said that she did not take these events very seriously because they interrupted the scholastic activities of her school.

16 *Anushasan ke bina vidhyarthi na to sabhya nagrik ban sakta hai aur na hi apne vyaktigat jeevan me safal ho sakta hai.*

17 During the Mandal and Ayodhya disturbances of 1990–1, boys from the Inter-College were said to have taunted young women en route from Bijnor town to the Degree College, and to have challenged them – especially those thought to be Muslims – to respond to greetings of 'Jai Shri Ram'.

18 Muslims particularly object to cross-dressing and dancing, explicitly seen as sinful in the Qur'an. The principal of a *madrasah* on the other side of Bijnor scoffed that he saw the children putting on a dance show inside a public school:

> So now I believe that all they do in that school is teach children how to dance, I don't think they offer any education! So they are teaching their children how to dance and we are teaching our children Qur'an Sharif.

19 Ragging is illegal in Uttar Pradesh.

References

Amar Ujala (2001) 'Nakal karne se rokne par shikshak se marpeet' [In stopping copying, beaten by student] 7 January

Bijnor Times (2001) 'Shikshakon se marpeet ka silsila abhi rooka nahin' [The tradition of beating by students is not yet stopped] 8 January

139

Bayly, C.A. (1983) *Rulers, Townsmen and Bazaars*, Cambridge: Cambridge University Press

Billig, M. (1995) *Banal Nationalism*, London: Sage Publications

Bridge, G. and Watson, S. (2000) 'City differences', in Bridge, G. and Watson, S. (eds), *A Companion to the City*, Oxford: Blackwell

Castells, M. (1994) 'European cities, the informational society and the global economy' *New Left Review* 204 1–30

Corbridge, S. and Harriss, J. (2000) *Reinventing India: Liberalization, Hindu Nationalism and Popular Democracy*, Cambridge: Polity Press

Drèze, J. and Sen, A. (2002) *India: Development and Participation*, New Delhi: Oxford University Press

Ennew, J. (1994) 'Time for children or time for adults?', in Qvortrup J., Bardy, M., Sgritta, G. and Wintersberger, H. (eds), *Childhood Matters: Social Theory, Practice and Politics*, Aldershot: Avebury

Freitag, S.B. (1989) *Collective Action and Community: Public Arenas and the Emergence of Communalism in North India*, Berkeley, Los Angeles and London: University of California Press

Healey, P. (2002) 'On creating the "city" as a collective resource' *Urban Studies* 39(10) 1777–92

Jeffery, P.M. and Jeffery, R. (2006) *Confronting Saffron Demography: Religion, Fertility and Women's Status in India*, New Delhi: Three Essays Collective

Jeffery, R., Jeffery, P.M. and Jeffrey, C. (2005) 'Social inequalities and the privatisation of secondary schooling in north India', in Chopra, R. and Jeffery, P. (eds), *Educational Regimes in Contemporary India: Essays on education in a changing global context*. New Delhi, Thousand Oaks and London: Sage Publications

——(2006) 'Patterns and discourses of the privatisation of secondary schooling in Bijnor, UP', in Kumar, K. and Öesterheld, J. (eds), *Education in Modern South Asia: Social and Political Implications*, New Delhi: Orient Longman

Lynch, K. (1990) 'Reproduction: the role of cultural factors and educational mediators' *British Journal of Sociology of Education* 11(1) 3–20

Kearns, G. and Philo, C. (1993) 'Preface', in Kearns, G. and Philo, C. (eds), *Selling Places: The City as Cultural Capital, Past and Present*, Oxford: Pergamon Press

King, A.D. (2000) 'Postcolonialism, representation, and the city', in Bridge, G. and Watson, S. (eds) *A Companion to the City*, Oxford: Blackwell

Kumar, K. (1991) *Political Agenda of Education: A Study of Colonialist and Nationalist Ideas,* New Delhi: Sage Publications

Kumar, N. (1996) 'Religion and ritual in Indian schools: Banaras from the 1880s to the 1940s', in Crook, N. (ed.) *The Transmission of Knowledge in South Asia: Essays on Education, Religion, History and Politics*, New Delhi: Oxford University Press

Mishra, P. (1995) *Butter Chicken in Ludhiana: Travels in Small Town India*, New Delhi: Penguin India

Orsini, F. (2002) *The Hindi Public Sphere, 1920–1940: Language and Literature in an Age of Nationalism*, New Delhi: Oxford University Press

Philo, C. and Kearns, G. (1993) 'Culture, history, capital: a critical introduction to the selling of places', in Kearns, G and Philo, C. (eds) *Selling Places: The City as Cultural Capital, Past and Present*, Oxford: Pergamon Press

Sassen, S. (2000) 'Analytic borderlands: economy and culture in the global city', in Bridge, G. and Watson, S. (eds) *A Companion to the City*, Oxford: Blackwell

Tyagi, R.K. (2001) 'Vidhyarthi jeevan me anushasan ka mahatv' [The importance of discipline in the life of the student], *Jwala Magazine* 29–30

7

THE POLITICS OF GENDER, CLASS AND COMMUNITY IN A CENTRAL CALCUTTA NEIGHBOURHOOD

Henrike Donner

Introduction

This chapter explores the way in which gendered spatial practices constitute a particular socio-spatial configuration – namely, the urban neighbourhood. It focuses on the views and experiences of middle-class women in a Central Calcutta neighbourhood, and describes how local identities are constructed in relation to gender through everyday practices. Rather than looking at the space constituting the neighbourhood as the backdrop of meaningful social relations, the chapter highlights how spatial concepts and practices (re-) produce hierarchies, class and ethnic identity through behavioural norms and the provision of metaphors and categories, and explores different contexts within which the neighbourhood is appropriated and negotiated by middle-class women on an everyday basis.

Urban anthropologists often use the terms 'locality' and 'neighbourhood' interchangeably to denote their site of fieldwork, but rarely look at the neighbourhood as 'a relational rather than a categorical concept' (McDowell 1999: 101) A closer look at the meaning of locality demands new perspectives in anthropology because, as Henrietta Moore writes, globalisation subjects the local to a double movement: 'Cultures are becoming both deterritorialised and reterritorialised: they are no longer predicated on particular spatial co-ordinates, but neither are they adrift from the particularities of lives lived' (Moore: 1999: 11–12).

In this chapter, I explore how middle-class women's views and experiences of the urban neighbourhood reflect such movements, and how they are shaped by gender-specific discourses on the public sphere and shared communal histories as well as class-based notions of respectability. The historical importance of changing attitudes towards women's education, employment and modern family life have been discussed in much detail in relation to the Calcutta middle classes (Broomfield 1968; Borthwick 1984;

Engels 1996), which has lead to an emphasis on women's participation in distinctly modernist spaces such as education, cultural production and progressive movements including the nationalist era. Middle-class women's experiences of urban India have therefore been highlighted in relation to the categories of the 'home' and the 'world' in contexts where the construction of ideologies of private and public spheres is of particular importance (Bannerjee 1989; Chatterjee 1993; Chowdhury 1998). But in spite of the renewed interest in urban South Asia, these gendered urban geographies have gained little attention. This chapter discusses the relation between gender and the urban neighbourhood as a prime site for class-specific practices of identity formation through middle-class women's everyday discourses on spatial divisions and the related practices.

I suggest that the neighbourhood represents a particularly interesting 'field' because of its importance as an arena within which various interpretations of gender ideologies in relation to class- and community-based identities are played out. In what follows, I want to explore two related questions – namely, how a specific neighbourhood is constructed in relation to women's mobility through idealised representations as well as lived experiences by middle-class women, and in which way group-based divisions establish the neighbourhood in these women's lives.[1]

The neighbourhood

The *para* (neighbourhood) we are concerned with is part of the wider area called Taltala, which in Central Calcutta developed with the expansion of local wholesale markets and colonial administration throughout the 19th century. In the 1870s, wealthy merchants and businessmen built their city residences here, and more and more affluent traders belonging to Hindu and Muslim communities constructed impressive residences amid slum settlements (*bastis*). Both the settlements of the poor and the residences of the affluent drew migrants into the area, which soon boasted the signifiers of modernity – notably, schools, a drainage system and political organisations.

The neighbourhood we are concerned with here developed during the colonial period at the border of the 'White town', the preserve of Europeans, and is located in the municipal Ward 58. According to the 1991 Census, the overall Ward had a population of 78,565 persons, out of whom 44,195 were male and 34,370 were female. I selected this area for my initial fieldwork of 18 months because of its heterogeneity, but the neighbourhood itself is predominantly populated by Hindus, while the wider area within which it is located is dominated by poor Muslim households. Thus, most of those interviewed in the neighbourhood belong to the Bengali-speaking middle-class Hindu minority, but in the neighbouring slums Hindi-speaking Muslims are the dominant group. Other communities present in the Ward and the neighbourhood include Bengali-speaking Christians, and Hindi-speaking Hindus of north-western origin, South Indians and Anglo-Indians.

The vast majority of the women I worked with belonged to middle-class households in the neighbourhood and, although I first gained access to the neighbourhood through an introduction to the local councillor, I gradually met more residents in informal contexts – for instance, in the course of religious festivals and political meetings. In most instances, the women I came to work with were introduced by a relative or friend, and these networks were utilised to identify more respondents throughout the research process (see Donner 2006). Because my point of entry into the neighbourhood was through introduction by a Bengali Hindu woman, Bengali Hindus came to make up the majority of my contacts, but I also maintained links with a number of Bengali-speaking Christian and Hindi-speaking Marwari households.[2]

The households in this sample are defined as middle-class by virtue of their dependence on one or more salaries from male white-collar employment (see also Debi 1988), but incomes vary greatly and material lifestyles as well as financial security of households range from the struggling lower middle-class widow living in rented accommodation to the affluent doctor, whose family own a three-storey house they share with his parents and his brother's family. The male breadwinners in these households may be in government jobs, may be accountants, doctors or clerks, or may run small businesses, but married women are usually housewives with only a few exceptions ever having been in employment.

By describing themselves as middle-class, the women did not so much refer to occupations and incomes, but shared values, educational strategies and, very importantly, shared ideologies related to gender roles and family life. It is this value system, rather than economic standing, which unites the Bengali middle-class in Calcutta in relation to working-class households and distinguishes this sizeable minority from the very small group of upper class households.

Like the wider area, the neighbourhood itself emerged as a mixed locality, with middle-class families and slum dwellers often living in the same streets. It is referred to by its inhabitants as Doctor's Lane *para*, named after the narrow lane running from West to East through its centre. In common with the neighbourhoods to the North, which are situated within the boundaries of the former 'Black town', it is a predominantly Bengali locality. It is significant that in local discourse the neighbourhood is represented as a Hindu *para* surrounded by Muslim localities and, although few of the interviewed middle-class women ever venture there, all of them started their descriptions of the *para's* boundaries at the Western end of Doctor's Lane. This marks the entry into a Muslim slum and is described by the women interviewed as a 'no go' area for respectable women. Like its Western boundary, the *para's* Southern borders are identified in terms of the communal divide between Hindus and Muslims and, throughout our conversations, middle-class Hindu and Christian women highlighted slums as indicators of spatial boundaries as well as social divisions. Middle-class women also routinely cited Mirza Ghalib Street and the adjacent lanes as the Southern border of the *para*, and emphasised that, because the *bastis* here are notorious hubs of illegal activities, middle-class men and women rarely visit this part of the neighbourhood. In the course of our conversations, it was stated repeatedly that not only young girls but middle-class women in general avoided walking in this direction, and that they entered or left the neighbourhood from the Eastern and Northern sides, where two busy roads are plied by buses, scooters and taxis. Although this neighbourhood was not planned or built around a centre, a couple of small lanes off the main roads function as 'gates' to the neighbourhood in more than one sense, and lead towards the inner part consisting of residential buildings and workplaces. Crucially schools, churches, temples and nursing homes, as well as a well-stocked market, situated outside or at the borders of the neighbourhood are frequented by middle-class women and their families on a daily basis.

To the untrained eye, the inner parts of the *para* may appear as a maze, with its mixture of residential and commercial use of the same buildings, and small workshops situated on the ground floor of middle-class residences as well as the front rows of slums. These direct the attention of a casual observer away from the residences of middle-class families, which are mostly three stories high, colonial-style brick structures, sometimes well maintained but more often than not in different stages of decay. Visitors rarely take an interest in the beautiful architecture of these buildings, because so much more is going on in the streets, where workers hang out and *basti* dwellers perform domestic tasks due to lack of space inside their huts.

The vast majority of middle-class residents in the neighbourhood live in houses that were built around the middle of the 19th century and were designed as multi-storied buildings around a courtyard. Today, the once spacious rooms provide accommodation for numerous descendants of their founders, and the ground floor is often rented out to tenants, many of whom came as refugees after 1947 from East Bengal. They also occupy some of the houses formerly owned by middle-class Muslims, who moved southwards into Muslim neighbourhoods or left for East Pakistan at around Partition time.[3]

Mapping the neighbourhood

Among the women I worked with, the neighbourhood was routinely described in relation to other significant places – for instance, places of work, consumption or worship – and the neighbourhoods where married women grew up. Thus, comparisons, either with other neighbourhoods or imaginary maps of the city, were introduced while talking about the specific *para* and its significance in women's lives. Among the most prominent features of the places mentioned were behavioural codes related to different localities, which in the descriptions linked gender, group-based identities and various spaces. It has been emphasised by many scholars that in South Asian societies women's bodies and therefore their movements are a symbolic manifestation of group boundaries, in a metaphorical as well as a practical sense (Sharma 1980, Jacobson 1982). Differences between groups, expressed in terms of imaginary and real concerns with purity and pollution, are emphasised to express such communal identities and class boundaries, and are extremely significant in relation to the conceptualisation of the neighbourhood in the given context. In Calcutta, concerns about class and ethnic identity dominate the discourse on the local, and determine how social norms governing women's mobility are enforced in relation to material conditions, which, as Blaustein observes, 'respond to and produce conceptions about, and lived experiences of sexual difference' (2001: 15).

This is apparent in the accounts of local life and architectural forms which always draw on two prototypes of localities in the city – linking the character of both to gender ideals. Neighbourhoods such as Doctor's Lane are generally described as 'traditional' in relation to other places, which are in turn seen as 'modern' (see Figure 7.1).

Prototypes of the latter kind are the *paras* that came into being with partition and the massive influx of East Bengali refugees into the city, who settled at the fringes and over the last 30 years became increasingly affluent (see Figure 7.2).

Figure 7.1 Mixed housing in Taltala, central Calcutta

Figure 7.2 New development in Rajarhat, at the outskirts of the city

As Manas Ray (2002) pointed out with reference to these refugee colonies, it is here that 'modern' neighbourhoods emerged, because these colonies gradually became home to a largely successful, upwardly mobile middle class, which modernised the 'vernacular' through the introduction of new social, educational and architectural patterns containing the neighbourhood. Among these patterns, new possibilities of gendered behaviour in the neighbourhood and the city emerged – for instance, through female employment, education and women's involvement in politics. In the course of this transformation, the 'new modernity' emerged through the lives of refugees, while *purono kolkata* ('old' Calcutta) became more localised and permanently fixed in the Central and Northern neighbourhoods, by now almost engulfed by new developments. They emerged as 'traditional', and are often described as localities with 'true Bengali culture'. For those speaking of them, it is clear that this implies adherence to norms of gendered behaviour, which include less education for young women, married women's domestic roles and a preference for joint family life. In short, restrictions of women's mobility and education, specific marriage patterns and neighbourhood organisation make up characteristics of specific neighbourhoods in the city.

These contrasting images are also propagated by the media, where advertisements, TV serials and movies feature the happy family in their modernist home combining traditional family values with excessive consumer strategies. But in real life all middle-class residents of the Doctor's Lane *para* have visited apartments and new 'developments' elsewhere, and many have relatives living in these more 'modern' localities. Talking about the advantages and disadvantages of life in a 'traditional' *para* like Doctor's Lane, many women pointed out that low rents, proximity to schools, temples, churches and markets as well as ample supplies of servants from the nearby *bastis* influenced their decision to stay in Taltala. The latter point is perhaps more significant than it may seem, because all households included in the sample employed servants to assist with specific tasks, and even the least affluent employed one so-called part-timer. In the better-off households and in smaller units, full-time maids – often children – lived with the family and performed a wide range of tasks, ran errands and kept the housewives company while their men and children were away. Because many of the urban poor living in the area prefer to work in the locality, middle-class households can maintain patron-client relationships with particular families, which accounts for the very low wages paid.

Apart from these 'amenities of domestic life', a further frequently mentioned advantage of life in localities like the Doctor's Lane *para* is its assumed safety, which residents feel is enhanced by the fact that most families share their house with kin or tenants. Although the streets are not considered safe for women at night, and especially young girls are advised not to spend much time in the streets, the anonymity of modern neighbourhoods is associated with an increase in burglaries and threats to the safety of women. What may appear to be a contradiction – namely, that women are safe in a more heterogeneous area but have to carefully monitor their movements, whereas they can move more freely in homogeneous middle-class neighbourhoods, but often feel less safe within the house – was closely related to the way local discourses of class-based identities and the norms of gendered behaviour in the neighbourhood interact. In the view of those interviewed, modern neighbourhoods are often seen as unsafe, and they therefore prefer the 'old' neighbourhoods with their lack of privacy, shortage of space and minimum of modern fittings in the houses. But where proximity to neighbours may make a neighbourhood safe, it figures also as one of the main disadvantages of life in the older parts of the city. It came out clearly in the interviews that the 'traditional' neighbourhood is not seen as a very popular place for socialising among women, and the accounts of middle-class women generally lack a positive sense of community.

However, the alleged impact of the neighbourhood on the personal lives of women extends much further, and the interviewees emphasised the effect a locality has on family values. In their view, the 'modern' *para* is dominated by the ideology of the nuclear family, exemplified in the layout of the prototypical apartment, a view held in spite of the *de facto* prevalence of a nuclear-extended residential pattern in many such localities. In Taltala, a typical house dates back to the 1880s and was designed for the extended family of a businessman, whose sons and their families partitioned and refurbished it numerous times, so that the basic layout may be barely discernable. Today, the smaller units are occupied by members, who at one point belonged to a 'joint' family, and in some cases relatives still share all the rooms. But, while more nuclear families exist than one would admit, the layout, occupation and use of space is seldom as self-explanatory as in a modern two-bedroom apartment. Thus, whereas the houses with their balconies, rows of windows and heavily decorated entrances look more or less alike from the outside, and the interiors were once comparable in that galleries surrounded a courtyard that could be accessed through one central gate, the number of units and the distribution of rooms in this kind of house is flexible. Further-more, while living spaces are clearly separated in middle-class residences, workshops, shops and offices are often located on the ground floor or in the courtyard, as indicated by signboards, benches and chairs, or a counter in the area of the *bhaikhanna*, the street-level veranda / reception room.

Residents of the Doctor's Lane neighbourhood highlighted the fact that the old houses provided an environment within which 'privacy' and conju-gality – both associated with the nuclear family – were subordinated to the wider interests of the extended family. To remain in this traditional environ-ment by marrying into such a family was largely seen as desirable, and in more than one instance represented the conscious decision of a young educated woman, explicitly not seen as a function of financial circumstances. The cultivated conservatism displayed was realised through gendered behaviour like the limited mobility granted to young girls and recently married women, and an expressed preference for 'joint' family life. Many young married women and middle-aged mothers were proud of the way their in-laws' family reflected what they saw as 'traditional Bengali culture'. In their view, while the nuclear family provided a solution to those who wanted to leave behind the tensions arising from joint living, it also gave rise to particular anxieties: first, the fear of abandonment in old age, and, second, the fear of violence by outsiders – in particular, people working in the house.

In more than one sense, the locality provides women with a wider sense of belonging, which, as discussed in the following section, is created through gender-specific practices which highlight group boundaries, reproduce middle-class status and define women's engagement with neighbours as part of moral communities.

Mobility in the neighbourhood

In Sylvia Vatuk's 1970s study of a *mohalla* (neighbourhood) in the North Indian city of Meerut, different degrees of co-operation between neighbours were based on distinctions between members of the same kin group, caste and class, and these shared identities implied various codes of conduct, terms of address and types of interaction (Vatuk 1972: 149).

Middle-class men and women in Central Calcutta were equally concerned about communal boundaries when describing relationships with their neigh-bours, and referred to ethnic and religious identities to paint the more generalised picture. However, in contrast to Vatuk's observations in Meerut, it became evident in the course of the conversations that women did not usually consider their *para* in Central Calcutta as a public space that allowed for familiarity and co-operation *per se*, let alone kin-like relations. Referring to its heterogeneous composition, middle-class women described the *para* as a hostile environment, citing its heterogeneity, the presence of 'lower class' men in the streets and the damaging effects of gossip as reasons for their views. In more than one case, a middle-aged housewife stated that ideally a respectable woman would not go out without good reason, and it became apparent during the period of fieldwork that most young, recently married women and the elderly remained indoors for several days in a row. Depending on the age of the woman concerned, the reasons for this restricted movement in the 'locality' was related to propriety, as in the case of young girls, who in most instances were not allowed to roam the neigh-bourhood unless accompanied by an adult. In the case of women and girls, 'moving around' is only acceptable on special occasions – for instance, during the *Durga puja* festival, when groups of girls and boys walk the streets and visit the little park in the centre of the *para*. Although girls as well as boys have friends in the *para*, the only purposeful movement in the neighbourhood is going to or coming from school and visiting relatives. These restrictions are dressed as a concern for the safety of children, but partly stem from parental fears about 'affairs' and love marriages, which occur frequently in this locality. But whereas daughters as girls from the neighbournood may still be well connected, more rigid restrictions are imposed upon newly married daughters-in-law, whose social relations are ideally limited to the homes of their in-laws and a narrow circle of affines. Only in cases where a love marriage took place in the neighbourhood itself would young, married women move freely within the *para*. They themselves and elderly mothers-in-law observed that therefore such matches have many advantages for the women concerned, and are least favoured by mothers of young men (see Donner 2002).

Once a married woman becomes a mother, she will be more visible in the neighbourhood because schooling requires her involvement with public institutions. From the age of two, children are accompanied to and from schools and tuition classes, and mothers have to perform many education-related tasks, which bring them into contact with a wide range of people (see Donner 2005). Some middle-aged married women experienced their role as 'good mothers' as an opportunity to expand their networks inside and outside the *para*, and welcomed the degree of mobility mothers of school-going children enjoy, but the vast majority in my sample of married women still limited their personal relationships with neighbours and friends and presented themselves as dutiful housewives with limited control over their time and movements. Consequently, elderly women, who are themselves no longer responsible for the daily chores related to education, are likely to withdraw from the public sphere altogether, and many devote more time to food preparation and religious activities than the cultivation of relationships within the neighbourhood.[4]

Links with the 'outside' world beyond the immediate circle of relatives and the household are obviously problematic for women before marriage, but even among those who go out daily and are largely independent, few maintained that their own neighbourhood offered much in terms of social-ising. Only those who remained unmarried stated that the public sphere offered freedom and interacted voluntarily with women and men from a wide range of backgrounds.

What these discourses on women's mobility at different stages in their lives aptly demonstrate is that concerns with the sexuality of women in general are not the determining factor for women's mobility in these urban contexts. Rather than the generalised distinction between male / public and female / private / domestic spheres put forward in conversations, or the control of women's sexuality emphasised in much of the literature, it is the role of married women as mothers and homemakers that determines how a woman relates to the neighbourhood and describes her involvement with different groups.

Community activities and the public sphere

In Vatuk's account of the way white-collar migrants organised their lives in a middle-class neighbourhood of Meerut, women's involvement with their neighbours and the wider community was mostly informal. But in the case of Calcutta in the 1990s, more organised collective activities through which the neighbourhood is reaffirmed – namely, political work and religious festi-vals (*pujas*) – play an equally important role.

The Ward as a whole, and the majority of the middle-class families in the neighbourhood I visited, supported the Congress party – then about to split – during the elections in 1995, and the fact that the councillor resided in the neighbourhood was an expression of its political significance. Women, who were actively wooed by all parties during the first municipal elections with reservations for female candidates, could be party members and develop activities through the Congress party's women's group, the *Mahila Samiti* (Women's Committee) (see Donner 2006). But only five of the women I knew well were active members of this organisation, whereas all middle-class women knew of it and most were acquainted with one or more of the activists. In the course of our conversations, it became quite clear that – unlike other neighbourhoods – Doctor's Lane was not a locality where middle-class women liked to become involved in party politics. However, because the *Mahila Samiti* was seen as a women's organisation akin to a charity, most acknowledged its existence as necessary and worthwhile. The committee met twice a month and had two main tasks – namely, the resolu-tion of disputes involving women, and electoral campaigning. In this locality, like in other neighbourhoods of Calcutta, political parties are routinely involved in domestic conflicts, mostly evolving around disputes over dowry, domestic violence, divorce and separation, and the custody of children. If the complainant is female, the local party will normally refer her to a local *Mahila Samiti*, which will decide how the party should resolve the issue.

In this locality, the meetings of this committee were held in the house of one of the members and were attended by a dozen, mostly middle-aged women, who assembled in the parlour (*bhaikhanna*) of this residential building.

While all women in the committee where from middle-class families, although most would have been defined as lower, rather than upper middle class, the complainants during the sessions I attended belonged to poor families. On being asked, the committee members explained that 'respectable' middle-class women do not approach the *Mahila Samiti* for help. It was suggested that middle-class women in general were less prepared to 'open up' and speak about their problems in public, and that if any of them decided to do so this would spoil her reputation. Thus, although none of the women denied that problems like domestic violence, dowry demands and problems with separation and divorce occur among the better-off, middle-class women are expected to relate to the political arena in a different way – namely, as representatives rather than complainants. It also became clear in the course of fieldwork that even this formal involvement had its limits.

Apart from the resolution of disputes, the committee was also actively involved in pre-election canvassing, which consists mainly of all-important house-to-house campaigns. Although the local Congress filed a female candidate, who was married and from an affluent family, unlike her male counterparts, she did not take part in public meetings and functions. Even the necessary canvassing was – in her own view – too problematic, as it would involve contact with lower class voters and, in particular, Muslims in the nearby slums, and so she employed a couple of desperate young middle-class women to complete her rounds for her. As is evident from this example, women from the well-to-do families in the neighbourhood do get involved in politics, but because the 'mixture' is not 'good', their activities may take place in the parlour. Typically, even members of the *Mahila Samiti* avoided visiting the party offices, which were allegedly full of *goondas* (ruffians), but at the same time managed to support the party in numerous ways and helped to win elections.

The same can be said for middle-class women's participation in religious festivals or communal *pujas* – most notably, their involvement in the community *pujas*, during which local committees or clubs, consisting entirely of men, order images of the deities, install them in public places and invite the local residents to worship. In old neighbourhoods like the Doctor's Lane *para*, community *pujas* were first organised on the basis of caste. Today, class is more important than caste divisions, and hence two *pujas* may be organised within 50 metres of each other: one by working-class men, who arrange for a middle-class guest of honour; the other by their middle-class neighbours. Fernandes' observation (1997) that hegemonic middle-class discourses on class relations are reproduced through these festivals is confirmed by the way they were organised and interpreted in this mixed neighbourhood. However, a further hierarchical implication of this pattern is that, because the Bengali Hindu middle-class households in the locality have to extend a degree of co-operation to their working-class neighbours, this in turn limits the involvement of middle-class women in these *pujas*. Interviewees were explicit about this effect and emphasised that, unlike in other *paras*, here 'respectable' women are only involved as worshippers on specific days during the festival, mostly on the eighth 'day' (*osthomi din*) of *Durga puja*, when women from all households bring offerings to the goddess and receive her blessings in return. This remained the only act of collective worship involving women during this *puja*, and few were interested in the ritual departure of the goddess, which in other *paras* is attended by many women because the goddess is often imagined as a married woman / daughter leaving her parents' house. Although the majority of the women interviewed in this neighbourhood were well aware that middle-class women in other localities play a major role in the organisation of the *puja*, they confirmed again and again that this was too dangerous and inappropriate in a heterogeneous locality like the Doctor's Lane *para*.

More generally, the activities of middle-class women, which brought them in direct contact with neighbours and unrelated persons, were situated in the domestic sphere, where they contributed food to festivities and performed the rites of hospitality on many occasions. In many instances, the serving of food and the variety of lifecycle rituals and *pujas* performed in the more affluent households pose problems for these women. This was the case when their husbands and brothers invited clients, customers and workers into the house, and middle-class women, who are concerned with symbolic boundaries, found that such visitors, especially when they belonged to a variety of backgrounds but came from the neighbourhood, difficult to deal with. Where, for instance, the wife of a businessman employing local artisans had to invite 'these people' (many of whom happened to be Muslims) for a feast into the house, she made sure that her maidservants served the workers in the main living-room, while relatives and special guests of honour were seated in the bedroom. While new apartment houses often provide designated spaces for such festivities on the more neutral roof terrace, in these old neighbourhoods it is the duty of those employing people from the *para* to invite them into the house on special occasions. It was this unease related to the exposure of middle-class women to persons belonging to 'other' classes and sometimes communities prevented middle-class women from being involved in politics and community *pujas* in the locality.

Although generally women born in a neighbourhood feel more at home than those who enter as newly married wives, adherence to the norms of restricted mobility and specific codes of conduct is expected from all. The perceived threat to the reputation, physical purity, and safety, is clearly represented as a result of the history and composition of this neighbourhood.

As explained above, formal political organisation as well as community worship among Hindus are public displays of these divisions rather than the unity among neighbours. In the lives of its middle-class inhabitants, its heterogeneity creates a very specific sense of local identity, and a strong emphasis on class differences.

The community of neighbours

In an environment where public places for the exclusive or shared use of middle-class women barely exist, the majority feel ambivalent about their relationship with the local 'community'. Given the importance of *lajja* (shame) related to the female body and sexuality, which is extended to symbolise the reputation of the wider kin group and community, they perceive the neighbourhood first as a site of practised self-discipline. Middle-class women's representation of the prevalent socio-spatial relations, the structure and the architecture of the neighbourhood evoke the imagery of the panopticon, with its facilities for control suggested by Foucault (1979). In the course of my conversations, it became clear that women are constantly aware of the fact that public space in the *para* is dominated by men, and that those who fail to adhere to the norms become the target of criticism and gossip. It was stated again and again that neighbours observe each other's movements and comment on offensive behaviour to third parties, and that the surveillance by others is supported by architectural features like courtyards, verandas and balconies. But while they are the objects of control, middle-class women, who often spend most of their time at home, are also crucially involved in monitoring others, although we need to be reminded that unlike their male counterparts they easily become targets of malicious gossip themselves. Their role, however, is not restricted to the observation of others from the comfort of their homes because, as Dickey observes with reference to middle-class women in Madurai, housewives crucially control what kind of information leaves the house – for instance, through servants (Dickey 2000). This rigid separation of the inside and the outside spheres and the practises distinguishing the home, the streets and urban public space reproduce the street in this neighbourhood as the realm of the working class, which does not merit particular care or respect by middle-class residents (Kaviraj 1997). Consequently, the public space in the neighbourhood is represented as filthy and morally problematic and, unlike in Delhi or Mumbai, environmentalist discourses have had little impact on Calcutta's heterogeneous neighbourhoods (Baviskar 2002). With reference to this kind of morality, the emerging bourgeois consciousness reflected in the initiatives to beautify a street corner are often met with resistance by the less affluent, who outnumber the guardians of civility and manners by far.

It was in talk about specific neighbours that the rigid distinction between different spheres, of a 'home' and a 'world', was most difficult to impose. In order to maintain middle-class domesticity, all households had to maintain relationships with lower class households, whose members provided essential skills and services. It was therefore not the case that middle-class women did not interact with persons from different backgrounds but they were concerned about displaying knowledge of these links in public. Whereas middle-class men can often be seen having intensive discussions with slum dwellers in the streets and join people from all walks of life in the tea stall, middle-class women do not communicate directly with the poor in the neighbourhood, nor do they ever visit the homes of maidservants and service providers to call them to their houses, but instead communicate their need for a specialist through intermediaries like shopkeepers.

If this pervasive discourse on class in many ways determines middle-class women's relationships in the *para*, the same cannot be said for contacts between women belonging to different communities like non-Bengali Hindus and Bengali Christians. Relationships between neighbours belonging to different *jatis* – ethnic or religious communities – were generally vague and limited to occasional visits and formal food exchanges during festivals. In many instances, these contacts were mediated by men, which enhanced the comparative isolation of the many female-headed Christian middle-class households in the neighbourhood. Although love marriages between members belonging to different communities occurred frequently – and mixed matches were much more common here than in the 'modern' neighbourhoods elsewhere – middle-class women found it very difficult to talk about inter-community relations in the neighbourhood and it was obvious that, even where a house was occupied by families belonging to different groups, they avoided contact as far as possible. Overall, co-operation between households belonging to different ethnic groups was very limited, and close friendships between women belonging to these families were rare.

Conclusion: Representation and the everyday

In spite of the ambiguous feelings expressed by the women interviewed, the restrictions of women's movements and the preoccupation of the middle class with the reputation of the family, all the women I spoke to moved in public spaces and some had ambitions to be active players in the public sphere. All interviewed agreed that the neighbourhood as a primary site of contact with people not belonging to the family group was problematic in many ways, but they also insisted that women were able to move freely, albeit only on specific routes, as part of specific groups and for stated purposes (i.e. as pupils, working women, customers, mothers). Rules and regulations governing the mental map of the city or the neighbourhood are constantly negotiated, and transform a place into a space through gendered practices. Since the neighbourhood is not an administrative unit, it only exists in the form of narratives, which are transmitted orally between generations. By living in the neighbourhood, women reproduce the boundaries between groups based on class or ethnicity in everyday movements, contacts, dealings with neighbours, servants and their advice to children. While all these practices were modes of community building as well as self-realisation, a small minority appropriated alternative models of the self. Whereas all women engaged actively with the 'outside' beyond the immediate household as part of a family, some transgressed the narrowly defined path of appropriate behaviour through their participation in political groups or specific friendships, which were unrelated to their role as homemaker. There are indeed many examples of common and not so common tactics to overcome the restrictive aspects of narratives of the neighbourhoods presented earlier, which are after all '*strategic* representations offered to the public' (de Certeau 1984: xxiii). But however variable the interpretations of these maps may appear in everyday interaction, few middle-class women consciously violate the rules related to these flexible but nevertheless gender-, status- and age-specific roles in the context of neighbourhood relations.

This is partly the legacy of 19th-century upper caste traditions of female seclusion, which shaped the modernisation of gender relations among the urban middle classes, and provided a rigid re-interpretation of separate spheres. Towards the end of that period, the ideology of 'two domains' gained momentum in urban areas. Charting this development in the context of colonial Bengal, Partha Chatterjee observed that:

> Applying the inner / outer distinction into the matter of concrete day-to-day living separates the social space into *ghar* and *bah{imacr}r*, the home and the world. The world is external, the domain of the material; the home represents one's inner spiritual self, one's true identity. The world is a treacherous terrain of the pursuit of material interests, where practical considerations reign supreme. It is also typically the domain of the male. The home in its essence must remain unaffected by the profane activities in the material world – and woman is its representation. And so one gets an identification of social roles by gender to correspond with the separation of the social space into ghar and bahir.
>
> (1993: 120)

This development, together with a significant rise in the age of marriage and the decrease in the number of children such women were expected to raise, changed the actual work of housewives, although the spread of women's education and female employment varied greatly between regions and ethnic communities. Thus, while the division between the outside and the inside of the house and the description of women's role as homemaker are derived from the colonial legacy of separate spheres, contemporary gender relations and representations of respectability vary, and what such spatial metaphors as inside-outside actually imply in different historical and regional settings today has to be established in the case of each locality.

We have seen how the neighbourhood is crucially not only a place where such notions are played out, but is constructed through the spatial practices women narrate: the avoidance of specific forms of contact and mixing, and the withdrawal of middle-class women from public spaces – notably, politics and religious activities. However, their enactment of the role of mother and housewife, which allows for increased mobility and contacts outside the neighbourhood, does emphasise their important role in the establishment of group boundaries through spatial and social segregation of the home and the outside world. In this specific urban setting, the neighbourhood appears as a space realised equally through design, a history of communal segregation and contemporary domesticities. All these factors support the middle-class notion that this particular neighbourhood is a problematic place for women, which has become a characteristic of comparable localities in the city and naturalises gendered spatial practices as part of the character of a neighbourhood. Although communal divisions are present, it appears that class relations govern behavioural codes and spatial strategies in this locality, and that class-based gendered identities are inscribed in the notion of the neighbourhood. Compared with other spaces in the city – in particular, 'modern' homogeneous middle-class neighbourhoods – the *para* is not a place where these women take part in a 'modernist' vision of the community. Depicting the neighbourhood as a place of surveillance and control without ever providing a generalised, positive notion of participation, women and men restrict access to the *para*, which is importantly a space where exclusion produces communal and class-based identities.

The analysis of the neighbourhood through gendered practices rather than communal identities or class structure allows us, according to Fernandes, to transform 'the spatial representation of categories (. . .) from a static frame of analysis or technique of mapping to a dynamic process and critical aspect of the genealogical approach to social categories' (1997: 163). Middle-class women do participate in public but engage in spatial practices that reproduce social categories of class and community locally. These categories or groups, which are presented as natural composite parts of the locality, are not only presented but reaffirmed through narratives of the neighbourhood and the field that this discourse opens, present in the routes chosen to reach a specific bus stop, talk about marriages past and present, and exchanges between neighbours.

Acknowledgements:

The research on which this article is based was supported by two grants from the Economic and Social Research Council (ESRC). Different versions of this article have been presented during seminars at the London School of Economics and Political Science, the University of Sussex and the University of East Anglia. I am grateful for suggestions received on all these occasions and the detailed comments on earlier drafts by Nandini Gooptu, Chris Fuller, Geert De Neve, and Hendrik Wittkopf.

Notes

1 Fieldwork was conducted between October 1995–April 1997 and October 1999–August 2000. I use Calcutta instead of the more recent Kolkata because much of my data was collected before the process of renaming the city gained publicity.
2 Members of a north-western business community.
3 A few buildings were described as 'exchange houses' which denotes that these houses belonged to Muslims and were exchanged against properties owned by Hindus in East Bengal after Partition. The history of these exchanges remains to be written.
4 It is also apparent from the importance given to outward signs of these roles, which indicate the legitimacy of women's movements. Mothers on their way to school carry water bottles and snacks for their children, pupils wear uniforms and bags, shoppers carry bags or are accompanied by a servant, while working women adhere to the dress code by wearing clothes that are distinct from what is worn at home.

References

Banerjee, Sumanta (1989) *The Parlour and the Street: Elite and Popular Culture in Nineteenth Century Bengal*, Calcutta: Seagull Books
Baviskar, Amita (2002) 'The politics of the city' 516 *Seminar* 1–6
Blaustein, Jessica B. (2001) 'Critical dwellings: foregrounding space in the feminist picture', in Currie, G. and Rothenberg, C. (eds), *Feminist (Re)visions of the Subject: Landscapes, Ethnoscapes and Theoryscapes*, Lanham, MD: Lexington Books
Bose, Nirmal Kumar (1968) *Calcutta 1964: A Social Survey*, Bombay: Lalvani Publishers
Borthwick, Margret (1984) *The Reluctant Debutante: The Changing Role of Women in Bengal 1875–1927*, Princeton, NJ: Princeton University Press
Broomfield, John E. (1968) *Elite Conflict in a Plural Society: Twentieth Century Bengal*, Bombay: Oxford University Press
Chatterjee, Partha (1993) *The Nation and Its Fragments: Colonial and Postcolonial Histories*, Princeton, NJ: Princeton University Press
Chowdhury, Indira (1998) *The Frail Hero and Virile History: Gender and the Politics of Culture in Colonial Bengal*, Delhi: Oxford University Press

Debi, Bharati (1988) *Middle Class Working Women of Calcutta: A Study in Continuity and Change*, Calcutta: Anthropological Survey of India

De Certeau, Michel (1984) *The Practice of Everyday Life*, Berkeley, CA: University of California Press

Dickey, Sarah (2000) 'Permeable homes: domestic service, household space, and the vulnerability of class boundaries in urban India' 2(2) *American Ethnologist* 462–86

Donner, Henrike (2002) 'One's own marriage: love marriages in a Calcutta neighbourhood' 22(1) *South Asia Research* 179–94

——(2005) 'Children are capital, grandchildren are interest: changing educational strategies and kin-relations in Calcuttan middle-class families', in Assayag, J. and Fuller, C.J. (eds), *Globalizing India: Perspectives from Below*, London: Anthem Press.

——(2006) 'Reflections on gender and fieldwork in the city', in De Neve, G. and Unnithan-Kumar, M. (eds), *Critical Journeys: The Making of Anthropologists*, Aldershot: Ashgate.

Engels, Dagmar (1996) *Beyond Purdah? Women in Bengal 1890–1939*, Delhi: Oxford University Press

Fernandes, Leela (1997) *Producing Workers: The Politics of Gender, Class, and Culture in the Calcutta Jute Mills*, Philadelphia, PA: University of Pennsylvania Press

Foucault, Michel (1979) *Discipline and Punish: The Birth of the Prison*, New York: Vintage

Jacobson, Doranne (1982) 'Purdah and the Hindu family in central India', in Papanek, H. and Minault, G. (eds), *Separate Worlds: Studies of Purdah in South Asia*, Delhi: Chanakya Publications

Kaviraj, Sudipta (1997) 'Filth and the public sphere: concepts and practices about space in Calcutta' 10(1) *Public Culture* 83–113

McDowell, Linda (1999) *Gender, Identity and Place: Understanding Feminist Geography*, Cambridge: Polity Press

Moore, H.L. (1999) 'Anthropological theory at the turn of the century', in Moore, H.L. (ed.), *Anthropological Theory*, Cambridge: Polity Press

Ray, Manas (2002) 'Growing up refugee', 53(1,2) *History Workshop* 148–79

Sharma, Ursula (1980) 'Purdah and public space', in de Souza, A. (ed.), *Women in Contemporary India and South Asia*, Delhi: Manohar

Vatuk, Sylvia (1972) *Kinship and Urbanization: White Collar Migrants in North India*, Berkeley, CA: University of California Press

158

8

ANONYMOUS ENCOUNTERS

Class categorisation and social distancing in public places

Kathinka Frøystad

'Just by looking at a girl will I know whether she knows English or not.'
Nodding towards the girl behind them in the train compartment, this was
how an army officer assured my colleague that the girl would not be able to
follow their English conversation.[1] Evidently, the girl's physical features,
dress and behaviour indicated that she did not know English, presumably
because it revealed her low-class status. This remark is a striking example of
the phenomenon examined in this chapter: the class positioning of strangers
in public places and the forms of distancing that this positioning results in,
including withdrawal from public places and the production of enclosures in
which the people present are as homogeneous as possible. While these forms
of distancing exist in many stratified societies, this chapter explores how and
why they occur in an Indian urban context, and argues that they are rooted
in notions of class that entail implicit assumptions of caste.

The exploration will lie at the intersection of three separate, but interrelated, fields of research. One is Erving Goffman's work on public places
(Goffman 1963) – that is, places where people encounter strangers. The
multitude of such places is one of the features that characterise urban
contexts, whether in India or elsewhere. For Goffman and the urban anthropologists who followed in his footsteps, the main criterion of a public place
is that access is unrestricted (Goffman 1963: 9; Earnes and Goode 1977:
218–19). While such a notion may be useful for delineating public places as
Weberian ideal types, I suggest that it is more fruitful to think of access as a
matter of degree. Many urban spaces that bring strangers together are regulated by means of tickets (such as in trains and cinemas), membership (such
as in clubs), invitation cards, physical boundaries, armed guards or darkened
windows. In India, middle-class people – and women in particular – tend to
feel uncomfortable in places where access is entirely unrestricted and where
they encounter people who differ widely from themselves in terms of class,
caste and lifestyle. It is this discomfort, I will argue, that favours the emergence of restricted spaces which 'homogenise' the people present. While

some urban 'enclosures' are permanent, this chapter will also examine enclosures of a more mobile and temporary kind. In the latter case, the public character of a place is not only a matter of degree, it can also be a processual feature.

The second field of inquiry pertains to how people 'class-ify' the strangers they encounter – that is, how they recognise a stranger as being either of roughly equal status to themselves, or as belonging to a different, most often inferior, social segment. This process has been examined in several Indian settings already. James Sebring, who studied how teashop owners in Almora identified the caste background of their customers in the 1960s, argued that the most important traits were the customers' verbal and non-verbal behaviour, skin colour, height and nose structure (Sebring 1969: 201). Reflecting on how people in Madurai made class judgements in the 1980s and 1990s, Sara Dickey writes that 'they identify differences in clothing, food, hygiene, manners, sophistication, education, intelligence, language, mutual support systems, and attitudes toward money and consumption' (Dickey 2000: 466). Speaking about class identification in movies, Filippo and Caroline Osella argue that in Mani Ratnam's celebrated film, *Bombay*, the hero came across as a bourgeois high-caste Hindu partly because of his horizontally striped jersey shirt, whereas the man dancing the passion scenes was identified as working class because of his 'extremely curly hair, darker skin tone, street-style baggy clothes and lubricious dancing' (Osella and Osella 1999: 1000; 2000: 121). Many of the traits mentioned in these studies come into play in the case I will examine in this chapter as well. These similarities suggest a strong continuity with the recent historical past, between different parts of India and across rural and urban settings, although to classify strangers according to such traits is at once more complex and more frequent in urban settings. In this chapter, I will explore the positioning of strangers in public places further, and I will argue that it rarely pertains to *either* caste *or* class, as the earlier studies seem to suggest, but tends to blur and conflate these principles of differentiation.

The third field of inquiry that this chapter relates to is the kind of research that approaches classification through local idioms and their connotations. Gerald Berreman found that, in Dehra Dun, labels based on religious, regional, linguistic and phenotypical criteria were used interchangeably with referents to caste, employment and economic background, thereby completely defying the classificatory consistency assumed in most scholarly texts (Berreman 1972; 1975). Edwin D. Driver, who explored the use of the class idiom in Madras, found that his respondents tended to position themselves as 'lower class' and 'middle class' but rarely as 'upper class', or employed the more refined distinctions between 'upper middle class' and 'lower middle class' (Driver 1982; Driver and Driver 1987). Sara Dickey argues that in Madurai only the more affluent people use the terminology of class. Her poor informants, in contrast, tended to categorise themselves as either 'poor people', 'labourers' or 'people who have nothing', while lumping together those who were more privileged than themselves as 'rich people' or 'big people' (Dickey 1993: 8). Rachel Tolen, who studied master–servant relationships in a railway colony in Madras, reports that the railway employees referred to their domestic servants as 'outhouse people' and 'poor people' whereas the servants referred to their employers as 'bungalow people' and 'rich people', thereby suggesting a combination of spatial and economic referents (Tolen 2000: 67). In sum, these studies reveal the existence of several idioms related to class. Many of them are used almost interchangeably, as in the urban neighbourhood where I conducted fieldwork. But the idioms that most frequently cropped up here, when strangers were assessed in public places, were the terms *chote log* (small people), *acche log* (good people) and, less frequently, *bare log* (big people). Despite their close relation to the class concepts mentioned earlier, I will argue that the two former terms – 'small people' and 'good people' – bring out particularly clearly the implicit assumptions that link class with caste, at least when used by people who claim to belong to a 'good' family.

None of these issues had been in my mind when I planned my fieldwork. On the contrary, they arose gradually, almost inductively, from my stay with upper-caste Hindus in Kanpur, Uttar Pradesh. However, before we move on to the ethnographic section, it will be necessary to provide a brief introduction to the neighbourhoods in which I lived during fieldwork.

Mohanganj and its inhabitants

'Mohanganj' is a synthesis of three of the neighbourhoods I lived in during my stays in Kanpur. These neighbourhoods are located in different parts of the city, but all are somewhat remote from the city centre and dominated by upper-caste Hindus, with scattered clusters of Muslim and low-caste Hindu residents. A locality like Mohanganj has at its centre the market, which provides everything the residents need for day-to-day living. It consists of rows of fruit and vegetable vendors with their carts, small general stores and a bakery, as well as small shops selling picture frames, sweets, sandals, stationery, cassettes, watches and gifts. Close by, one can find roadside temples, a hairdresser, a beauty parlour, a tiny post office, a travel agent providing unauthorised booking of railway tickets, a branch of the State Bank of India, a sleepy police station and a variety of eateries. In the bylanes, *pan* sellers, *dhobis* (washermen) and tailors sit side by side with those who manage the public phone booths. Further ahead are the residential streets. Closest to the market are the three-storey apartment buildings constructed during the rapid population increase Kanpur experienced in the 1940s. Beyond the apartment buildings, there are bungalows, some of which are neatly maintained and surrounded by green gardens, others that are falling apart. In between these bungalows, one can also find relatively recent

161

eight-storey apartment buildings, which were constructed from the late 1980s onwards, and some vacant plots used for makeshift houses or garbage disposal.

My informants lived in apartment buildings or bungalows with their joint or 'semi-joint' families, and belonged to Brahmin, Punjabi, Khatri or Baniya communities.[2] All the families had lived in Kanpur for at least three generations and, apart from the children and a few elderly women, all informants had been educated to Class 10 or above. Most of the men and young women held bachelor degrees from one of the local colleges. Most of the men were businessmen. One owned a hotel, another ran a factory producing chemicals, a third had wholesale business for rice and textiles, a fourth managed a leather export house, a fifth was a building developer, and a few were unemployed. Almost all the married women were housewives, but many unmarried women who had finished their own education worked as teachers in schools or provided tuition from home. The general standard of living in these households was far higher than that of the working class in Kanpur but, with incomes varying from Rs 3,000 to Rs 7,000 per earning member in the early 1990s, these households were nevertheless not part of the local elite. Despite their aspirations to upward mobility, most of the men seemed unwilling to devote more than three to four hours a day to work, something that made them vulnerable to instability in the local economy and caused a high degree of insecurity within the households.

'Good', 'small', 'big' and other idioms of class

To illustrate the categorisation of strangers in public places, let me open with an incident from my stay with my Brahmin host family, here called the Sharmas. One evening in 1997, like most other evenings, the men were playing cards with their friends while their wives were watching a TV serial and the young ones were sitting around doing nothing in particular. Suddenly one of them suggested: 'Let's go for an ice cream!' Billu, the eldest son in the family, agreed to drive, and his 30-year-old wife, their daughter, his two female cousins and I squeezed into their Ambassador and headed for the ice-cream stalls in Mohanganj market. Billu ordered five 'Tooty Frooties' through the car window and, while waiting for the ice creams, Billu and his cousin Gurhiya looked for familiar faces. Suddenly, a white shadow passed the car windows, stopped and blocked their view. It was a skinny old woman, limping, with a slightly bent forward position, dressed in a white, torn cotton sari. She joined her hands humbly together and held out her hands, but said nothing. Billu put his hand in his pocket to search for some coins. Seeing his gesture, his cousin Gurhiya shouted 'Don't give!', but it was already too late. Billu had just put a coin into her hands. The old woman joined her hands together in gratitude and proceeded to the next car. Billu's three-year-old daughter, Dimpie, who had watched silently, asked 'Who is she?' Almost in unison, Gurhiya and Dimpie's mother replied that the woman was a *gandi aurat* (bad / dirty woman). Dimpie seemed satisfied with this explanation but, half-way through her ice cream, she asked '*Gandi aurat kyon ai?* Why did the bad / dirty woman come?' Her mother, in an attempt to curtail further questions, snapped '*tumko lene ai*' (she came to fetch you). At this, Dimpie fell silent and lay quietly in her aunt's lap until we reached home, obviously thinking hard about what she just heard. But she did not ask further questions, and there was no one who mentioned the beggar woman again.

In Kanpur the words *gandi* (f) and *ganda* (m) were used to describe a whole range of objects, actions and people that were negatively valued. In this particular incident, it also seemed to function as a class label. The woman was a stranger, and the Sharmas knew neither her specific caste background nor her occupation, if she had any. And yet they immediately positioned her as being of a roughly similar status to the low-caste or ex-untouchable Ahirs, Valmikis (Bhangis) and Dhobis they employed as domestic servants to wash their floors, bathrooms and clothes (Frøystad 2003), a positioning process based on more complex similarities than her work as a beggar. Before disentangling the traits that enabled such labelling, let me provide an overview of the other class labels that my upper-caste acquaintances in Mohanganj used.

Like Dickey's better-off informants, upper castes in Mohanganj distin-guished between three broad categories of people. Those they considered inferior were occasionally referred to as *gande log* (bad / dirty people), as in the earlier incident. This group could also be referred to as *jo parha-likha nahin* (literally 'those who cannot read or write' – illiterates) or as 'the illit-erate class' or 'the masses' (in English). Most commonly, however, they were referred to as *chote log* (small people). Whatever the label used, this category consisted of people who looked relatively poor, and whom the upper castes automatically assumed to be of low-caste or ex-untouchable origin – the difference between the two categories did not seem to matter much to them. People that my upper-caste acquaintances considered to be at their own level – in terms of economic standing, caste, lifestyle and so on – could well be referred to as 'middle class' or even 'upper middle class', but the most common referent was *acche log* (good people), which also was the term they applied to themselves. In addition, there was a third category, namely *bare log* (big people). This term did not necessarily refer to people they thought of as 'better' than themselves. What made people big in the eyes of my upper-caste informants was either money or influential positions and connections – features that could be further described through labels such as *karorpatis* (multi-millionaires), *amir log* (rich people), 'VIPs' or the hybrid term *VIP log* (VIP people).[3] Given that the 'big' category was of a different order from the 'good' and 'small' categories, class was evidently construed in a more complex way than by positioning others below, on a par with, or above themselves, as Dickey suggests was the case in Madurai.

In this chapter, I will concentrate on the two first categories, which I refer to as *acche log* and *chote log* or their English equivalents hereafter.[4] Both terms, as well as the *bare log* label, were used far beyond Mohanganj and Kanpur, but have not yet been adequately studied in their own right. To exemplify how these idioms were used as class labels, let me cite from some murder reports that appeared in the local edition of *The Times of India*, the most commonly read English daily. One report describes an unidentified victim, a young man about whom little could be said because his body was found decomposed. This did not preclude the journalist from class-ifying him, which he did as follows: 'Clad in blue T-shirt and a pair of black trousers, the deceased appeared to belong to a good family.' The same newspaper also reported another murder case, which concerned a young girl who had been raped and killed. She was described and positioned as follows: 'The victim, hardly 20 years of age was found clad in a pink shalwar suit, and had short hair and gold finger rings. Her fair complexion and sharp features indicated that she was from a good family background.' A third report described a male victim as 'clad in cream-coloured trousers and shirt', continuing that 'sporting both a beard and a moustache, the man had a wheatish complexion and apparently hailed from a lower-middle-class family'.[5]

As suggested by these newspaper articles, clothing and complexion were crucial indicators of class, which were also more widely used to position individuals in anonymous encounters in the city. But while the reports suggest that the journalists virtually ticked off various features, class positioning in public places tended to occur in the way Eleanor Rosch (1978) and Maurice Bloch (1991, 1998) suggest. Rather than consulting a mental catalogue of essential 'good' or 'small' features, strangers were immediately compared with the prototypical mental image of a 'good' or 'small' person, a process so rapid that it instantly ranked strangers somewhere on a continuum between the two ends of the 'good' and 'small' categories. Yet not a single person I met was able to explain this process or the categories employed, because the knowledge on which it was based was largely inarticulate. Being deeply internalised, however, it influenced the behaviour of actors in a number of ways. On the basis of the subtle everyday remarks and distancing practices I observed in Mohanganj, I will now attempt to unpack some of the most important markers involved in the class positioning of strangers in public places.

Markers of class and their relationship with caste

The markers of class that my acquaintances in Mohanganj most commonly used included complexion, clothing, body shape, movement and speech. It was widely believed that members of the upper castes, and Brahmins in particular, were fairer than members of the lower castes. Yet as everybody knew, the congruency was far from absolute. Once I was told about a Scheduled Caste man who 'was so tall and fair that if he told anybody that he was a Scheduled Caste, people would laugh in disbelief.' Likewise, a Barhai (carpenter) migrant to Kanpur told me that, while his first child was *kala* (black) like himself, his next two children were so fair that all the Barhais in his native village near Azamgarh joked that his wife must have taken some secret trips to *phoren* (abroad). Despite such jokes, the two children were considered handsome and their parents lucky. In turn, an upper-caste couple with dark-complexioned offspring were considered unfortunate and pitied, and several upper-caste men who happened to be of darker complexion than their family members and friends, were nicknamed Kallu (Blackie). After one of my female informants gave birth to a son, her very first question was '*kala nahi hai, na?* (He is not black, is he?)' Later, she explained that in a dream she had before giving birth she lay in bed and noticed that a ten-year-old *kala* boy stood by her bedside. Although she had never seen him before, she instantly knew that he was her son, and spent what remained of her pregnancy worrying that the dream had foretold the birth of a dark-skinned son. The fear, disbelief, discomfort and teasing that surrounds the birth of dark-complexioned children to upper-caste parents, I suggest, confirm the strong associations between fairness and an upper-caste background on the one hand, and dark complexion and low-caste background on the other.

Other factors being similar, this association between caste and complexion led my upper-caste informants to expect dark-skinned strangers to belong to one of the low castes and fair strangers to belong to one of the upper castes. This association was also manifest in an old proverb which states that 'One should never trust a black Brahmin', who, as the story goes, might turn out to be a Chamar in disguise – that is, belonging to a community that seemed to epitomise untouchability for the upper castes in Kanpur. Although none of those I met believed in this proverb, it might well have served as a word of caution to Brahmins in the past.

Among the Brahmin men I met during my fieldwork, a few were dark-skinned. As if to compensate for their dark complexion, they were always impeccably dressed in high-quality pants and striped, branded shirts, whereas other, fairer, upper-caste men often sported the cheaper, unbranded shirts, pants or the traditional *kurta-pajamas* (knee-long shirt over loose trousers) made from inferior-quality cloth. While living in a poor neighbourhood in 1993, I was drawn into something I interpret as a reverse compensation strategy. My next-door neighbours were Brahmins, and their seven-year-old daughter frequently asked me to point out the most *gori* (fair) person in the courtyard. My own Nordic skin was too fair for the local complexion scale, so the winner was always the girl herself and, by making me say so again and again, she evidently confirmed her own self-worth. I gathered that to her and her parents complexion was probably more important than to other members of the upper castes because, everything else being more or less similar, there was little else to distinguish her from her low-caste neighbours.

Given the association between fairness and upper caste background, fairness was something that my upper-caste acquaintances actively cultivated. Those unable to protect themselves from the sun normally dressed in clothes that covered the entire body in order to stay fair. Often Billu, who wore short-sleeved shirts even for long scooter rides, was rebuked by his wife for becoming 'ugly' and was asked to use long-sleeved shirts to protect his skin. Some people, including a few men, had started to use the sun-block creams that became available in Mohanganj market in the mid-1990s, and young girls applied complexion-lightening powder when dressing up for a party. However, the facial bleach offered by the beauty parlours was reserved for special occasions such as weddings, or for women whose complexion did not reflect their status. Complexion, then, was more than a biological given: it was something to be actively preserved or even created. But remaining inside and using costly cosmetics were beyond the means of the urban poor, so fairness was also a result of economic standing. This indicates an intricate blurring of genetics and economic status, which in turn contributes to the local conflation of caste and class.

Another feature that helped to assess the class and caste background of strangers was clothing. Rather than simply referring to quality and branding, it was primarily the maintenance, fitting and fashion of a stranger's dress that were important. While my upper caste friends and informants dressed up in spotless clothes at least once a day, most 'small' people were unable to do so. Not only did they have fewer clothes to circulate, they could neither afford high-quality laundry powder nor the services of a washerman, and were too busy making ends meet to tend to their clothes every day. Maintenance also entailed getting clothes ironed and cotton saris starched. Wearing an unstarched cotton sari, a woman explained, would make her look like a domestic servant. Furthermore, my upper-caste acquaintances made it a point to get their white clothes bleached, in contrast to the white clothes of 'small' people, which turned grey and became stained as the months and years went by.

The emphasis on maintenance also spoke about the flow of clothes from middle-class homes to the households of domestic servants. Many 'small' people wore hand-me-down clothes that were too wide or too long. In the case of saris, this flow was evident in the combinations between saris, blouses and petticoats, which would be carefully selected by middle-class women, but had to be combined in often awkward ways by the less affluent. Rarely was a maidservant given the matching blouse alongside an old sari, and thus a woman could often be recognised as 'small' by the odd pairing of her sari and petticoat, and the ill-fitting blouse worn beneath the former. Furthermore, fashion served as a status marker among the younger cohort of unmarried girls. Those from more affluent homes did their best to keep up with the ever-changing *salvar-kurta* fashions, and clothes that had gone out of fashion were first downgraded to 'inside' clothes and thereafter handed down to servants. Dressing up like 'good' people was possible for anyone with sufficient means, including low castes and Dalits who had ascended to a middle-class standard of living, something my upper-caste acquaintances were fully aware of. In public places, however, they had no means to 'test' the caste background of the strangers they encountered. Other markers being equal, they simply assumed that a stranger dressed like a 'good' person was likely to belong to one of the higher castes and therefore would be 'one of us'.

Another visual marker of social status, which was assessed when strangers encountered one another in public places, was the height of a person. The average upper-caste person was assumed to be taller than the average low-caste person. Consequently, being tall was interpreted as a marker of possible 'good' pedigree and upper-caste status. Statistically, this assumption is likely to contain some truth since the average height of a population is affected by its standard of living and diet over long periods of time. But several of my upper-caste acquaintances were shorter than their stereotypical image of an upper-caste person. While the women among them could use high heels to appear taller, short men had to resort to gluing an extra sole under their shoes. A Khatri medical doctor, who looked short even when wearing his 'platforms', was humorously referred to as 'child labour' by some of his friends.

Even more significant than height was how a person, be it a man or a woman, moved about in public. Like other 'good' people, my upper-caste acquaintances used a vehicle whenever they could – even if they only headed for the corner shop. A vehicle did not only offer protection from the sun and the dust, but also from the heterogeneous collection of strangers they were exposed to outside their homes. Different means of transport were accorded different degrees of respectability. Buses and *tempos* – rusty vans that officially took six passengers at a time, but normally transported eight or nine – were so intensely despised by my upper-caste acquaintances that they never used them. On the rare occasions when 'good' people walked about in public places, their movements were governed by strict norms as to when, where and how they should walk. When walking to the market in the evening, they moved slowly, in a controlled and dignified manner. It was as if they deliberately employed their walk to dramaturgically contrast the swift movements of the vegetable vendors, rickshaw drivers, newspaper boys, milkmen, labourers, servants, sweepers and shop owners they encountered on the streets. Thorstein Veblen's observation that 'conspicuous abstention from labour' was an 'index of reputability' in nineteenth-century Europe (Veblen 1931 [1899]: 38) seems to hold true for contemporary India as well. Brisk walking was something my upper caste informants reserved for exercise, an activity that was restricted to the early mornings. At this time of the day, the exposure to the sun did not cause a tan, the temperature was moderate and the air was fresh and less polluted. Moreover, morning walks were rarely conducted in the streets, but located to parks, open fields or one's own home compound. Even though the time and place of morning walks were largely determined by practical considerations, the location and timing enabled the walkers to communicate that they walked out of choice rather than compulsion.

Only two of my upper-caste contacts were morning walkers, and many were overweight due to lack of exercise and preference for fried, oily or heavily sweetened food. In a polemic comment about the link between caste, occupational patterns and dietary habits, the low-caste scholar and activist, Kancha Ilaiah, describes the typical Brahmin priest as having 'an overgrown belly [with] his unexercised muscles hanging from his bones' (Ilaiah 1996: 22). Although Ilaiah undoubtedly overstated the congruence of bodily and dietary differences with caste, his view conforms to the associations made by the residents of Mohanganj, who, other markers being equal, assumed that skinny persons were 'small' and plump ones were 'good'. This association between body shape and social status was also reflected in the local notion of the ideal body, which would have been described as moderately sturdy in Europe, but which was referred to as 'healthy' in Kanpur (cf. Osella and Osella 1996). The only exception seemed to be young brides-to-be, who ideally should be slim and frail.

The lack of exercise and preference for sweet and oily food made 'good' people in Mohanganj prone to lifestyle diseases such as diabetes, high blood pressure, angina pectoris and arthritis. Strangely, the presence of these diseases did not seem to worry them, in spite of the many reports about the risks of sedentary lifestyles and the concerns raised by medical doctors. On the contrary, diagnoses and prescriptions were so often discussed and compared, medication so frequently swallowed in front of visitors and complaints about 'high BP' (high blood pressure) so regularly voiced that diseases associated with a semi-affluent urban lifestyle appeared to have a certain conspicuousness about them. In contrast, none of those I related to in Mohanganj would be likely to mention publicly that he or she had contracted diseases such as tuberculosis or malaria, which were strongly associated with poor neighbourhoods and the 'small' people who lived there, just as infectious diseases like plague or cholera were associated with the poor in the early twentieth century (cf. Gooptu 2001: 74, 183). In the same way, lifestyle diseases were indicators of high status. Just like bodily stature and specific modes of movement, lifestyle diseases were almost solely understood as products of economic standing. The relationship between economic standing and attitude to bodily movements was associated by my upper caste acquaintances in the following way: other matters being equal, sturdy strangers who passed them in a car or on a scooter were assumed to be of 'good' status, while skinny strangers passing them speedily on foot were thought of as 'small' people.

The final marker of social differences that I will consider here is language. Following Steven Feld (1982) and Arjun Appadurai (1990, 1996), we may think of the public places in Mohanganj as soundscapes in which strangers are not only seen, but also heard. The linguistic ideal of my upper-caste acquaintances was the *mithi bhasa* (sweet speech) associated with the court culture of Lucknow, the erstwhile capital of Awadh state and seat of the local ruler, the Navab. Sweet speech was particularly renowned for its courtesies, epitomised in the term *'pahle ap'* ('you first'). In addition, sweet speech involved the use of a standard Hindi pronunciation, moderate volume, little gesticulation and minimal facial mimicry – especially in the case of women. Sweet speech often contained references to poetry, songs, scriptures or an English phrase or two that revealed a certain level of education and what was referred to as 'culture' or 'exposure'. Most of the features that characterised sweet speech were absent in the working-class dialects of Kanpur, which the 'small' people in Mohanganj spoke. In addition, working-class speech often revealed strong traces of the dialects spoken in the surrounding rural areas of eastern Uttar Pradesh and Bihar, where many of the recent migrants originated. Whenever the question of speech emerged in the course of a conversation, it did not take long before Atal Behari Vajpayee's name was mentioned. Vajpayee, a prominent Bharatya Janata Party leader and later prime minister, was lauded as a master of sweet speech and an excellent 'orator'. Because he was a Brahmin from Lucknow, Vajpayee's speech matched the linguistic ideals of my upper-caste informants perfectly. In contrast, low-caste politicians such as Mayawati, Mulayam Singh Yadav and Phoolan Devi were often criticised for their 'rude' and 'plain' speech, and people who spoke loudly and bluntly were often rebuked for 'speaking like Phoolan Devi' or talking 'just like Mayawati'. Speech, then, clearly served as an indicator of social background. Strangers who mastered the sweet speech and 'cultured' mode of communication were generally assumed to be of 'good' and upper-caste background unless their bodily stature, complexion or clothing suggested otherwise.

Combination and conflation

I could have continued the examination of class markers by looking at the relevance of straight and well-kept teeth, footwear, hairstyles and accessories such as spectacles, jewellery, watches and mobile phones. The local murder reports I cited earlier suggest that I could even have looked at the relevance of physical features like the shape of a nose. The markers discussed earlier, however, appeared to be those my upper-caste acquaintances depended upon most heavily when positioning strangers in public places. I will now draw on these markers to make three further points.

The first is to reiterate that the presence or absence of these markers was established all at once rather than separately, and the way this was done suggests the prevalence of prototypical categorisation. While the prototype of a 'small' person was someone who had all the 'small' status markers one could think of, the prototype of a 'good' person had all the possible attributes of a 'good' person. Of course, these prototypes were caricatures, but they served as ideal types or conceptual images that facilitated my upper-caste informants' navigation in social situations in which they encountered people whose social status could not be assessed more accurately. Within a second, each stranger was compared to the prototypical 'small' and 'good' man or woman and, depending on the balance of 'small' and 'good' traits, was placed somewhere along the continuum. The markers worked in combination rather than as distinctive categories, and none of them was essential. This enabled people to compensate for missing indicators and shortcomings, as the case of the dark-skinned Brahmin man or the poor but fair-skinned Brahmin girl demonstrated. As long as the number of 'good' markers was sufficient to prevent ambiguous positioning, they could safely afford to neglect the remaining traits.

My second point pertains to the peculiar continuity between markers stemming from genetic make-up (i.e. height and complexion) and acquired markers available to anyone with sufficient economic means (i.e. clothing, healthy plumpness, vehicle, etc.). At first sight, these seem to be of different orders, the former being more suggestive of caste positioning, the latter of economic standing. As noted earlier, however, genetic features can be manipulated – a dark complexion can be lightened up, and height can be increased by extra soles or high-heeled shoes. Thus, even genetic markers of 'good' status were in principle available to anyone with sufficient economic means. Yet, as Pierre Bourdieu (1984) has shown, a similarity in economic capital does not necessarily translate into similarities in style, because 'taste' and 'culture' are usually acquired over a lifetime. Even when the 'small' in Mohanganj dressed up in their best clothes for a wedding, my upper caste informants found the menswear too shiny and the women's choice of colours and textiles too gaudy (cf. Osella and Osella 2000). Similarly, more than a high income was required if the upwardly mobile and newly rich low castes wanted to pass as 'good' in the eyes of my upper-caste informants. With inherited markers open to manipulation and acquired markers often bearing the traces of the past, the distinction between markers based on economic means and genetic heritage was not as clear-cut as it may seem.

My final point concerns the conflation of class with caste as an element of social positioning in public places. In part, the blurring is the result of the continuity between inherited and acquired markers of social status, and stems from a tendency to assess both at once, without making such a distinction. But the conflation of caste and class may also be explained in terms of the expectations on the part of those who make status assessments. I have mentioned that my upper-caste acquaintances almost inevitably assumed 'small'-looking people to be of low-caste origin and the 'smallest'-looking among them to be of untouchable background. These assumptions applied even though they were perfectly aware of the existence of high-income persons of low-caste background and poor persons of upper-caste origin. When such cases were mentioned in conversations without reference to known individuals, my friends and acquaintances expressed a combination of sympathy and disinterest for poor upper-caste persons, and anything from contempt to acceptance for upwardly mobile or affluent low-caste persons, depending on the degree to which they had successfully appropriated the ethos and style of 'good' people. In public places, however, the upper-caste persons I lived with made no attempts to distinguish middle-class persons of low-caste background from middle-class persons of upper-caste background, or poor persons of upper-caste background from poor persons of low-caste background. Had I asked my informants to thoroughly scrutinise the strangers they encountered, they might have tried to make such distinctions, but generally they did not do so. This, I suggest, was because class positioning was something they did when their main attention was directed towards something else, such as steering clear of the pigs in the street, discussing politics with a relative or pondering how many extra packets of milk to buy. Having positioned a stranger as 'small', my upper caste-informants almost automatically thought of him or her as being of low-caste or untouchable origin. Such conflations were so common that my upper-caste acquaintances frequently referred to 'small' strangers as 'people of the Chamar type' or 'some Harijan or the other'. These labels, then, are best understood as class concepts expressed in the idiom of caste. As such, they represent the flip side of the caste-class conflation entailed in the terms *acche log* and *chote log*, which are idioms of class implicitly connotating caste origins.

Distancing and the production of enclosure

Having examined class positioning in public places and the blurring of class and caste it entailed, I am now prepared to examine the forms of social distancing produced in the process. As a point of departure, I will turn to Dipesh Chakrabarty's reflections on the conceptual boundary between the inside and the outside of the house. He describes the house as 'an inside produced by symbolic enclosure for the purpose of protection', while the outside, epitomised by the market, is an unenclosed space which 'acts as the meeting point of several communities' and 'a place where one comes across and deals with strangers.' (Chakrabarty 1991: 22–3). While the inside is guarded and enclosed, the outside and the strangers one encounters there are ambiguous and potentially dangerous. A consequence of this mode of thought, Chakrabarty continues, is that rituals of enclosure are reproduced in the outside itself (ibid. 25). For example, shopkeepers worship deities in their shops just like they do at home, and sweep the ground outside their shops just like their own courtyards are swept, while local traders often patronise one of the local temples, thereby expressing their long-term affiliation with the market.

Chakrabarty's thoughts on the inside / outside distinction and its implications for the production of enclosures in the outside are relevant for understanding the upper-caste use of public places in Mohanganj. In the following section, I will emphasise the gendered notions of the boundary between the inside and outside more strongly than Chakrabarty's discussion may suggest. Whereas he is concerned with enclosures that make public places more like home, I will focus on enclosures that 'homogenise' people who are given access to them. For upper-caste Hindus in Mohanganj, I suggest, public places appeared as an ambiguous and threatening outside partly because they involved strangers of 'small' and, by extension, assumed low-caste or untouchable background – people with whom interaction was firmly regulated in other settings, not least the upper-caste home (Frøystad 2003). The overall pattern suggested that the higher the percentage and density of 'small' strangers in a public place, the more pronounced the upper-caste discomfort became, and the more imminent was the need for some kind of distancing. In this section, I will look at four forms of distancing that were common in Mohanganj – namely, withdrawal from public places; mobile enclosures; permanent enclosures and temporary enclosures.

The first form of enclosure, withdrawal from public places, was most common among women. Among my upper-caste acquaintances, the women restricted their presence in public places far more than the men (see Donner in this volume). Apart from a female Baniya friend, the women I associated with in Mohanganj never left their homes unless they had a definite, legitimate purpose and someone (preferably a male relative) to accompany them. Old women hardly left home at all and delegated all practical tasks related to the 'outside' to younger family members or servants. Elderly women hardly ever expressed curiosity about life beyond their own homes and TV screens. As one of them rhetorically asked, '*Bahar kya hai?* (What's there (to see / do) outside?'. Girls and unmarried women were restrained in their movements through a fear of harassment, which was referred to as 'eve-teasing', the prototypical example being a group of rowdy youths teasing girls and young women through improper remarks, pulling their *chunnis* (scarfs) or pinching their bottoms or breasts. The risk of eve-teasing was considered highest in anonymous venues such as streets and markets – not because 'small' men were thought to be more notorious eve-teasers than others, but because such places enabled eve-teasers to escape without being recognised or caught. But having said this, even my middle-aged male acquaintances limited their presence in these places, as they expressed discomfort in the presence of too many 'small' people whom they did not know. In contrast, boys and young men belonging to the same households spent much of their leisure time with their friends roaming freely across the city on scooters. Most instances of eve-teasing I was told about or experienced myself involved such young men from apparently 'good' families visiting neighbourhoods in which they did not live themselves. To summarise the gendered nature of the inside / outside distinction, we can state that it was most significant for young and elderly women, and least significant for young, unmarried men.

In the remainder of this section, I will focus on distancing that involved women – not only because it was among them that it was most apparent, but also because first-hand observation of exclusively male movements in public places poses a methodological impossibility for a female anthropologist. As suggested earlier, one form of distancing consisted of staying away from public places in which one would be surrounded by *chote* strangers. This tactic of withdrawal was based on notions of respectability and safety. I often observed children and unmarried daughters in upper-caste homes standing at the gates of their compounds, watching the road curiously but never venturing out themselves. The withdrawal of young women was taken to the extreme by two unmarried Brahmin sisters, who even remained inside their home compound during their daily walks. Every evening, they passed the width and length of their apartment building, evidently without considering the possibility of leaving their home compound and walking along the road outside instead. The view that buses and tempos were 'dirty' resurfaced in Deepu Sharma's explanation for why she and her cousin Gurhiya never went to the movies. Although watching films was one of their favourite pastimes, she labelled the cinemas downtown 'dirty', partly because she feared eve-teasing, but primarily because she loathed the thought of having to sit alongside 'rickshaw drivers and the like', as she put it. Fortunately for these young women, the many TV channels, which had proliferated since the monopoly of the state-run TV station Doordarshan had been broken in 1992, reduced the need to visit public cinemas. In the same way, my upper-caste informants spoke of the congested old *muhallas* (neighbourhoods) downtown. These parts of Kanpur were normally referred to as *gande* (bad, dirty), not because their residents were considered to be *gande* or 'small' in the way those who lived in the ramshackle huts along the roads and railway tracks near Mohanganj were, but because the roads of the central neighbourhoods were so narrow that they were inaccessible by car. When my acquaintances went downtown by scooter or rickshaw, they used broad roads instead of taking the shortcut through these residential quarters. Women also often explained that these parts of the city were dangerous and, although the men did not phrase it that way, they were equally reluctant to enter these areas.

The next forms of distancing that I will look at all involved enclosures of some kind. Let me look first at the mobile enclosures. This term denotes nothing more mysterious than cars and other means of transport, but aims to capture the protection they offered from *chote* strangers outside rather than their ability to transport people or display their social status. Take, for example, those who used public transport to go to work. A female teacher had made it a point to make the school bus pick her up from right outside her house in the mornings and drop her at the same spot in the evenings. One of her elderly male relatives and a female Punjabi bank employee paid a cycle rickshaw driver a monthly amount to pick them up right in front of their respective bungalows – inside their home compounds. The elderly man was dropped right in front of the door of his retail shop, and the bank employee got down inside the fence that separated her bank from the road. Thus, all three were able to go from home to work and back again without taking a single step into the public street. Utilising door-to-door transport, they could move through public spaces without having to mix with strangers at all.

The protection that cars and other vehicles offered from the proximity of 'small' strangers was equally important when the destination was a public place itself. On the occasion of the outing mentioned at the beginning of this chapter, the Sharmas remained in their car while ordering, waiting for and consuming their ice cream. Indeed, the vendors' readiness to take orders from vehicles parked at the other side of the road turned the food stalls in Mohanganj into a kind of drive-in that protected the owners of cars from contact with those who had no vehicles at their disposal, as well as protecting their footwear, saris and *chunnis* from the dust in the street. Moreover, the cars provided their passengers with protection from the poor children and beggars who were hanging around in the market unless a beggar, like the old widow mentioned earlier, was bold enough to walk over to the row of cars. The tendency to remain in the car while eating in public was so pronounced that on one occasion we ate tomato soup inside a car packed with so many passengers that it was almost impossible to lift our spoons.

The 'protection' that a closed vehicle offers was also given as an explanation as to why my upper-caste acquaintances avoided travel in regular second-class train coaches. Whereas I occasionally found such train rides exciting, at least during the early stages of fieldwork, my middle-class friends in Mohanganj would never even consider travelling second class. A newly wed woman, who asked her husband for money to visit her parents in another town, but was told that he couldn't afford a ticket for the better, air-conditioned so-called AC class right then, took this as a severe insult and reason not to travel at all. When telling me about it afterwards, she fumed that '*My* parents *never* let me travel in anything but AC class!' The air-conditioned train compartments that my middle-class informants preferred were mobile enclosures in three ways. First, the AC-class fare, which is between three and four times higher than the second-class fare, ensured that most passengers were of a relatively high income group. Second, the railway staff did not let hawkers, ticketless travellers or other outsiders board the AC coaches at stations, in stark contrast to the 'porous' boundaries of the second-class coaches, which are invaded by mobile sellers at every stop. Combined, this increased the class homogeneity not only of the passengers, but of everyone present in the train compartment, with the exception of railway staff. Finally, the tinted windows of AC compartments made the mess and dirt of the outside vanish from the passengers' view. In addition to the speed and comfort of AC-class trains and coaches, it appeared that these aspects made the AC class a favourite choice among my upper-caste informants.

Distancing could also involve enclosures with fixed and permanent locations. A number of shops and restaurants in Kanpur had tinted windows, something that signified a certain exclusiveness. Like in air-conditioned train coaches, tinted windows protected the customers from the sun, heat and the gaze as well as the view of strangers outside. Other shops and restaurants had uniformed guards who kept 'small' people away. In these establishments, 'small' people were politely and discretely turned away, but the poorest ones could even be turned away from shops and restaurants without guards. In one such incident, a poor woman who entered a textile shop in Mohanganj was shooed away by the shopkeeper because he suspected that she wanted to beg, as he told me afterwards. Another kind of permanent enclosure is the club. Most of my middle-aged male upper-caste acquaintances were, or had been, members of the Kanpur Club or the Ganges Club. Although they considered these clubs to be too posh, modern and 'fast' to feel comfortable, many stated that they retained membership to enable their sons to use the tennis or badminton courts – a possibility that very few youngsters utilised at the time of my fieldwork. Membership also gave their daughters and wives access to the exclusive movie screenings that the clubs occasionally arranged, and where 'the crowd is "good"', as one of them stated. As it turned out, however, the increased number of TV channels reduced the interest in exclusive club screenings.

Temporary enclosures were the homogenising enclosures that, in contrast to clubs, shops and restaurants, only lasted for some hours, days or weeks. Temporary enclosures included a number of arrangements, like wedding parties, religious festivals and shopping exhibitions. The religious festival that best exemplifies temporary enclosures was the celebration of Durga Puja, which was organised by the Bengali community in the city, but which my non-Bengali acquaintances also enjoyed visiting. During the days of the festival, images of Durga are placed inside huge *pandals* (tents), which are erected in public places across the city, and, although admission is theoretically open to all worshippers and spectators, the crowd inside the tents tends to be dominated by neat, well-dressed and 'good'-looking people, in stark contrast to those roaming the streets outside. This was partly because worship of the goddess Durga requires nice and clean clothes, but also because a large proportion of the Bengalis in Kanpur are middle-class professionals. In terms of class, then, my upper-caste acquaintances were by and large surrounded by their own inside the Durga Puja *pandals*. In terms of regional identity they were not, but this caused no estrangement since the Bengalis who dominated this festival were middle class and seen in a positive light.

In stark contrast to the interest in what is essentially an adaptation of a festival from another region, my upper-caste acquaintances showed far less interest in the public Ramlila celebrations, although most of them worshipped Ram and his aide Hanuman more often than they worshipped Durga. This disinterest stems, I suggest, from the public character of the Ramlila celebrations. As they take place in unenclosed spaces and are visited by a heterogeneous crowd, my acquaintances did not feel comfortable there. The Ramlila celebrates and dramatises the victory of Lord Ram over the evil king of Lanka, Ravana. At the height of the celebrations, a huge effigy depicting a many-headed, devilish Ravana goes up in flames, an event accompanied by the sound of deafening crackers. For my acquaintances, watching the large Ramlila celebration downtown was out of the question because they held it to be frequented by too many 'rowdy' people, too crowded and entailed a high risk of eve-teasing. They did, however, watch the smaller Ramlila celebration in their own neighbourhood of Mohanganj. This event was not closed off with a huge tent like Durga Puja, but was located on a vacant plot surrounded by a low fence, which allowed my infor-mants and other 'good' families to watch the 'burning of Ravana' while standing on the street, next to their cars. From the street, we could see young men erecting and setting fire to an effigy that was at least seven metres high and had eleven elaborately painted heads. As far as I could make out from a distance, the young men involved were neither of a particularly 'good' background, nor particularly 'small'. But when I asked my upper-caste acquaintances if we could enter the enclosure, or at least move a little bit closer towards the action, they held me back by saying 'We better stay here'. Later I read in a local newspaper that in the city of Ayodhya the Ramlila celebration has become less relevant than the festival of Durga Puja.[6] In Mohanganj, however, it was only the *public* Ramlila celebrations that were losing out. Ramlila was still widely celebrated but, rather than attending the public celebrations, my upper-caste acquaintances arranged their own events inside their compounds or colonies, with their children and their school friends as masters of ceremony. The openness and heterogeneity of the public Ramlila celebrations made the 'good' people in Mohanganj 'privatise' the ritual by relocating it to their own home compounds.

Temporary enclosures turned the public character of certain urban spaces into a dynamic and processual feature. To illustrate how access to a given space may change over time, let me pause a little with the venue for the public Ramlila celebration in Mohanganj. The space in question was quite large and located between Mohanganj market and the main road. It was fenced off, but usually kept open. Both my map and the sign outside the gate defined the space as a park, although there was more dust than grass to be found. As a park, the space was used by a variety of people for different purposes. Muslims residing in an adjacent neighbourhood tended their goats there, students of a nearby school hung around with their friends, boys played cricket and hawkers sold their wares. However, during the festival, the park became an entirely Hindu-dominated space. Although the burning of Ravana attracted Muslim and Sikh spectators as well, they remained at the periphery side-by-side with the 'good' people of Mohanganj. Despite the 'Hinduisation' of the park during Ramlila, it did not transform it in terms of class, because the young men who dominated the Ramlila arrangement appeared to belong to the same segment as those who used the park at other times. In contrast, a shopping exhibition that was arranged in the park on a different occasion 'homogenised' the park in terms of class while retaining its religious heterogeneity. To illustrate this process while drawing together several other points I have made in this chapter, let me briefly describe a visit to this shopping exhibition:

One day, the Sharmas received five entry passes for a 'shopping *mela*' in the mail. The young ones were eager to go, particularly the girls and women who rarely left home. Having been given permission and some money from their fathers, uncles and in-laws, they persuaded a brother to drive them and left to change their clothes. An hour later they were ready, with nice clothes, done-up hair, and a discrete layer of powder and make-up. Carefully handling their saris and *kurtas*, they squeezed into the rusty Ambassador, and off we went. The shopping exhibition was only a mile away and, having parked the car as close to the entrance of the tent as possible, they proceeded slowly towards the entrance. Outside the entrance were a number of short and thin men wearing worn-out clothes, selling snacks and offering to look after the cars and scooters for a small fee. The Sharmas hurried past them, handed in the entry passes they had received and paid the entrance fee for the rest of the group. Once inside, they found themselves in a different world. Not only was the space brightly lit, it was also clean and neatly organised with several rows of stalls. The stalls offered everything from clothes to household gadgets, life insurance and subscriptions for cellular phones. One could also buy Pepsi, ice cream and snacks. The visitors strolled two-by-two or in groups, partly looking at the items on display and partly watching other visitors. Everyone appeared to have dressed up a little, and the presence of occasional turbans, *burqas* (Muslim dress covering the full body of a woman) and beards indicated religious plurality. The only people who did not appear to have dressed up were those who brought tea to the salesmen or picked up the garbage that the visitors had thrown on the ground. The number of women and young girls present was also higher than generally found in the markets and streets. The Sharmas moved from one counter to another, not only commenting on the goods for sale but also on the appearance of other customers. Having seen all the stalls twice but not purchased more than two brightly painted clay *murtis* (images of deities), they started their journey home.

The case of the shopping exhibition does not only demonstrate the temporary transformation of a park into an enclosure that was virtually homogeneous in terms of class; it also serves to summarise some of the subtle upper-caste values that promote the production of such enclosures.

Concluding remarks

The foregoing discussion is the result of my puzzlement over the extent to which my upper-caste friends and informants in the middle-class neighbourhoods of Kanpur limited their presence in heterogeneous public places such as streets, markets and parks. In the previous pages, I have examined how they protected themselves from such places, and why they did so. Their most restrictive strategy was to withdraw from public places altogether, but the most common solution was to create enclosures that made the insiders more homogeneous. In this chapter, I delineated three kinds of enclosures: the mobile, protective cocoons provided by cars and other vehicles, the permanent enclosures provided by venues such as clubs, and, finally, the temporary enclosures provided by the large tents used for shopping exhibitions, religious festivals and other arrangements. These enclosure types could probably have been delineated in othesr ways, and there are surely enclosures and other forms of distancing that I have not dealt with here. I believe, however, that those I discussed earlier were the ones that were most common in the neighbourhoods in which I did my fieldwork.

To understand what motivated middle-class strategies of distancing, I opened by examining on what basis my upper-caste informants could assume some strangers to be inferior and others to be on par with themselves. I found such positioning to rely on a number of markers including complexion, height, bodily stature, clothing, speech, movement, accessories and vehicle ownership. The strangers whom my acquaintances, on the basis of such markers, assessed to be their equals were normally referred to as *acche log* (good people), or as being 'of a good family'. In contrast, strangers who lacked these markers were often referred to as *chote log* (small people) or *gande log* (dirty people), depending on the context. My examination of these idioms and the markers they were associated with suggested that the local notions of caste and class were highly conflated, something that probably is a characteristic of the way strangers categorise each other in public places in urban India today.

By directing the attention to anonymous encounters and the use of urban public spaces, this chapter also provides a vantage point from which one may address the following questions: What is particularly urban about Indian neighbourhoods? And what is particularly Indian about urban neighbourhoods in India?[7] Obviously, the answer depends on the problem under investigation, the city and neighbourhood in which the fieldwork is located, and the kinds of people who inform the study. My fieldwork among upper-caste Hindus in Kanpur suggests that the urban characteristic would be that most public encounters occur between people who are complete strangers, something that makes people heavily dependent on visual criteria both when making class judgements of others and when attempting to communicate their own status. The particularly Indian characteristic of this process would be that the strategies of social distancing employed are flavoured and reinforced by notions of caste, which also spill over to the local constructions of class.

The analysis of class recognition and distancing in this chapter is a snapshot taken in the late 1990s. Whether these phenomena were stable or part of processes of change was difficult to ascertain empirically. Although my field visits to Kanpur occurred over a decade, they provide a dubious source of information about change because my interest in these issues did not arise until late into my fieldwork. Nevertheless, some of the broader developments that have marked Kanpur, Uttar Pradesh and India on the whole for some time now – in particular, economic liberalisation and the upward mobility of certain low- and middle-caste segments – enable me to end with some speculations as to how the phenomena discussed here may be about to change. First, the closure of the textile mills in Kanpur, which forced large numbers of textile workers into pulling rickshaws, selling vegetables or entering casual labour (see Joshi 1999, 2003), increased the presence of 'small people' in public places during the 1990s. This development seemed to intensify the upper-caste preference for enclosures, thereby creating a market for expensive multiplexes and other novel enclosure forms. Second, the growing availability of clothes, gadgets and brands that could communicate social status seemed to be enhancing the importance of taste and fashion at the expense of 'genetic' or more physiognomic status markers. Although this undoubtedly was making it easier for upwardly mobile low castes to pass as 'good' in public places, it was also making them more vulnerable to identification as low-caste parvenus who lack the cultured tastes associated with 'good' people. Third, the upper-caste awareness that a growing number of seemingly 'good' people actually are low-caste is bound to increase. Many persons of upper-caste background will probably not mind mixing with low castes as long as they share their living standard, taste and ethos. But upper-caste people who wish to avoid the proximity of these groups – most of whom would probably be women – will have to limit their presence in heterogeneous public places even more while prioritising enclosures that keep the number of low-caste persons down. This would shift the weight from enclosures regulated by tickets and other sellable tokens of access to enclosures based on pre-existing social ties. At the end of the day, however, these speculations on changes can only be ascertained through further empirical studies.

Acknowledgements

This chapter began as a chapter of my doctoral thesis, now revised and published as Frøystad (2005), which was funded by the Norwegian Research Council and the International Peace Research Institute, Oslo (PRIO). I would like to thank Henrike Donner, Geert De Neve, Véronique Bénéï, Akhil Gupta and other participants in the Urban Neighbourhood workshop, as well as Thomas Hylland Eriksen, Signe Howell, Anne Leseth, Pamela G. Price, Arild Engelsen Ruud, Anne Waldrop and Unni Wikan for useful comments on earlier drafts.

Notes

1   The colleague was Arild Engelsen Ruud, and I thank him for permission to refer to this incident, which occurred on a train in West Bengal.
2   I follow the local tendency to juxtapose communities defined in terms of *jati* (Khatris, Baniyas) and *varna* (Brahmins) with communities defined by geographical origin (Bengalis), a juxtaposition that confirms Berreman's point about the multiple criteria of local classification.
3   The abbreviation VIP (Very Important Person) is widely used in India. In Kanpur there is even a road – Parvati Bagla Road – that is locally known as 'VIP Road'.
4   Approaching local classification through verbal idioms renders it necessary to employ terms such as *chote log* and its English translation 'small people' despite their condescending connotations. It appears that basing the discussion on local idioms favours a decision of the kind Mendelsohn and Vicziany took when using the term 'untouchable' despite its derogatory connotations (Mendelsohn and Vicziany 1998: 2–5), rather than the kind of decision Gorringe (see this volume) took when limiting himself to a term that is more acceptable to the people it refers to.
5   The two first murder stories were reported in an article entitled 'Girl raped, murdered in Gomtinagar' in *The Times of India*, Lucknow, 20 September 1999. The third murder was mentioned in a report entitled 'Middle-aged man hacked to death' in the same newspaper on 5 May 2000.
6   'A tradition on its way out', *The Hindustan Times*, Lucknow, 15 October 1997.
7   These questions were formulated by Akhil Gupta in his concluding remarks to the workshop in the course of which I presented an earlier version of this chapter.

References

Appadurai, A. (1990) 'Disjuncture and difference in the global cultural economy' 2(2) *Public Culture* 1–24
——(1996) *Modernity at Large: Cultural Dimensions of Globalization*, Minneapolis, MN: University of Minnesota Press
Berreman, G.D. (1972) 'Social categories and social interaction in urban India' 74(3) *American Anthropologist* 567–86
——(1975) 'Research on urban social groupings' 10(1) *Journal of the Indian Anthropological Society* 39–54
Bloch, M. (1991) 'Language, anthropology and cognitive science', 26(2) *Man* 183–98

——(1998) *How we think they think: Anthropological Approaches to Cognition, Memory and Literacy*, Oxford: Westview Press

Bourdieu, P. (1984) *Distinction: A social Critique of the Judgement of Taste*, London: Routledge and Kegan Paul

Chakrabarty, D. (1991) 'Open space / public place: garbage, modernity and India' XIV(1) *South Asia* 15–31

Dickey, S. (1993) *Cinema and the urban poor in South India*, Cambridge: Cambridge University Press

——(2000) 'Permeable homes: domestic service, household space, and the vulnerability of class boundaries in urban India' 27(2) *American Ethnologist* 462–89

Driver, E.D. (1982) 'Class, Caste and "Status Summation" in urban South India' 16(2) *Contributions to Indian Sociology* (N.S.) 225–53

Driver, E.D. and Driver A.E. (1987) *Social Class in India: Essays on Cognitions and Structures*, Leiden: Brill

Earnes, E. and Goode, J.G. (1977) *Anthropology of the City: An Introduction to Urban Anthropology*, Englewood Cliffs, NJ: Prentice-Hall

Feld, S. (1982) *Sound and Sentiment: Birds, Weeping, Poetics, and Song in Kaluli Expression*, Philadelphia, PA: University of Pennsylvania Press

Frøystad, K. (2003) 'Master-servant relations and the domestic reproduction of caste in Northern India' 68(1) *Ethnos* 73–94

——(2005) *Blended Boundaries: Caste, Class and Shifting Faces of 'Hinduness' in a North Indian City*, New Delhi: Oxford University Press.

Goffman, E. (1963) *Behavior in Public Places: Notes on the Social Organization of Gatherings*, New York: The Free Press

Gooptu, N. (2001) *The Politics of the Urban Poor in early Twentieth-Century India*, Cambridge: Cambridge University Press

Ilaiah, K. (1996) *Why I am not a Hindu: A Sudra Critique of Hindutva Philosophy, Culture and Political Economy*, Calcutta: Samya

Joshi, C. (1999) 'Hope and despair: textile workers in Kanpur in 1937–38 and the 1990s' 33(1) *Contributions to Indian Sociology* (N.S.) 171–203

——(2003) *Lost Worlds: Indian Labour and its Forgotten Histories*, New Delhi: Permanent Black

Mendelsohn, O. and Vicziany, M. (1998) *The Untouchables: Subordination, Poverty and the State in Modern India*, Cambridge: Cambridge University Press

Osella, C. and Osella, F. (1996) 'Articulation of physical and social bodies in Kerala' 30(1) *Contributions to Indian Sociology* 37–68

——(1999) 'From transience to immanence: consumption, life-cycle and social mobility in Kerala, South India' 33(4) *Modern Asian Studies* 989–1020

Osella, F. and Osella, C. (2000) *Social Mobility in Kerala: Modernity and Identity in Conflict*, London: Pluto Press

Rosch, E. (1978) 'Principles of categorization', in Rosch, E. and Lloyd, B.B. (eds), *Cognition and Categorization*, Hillsdage, NJ: Lawrence Erlbaum Associates

Sebring, J.M. (1969) 'Caste indicators and caste identification of strangers' 28(3) *Human Organization* 199–207

Tolen, R. (2000) 'Transfers of knowledge and privileged spheres of practice: servants and employers in a Madras railway colony', in Adams, K.M. and Dickey, S. (eds) *Home and Hegemony: Domestic Service and Identity Politics in South and Southeast Asia*, Ann Arbor, MI: The University of Michigan Press

Veblen, T. (1931 [1899]) *The Theory of the Leisure Class: An Economic Study of Institutions*, New York: The Modern Library

9

CONFORMITY AND CONTESTATION

Social heterogeneity in south Indian settlements

Penny Vera-Sanso

The significance of neighbourhood reputations for the economic and social status of residents makes neighbourhoods a highly contested domain. This chapter explores two arenas of contestation: neighbourhood boundaries and struggles over which residents 'really belong'. The criterion of belonging discussed here is family conformity with the values by which a locality strives to be identified. Assertions of neighbourhood boundaries and of conformity, or the failure to conform, are made, whether explicitly or implicitly, during every interaction between people residing in a locality as well as during encounters between residents and local institutions. They can be seen in the siting of and access to infrastructure, in demands for contributions to temple festivals or neighbourhood upkeep, in invitations to participate in local domestic and neighbourhood functions and, most significantly, in inclusion in the daily exchanges between residents on which poorer people rely in order to meet their everyday needs. These contestations of belonging do three things. First, they provide the platform for residents to define the character of their neighbourhood. Second, they play a significant role in shaping and reshaping collective identities and gendered subjectivities. Third, they reveal and frequently reinforce social and economic inequalities.

Drawing on fieldwork undertaken in two socially heterogeneous settlements in the state of Tamil Nadu, this chapter argues that when a neighbourhood is socially heterogeneous (in terms of caste, class, religion or occupation) they are unlikely to find amongst themselves the commonality of background or experience that can underpin neighbourhood identity. Instead they must rely on the shared meanings generated in wider social fields in order to build the consensus on which neighbourhood identity depends. It is beyond the scope of this chapter to delineate the basis, conformity and contestations on which more socially homogenous settlements

182

generate neighbourhood identities; these can be seen in the work of Chandavarkar (1994), De Neve (this volume) and Gorringe (this volume).

After a brief discussion of the particularities of socially heterogeneous settlements and the need for residents to draw on discourses generated beyond the neighbourhood to frame their collective identity, this chapter examines discourses prevalent in Tamil Nadu before illustrating how these are used to define neighbourhood identities, shape contestations of belonging and constrain action and relations in socially heterogeneous settlements. It will become apparent that in this process it is not only neighbourhood identities that are shaped and reshaped but gendered subjectivities as well.

Socially heterogeneous settlements

Gupta and Ferguson argue that identity and locality are founded on exclusion and othering; that identity is an unstable relation of difference (Gupta and Ferguson 1997:17). This describes the mechanism by which identity is continuously shaped and reshaped; the question it raises is what impacts different socio-spatial forms have on identity formation.

Accounts of city formation suggest that Indian cities initially replicated village socio-spatial forms in terms of the segregation of castes and work specialisms (Rowe 1973). Socio-spatial changes consequent on twentieth century developments, particularly the expansion of the housing market, government resettlement, shifts in the urban economy and diversification out of caste-based, or family-based occupations have meant that, while some localities continue to be dominated by one caste or trade, many are now much more heterogeneous. It might be thought that residence in heterogeneous settlements would liberate individuals from the constraints and restricted opportunities to which villages and homogenous settlements give rise. However, it is argued here that it is precisely because people living in heterogeneous settlements are not constrained by the dense, overlapping networks that occur within villages and homogenous settlements that these residents are subjected to and subject themselves to functionally similar, if different, constraints. In urban contexts where people are less able to check the *bona fides* of potential employees, debtors, tenants and in-laws than they are in rural areas, neighbourhood reputation becomes an important marker of a person's or family's integrity, as well as of social status. Consequently, neighbourhood reputations serve either to augment or impede people's ability to realise the social and economic opportunities that urban living can offer. For this reason, neighbourhood reputation is a valuable resource which residents are anxious to shape and protect. However, it would be a mistake to regard residents' interest in their neighbourhood's reputation in instrumental terms alone; it is intimately related to their sense of themselves, not just in terms of their collective identity but also in terms of individual subjectivity.

While everyone is engaged in an iterative process of manipulating shared meanings to produce collective identities founded on exclusion and othering, people living in socially heterogeneous neighbourhoods have particular difficulties in identifying shared meanings and common others. The particularities of socially heterogeneous neighbourhoods are most clearly seen when compared with more socially homogenous neighbourhoods, such as those based on common caste or work (for examples see Chandavarkar 1994; De Neve, this volume; Gorringe, this volume). The residents of homogenous neighbourhoods share common histories and experiences as well as interests which extend beyond the neighbourhood. Consequently, they are both more likely to have neighbourhood-based reputations ascribed to them on the basis of their common caste or work identity, and more likely to have a kit of shared meanings, rooted in common experiences, on which to draw to define their collective identity. This is not to say that these shared meanings and experiences preclude the development of intra-neighbourhood differences, as Chandavarkar demonstrates. Nor am I suggesting that residents of homogenous neighbourhoods do not subscribe to identity-forming discourses operating beyond the neighbourhood. Rather I am arguing that because of their divergent social and economic positions, residents of localities with limited historical depth do not have the commonality of interest or experience, that is the raw material, with which to forge a common neighbourhood identity.

In order to serve the twin purposes of unifying disparate residents into a collectivity and of promoting a positive neighbourhood reputation, residents of heterogeneous settlements look to dominant wider discourses precisely because shared meanings need to be shared by residents and non-residents alike. Subscribing to shared meanings regarding what constitutes a positive identity, however, is not enough: these meanings have to translate into physical forms; residents need to be seen, or deemed, to be the kind of people they claim to be. The process is necessarily one of embodiment and performativity. In socially heterogeneous settlements this process includes a suppression or, more accurately, a re-definition of difference, in favour of a conformity which is frequently more apparent than real. As will be shown, the embodiment of discourses and the determination of whether an individual's behaviour should be seen as conforming to or flouting neighbourhood norms is inevitably gendered.

By collectively defining norms of behaviour and social relations, through a continuous process of contestation, not only do people in socially heterogeneous neighbourhoods assert and enforce criteria of belonging with varying degrees of success, they also shape subjectivities while both *producing* local – that is neighbourhood-based – identities and *reproducing* more collective forms of identification. They do this by framing neighbourhood norms within discourses of exclusion and inclusion operating in the wider social arena. The comparison presented here, between a squatter settlement in Chennai and a gentrifying neighbourhood in western Tamil Nadu, suggests that manipulation of shared meanings to produce both a sense of self and of collective identity in socially heterogeneous neighbourhoods is more contested and more readily draws on discourses circulating in larger social contexts than is likely to occur in more homogenous neighbourhoods.

The wider discourse

Drawing on fieldwork undertaken in two heterogeneous localities, a squatter settlement in Chennai, studied between 1990 and 1992, and an urbanising and gentrifying neighbourhood on the outskirts of a small industrial and administrative town in Coimbatur District, studied in 2000, this chapter describes how people living in heterogeneous neighbourhoods use discourses generated beyond the locality to control perceptions of their neighbourhood's character. It shows how these discourses are used to define neighbourhood identities, shape contestations of belonging and constrain action and relations within the settlements.

During both periods residents of the two localities drew heavily on concepts of respectable / decent behaviour primarily defined in terms of male-female relations; concepts which have long been at the root of patriarchal structures in South Asia (Chatterjee 1993; Engels 1999). While these concepts proved robust discursive tools for defining the character of each neighbourhood, and the extent to which each family was deemed to 'really belong', their framing differed over the two research periods. The framing for this discourse, within a Tamil / Dravidian identity between 1990 and 1992, or an unmarked 'common sense' in 2000, is tied to larger economic and political processes of change. The shift to a 'common sense' framing reflects the extent to which Tamil identity has been fractured and displaced by a move away from anti-North Indian rhetoric on the part of the Dravidian parties, by the rise of Hindu nationalism and caste-based parties in Tamil Nadu and by the opening up of the Indian economy which began slowly in the late 1980s and hastened post-1991. But it also reflects the extent to which Tamil identity marginalised communal difference, making it, as yet, unacceptable in Tamil Nadu for the majority to espouse a strident Hindu identity. Instead, concepts of 'decent' behaviour are currently naturalised as 'common sense' to which all respectable people, irrespective of communal identity, should subscribe. In other words, what is at stake here is not the values themselves but who is stigmatised when common values are appropriated to produce particularised collective identities.

For historical and political reasons, which will be discussed briefly later, cinema and television are the main channels by which Tamils encounter and engage with discourses generated in wider social and political fields.

The extent to which film has penetrated Tamil Nadu can be seen by its extensive presence: by 1986 Tamil Nadu had 2153 permanent and touring cinema halls, the second largest number in India (Pandian 1992). By 1961 the Census of India was reporting the watching of films as the most widespread entertainment in rural Tamil Nadu (Pandian 1992), and a mid-1980s study of urban Tamil Nadu found that even the poorer informal sector workers were attending cinema houses three or more times a month (Dickey 1993). By the late 1980s, a greater number of people had access to televisions than figures of ownership would suggest, facilitating further regular watching of Tamil films (Rajagopal 2001). In addition to government provision of community TVs in scheduled caste localities, it is common practice for those without televisions to watch a neighbour's set, or for families to hire equipment during religious holidays in order to watch back-to-back videos. In these circumstances, people often watch television films in the presence of a number of neighbours. Similarly, Tamil cinema-going is a group activity, with family, peers or neighbours. The experience of watching a film, whether in cinemas or on television, is a collective and participatory one in which the audience engages audibly with the movie, singing film songs, pre-empting and responding to dialogue and commenting on any aspect of the production. These practices of collective viewing and, in the case of video-viewing, editing of films by fast-forwarding and rewinding, give Tamil films both a strategic value and a means of demonstrating or putting forward moral positions. Tamil films are typically melodramas containing fighting, dancing (frequently sexualised) and comedic dialogue. Depending on who is watching individuals may fast forward sections they feel inappropriate – the sexualised dancing rather than male violence – or they may choose to emphasise a point by rewinding.

For collective viewing people prefer to watch what are known as 'family films' as they are deemed to provide moral lessons as well as entertainment. These films address the tensions people experience between, on the one hand, social conformity and duty to others, and self-direction and individual desires on the other; they do so by showing, with varying levels of subtlety, the consequences of what are construed as diverse moral paths.[1] Hence, filmic themes, narratives and imagery provide good source material on which people selectively draw in their negotiations and contestations with others. Further, because of collective viewing practices and the shifting positions of involvement and distancing with the content of the narrative and imagery, people are also engaged in what is literally an inaudible struggle with others over moral issues; they know how their co-viewers will connect what is happening on the screen with their own behaviour and contestations over how it should be judged. Thus, rather than absorbing in an unfiltered manner what they see on the big and small screen, Tamil informants recognise the discursive and emotional force of films and actively mine them to

CONFORMITY AND CONTESTATION

back particular definitions of what it means to be a man or woman in Tamil Nadu and what constitutes acceptable, and unacceptable, actions and inter-relations within their social contexts.

Tamil Nationalism

In 1990–92, the discourse prevalent in Tamil Nadu was a Tamil nationalist discourse, and it was this discourse that residents in the squatter settlement in Chennai drew on to define the norms of behaviour and social relations on which they hoped their neighbourhood's reputation would be based. For the first half of the twentieth century, political discourse was divided between the Congress Party's Indian nationalism and a Tamil nationalist discourse propounded by a series of associations which came together in the Dravida Munnetra Kazhagam, more commonly known as the DMK. In 1967, the DMK wrested control of the state from the Congress Party and since then Tamil Nadu has been in the hands of one or other of the two Tamil parties (the DMK and what is now known as the AIADMK, the All-India Anna Dravida Munnetra Kazhagam).

The history of the Tamil nationalist movement is a drawing-in of diverse sections of Tamil society under a culturalist and sons-of-the-soil banner. Beginning in the nineteenth century with an intellectual elite seeking to purify the Tamil language by ridding it of Sanskritic words, the move-ment went on to develop an anti-Brahminic stance. During this period, educated non-Brahmins argued for the distinctiveness, antiquity and merits of Dravidians as a racial and cultural group that existed before the incur-sions of the Aryans from whom Brahmins are said to be descended. In 1926 the Self-Respect movement was founded; it derived its popularity amongst the urban semi-literate and poor youth from its emphasis on egalitarianism and opposition to the Brahminic priesthood, Sanskritic scriptural authority, arranged marriages and concepts of pollution and caste hierarchy (Pandian 1987). Although today the rationalism of the Self-Respect movement continues to provide the basis for a counter discourse, the radical agenda alienated large sections of the population. From the 1940s onwards, the Dravidian movement dropped its rationalist stance and its opposition to Brahmins and caste hierarchy. Instead, it promoted an anti-Hindi, anti-North Indian stance and emphasised a common Tamil identity based on what became the essentialised 'Tamil' values of female chastity, male valour, motherhood and love of the Tamil language. By defining values that are widespread in patriarchal societies as Tamil, the Dravidian move-ment not only developed a broad base of political support throughout the state which overshadowed communal and caste differences, but also managed to engender a heightened sense of Tamil identity, even amongst the middle classes who generally shunned the Dravidian parties in favour of Congress.

Tamil political parties have made the film industry an integral part of the Dravidian nationalist movement in order to mobilise an illiterate population. They have used film to mobilise an anti-North Indian, pro-Tamil stance in order to oust the Congress Party from state politics. They did so by making films that emphasised Tamil culture, individualising class divisions (the bad landlord/employer versus the working-class hero) and representing collective action as ineffective without a hero/leader. Initially, that hero was MG Ramachandran, who later became the Tamil Nadu Chief Minister. Through his 292 films Ramachandran was portrayed as the epitome of Tamil manhood; he was presented as a man of the people, a saviour of the poor, the protector of women, a venerator of the Tamil language and mothers and a person of immense generosity and stature. Studies of the political use of Tamil cinema accurately point to its role in hindering the development of a class-based politics in the state (Pandian 1992; Dickey 1993), however, what has been missed by such accounts is the role that Tamil cinema had in spreading and deepening a Tamil nationalism that has, until recently, largely managed to paper over communal cleavages within the State.

It is not, however, film makers alone who determine the impact of films. As Gupta notes, 'what was internalized . . . (by the audience) . . . was not always the radical ideas (such as atheism, DMK communism and so on) but the cultural definition of what it meant to be a Dravidian' (1991: 208). It was not only the political parties which noted this. Irrespective of their political links, all film makers seeking box office success made films appealing to, and reinforcing, Tamil national identity; until the early to mid-1990s all popular Tamil films promoted the values of female chastity, motherhood and love of the Tamil language. In cinematic discourse, as in political discourse, Tamil women were being used as markers of difference and served as symbols of community, commonality and solidarity.[2]

Dravidian identity is founded on the concepts and metaphors of female chastity and motherhood. Building on the Pure Tamil movement of the nineteenth century, the Dravidian movement used the mother metaphor to enhance the link between language and identity. In doing so it emphasised the centrality of both motherhood and purity for women (who were collectively addressed by Ramachandran in his political speeches as the *tay kulam*, literally the 'mother community') and the role of men as protector of their mother, and what became known as *tay Tamil* ('mother Tamil' is the name used to distinguish pure Tamil as opposed to everyday Tamil, which incorporates non-Tamil words and sounds). Under this framework, female purity and chastity (*karpu*) are seen as having a spiritual power which demands and ensures justice and victory and is therefore an object of veneration by men and women. While chaste mothers produce valorous men, unchaste mothers do not. Hence, unchaste women are presented as traitors to the culture and unrealised souls (Lakshmi 1990) as well as the source of male inadequacy. In addition, the man who does not protect the mother is emasculated. Not only did this discourse evaluate women in terms of their purity and chastity, locating them in a domestic, reproductive role, and positioning men in the public sphere as protectors and avengers of the mother (i.e. women), mother tongue and domestic sphere, it also sought to define gendered subjectivity and managed to do so with remarkable success, although the form varied by class. Tamil masculinity in working-class families was strongly associated with the capacity and readiness to use physical force to protect and avenge the domestic sphere while intellectual, economic and political force defined Tamil masculinity in middle-class families.

In films, these ideas found expression in plots in which sons protect and venerate their mothers, and women are victims and in need of the protection and guidance of men. The latter protect women from both sexual harassment and their own sexuality which, left to its own devices, would lead them into impurity – a development of the implicit theme that chastity is powerful precisely due to the moral strength required to suppress individual desire. Hence marriage is presented as the only option for women and the *tali* (the symbol of marriage) is the mark of female respectability. In these self-consciously Dravidian films, for women western clothes, ideas and education are presented as synonymous with sexual availability and superficiality, while the sari and an education appropriate to Tamil wifehood and motherhood indicates spirituality, purity / chastity and being civilised and Tamil. Unlike the early Self-Respecters who argued for widow remarriage, these films made it quite clear that female purity means not only that legitimate sex should be strictly limited to spouses, but that a woman should only have one sexual partner. Hence, remarriage or the marriage of a woman raped by another was presented as abhorrent to the woman concerned for it declares that 'her desire had taken precedence over her spirituality' (Pandian 1992: 90).

By 1990, Tamil values were endemic in all fields of discourse to which Tamils were exposed on a regular basis. This is not only due to the widespread consumption of films and the interconnections made between film and politics, but also to the way Tamil films dominated public space through large bill board hoardings, Hindu temples' penchant for amplifying Tamil film music and the pirating of film star images by tailors, barbers, auto-rickshaw owners and other small traders. This iteration of Tamil values, either in full or in their attenuated, associational form, kept these values foremost in people's minds. It provided a structured framework for developing a gendered identity and, for defining norms of behaviour and social relations by which families' reputations could be judged. In the early 1990s, it was precisely because residents of socially heterogeneous localities lacked widespread commonalities of social and economic experience that they used these standards to define which families 'really belonged' to their neighbourhood.

Fracturing of Tamil Identity

The Dravidian movement's dilution of the emancipatory politics of the Self-Respect movement in favour of a Tamil identity based on the values of motherhood, chastity, valour and a common culture and language facilitated and legitimated female subordination, reducing the potential earning capacities of poor households and placing the main burden of family provision on men (as will be argued later in the chapter). While this emphasis on a Tamil identity has undermined Dalit and class-based solidarities, it has been inclusive of communal minorities and, until the late 1990s, served as an ideological cordon protecting Tamil Nadu from the full consequences of Hindutva politics. Yet, by the year 2000, the salience of Tamil identity was clearly being undermined by economic and political processes that took root several decades before but are only now bearing fruit. Ironically several of these processes were and are being promoted by the Dravidian parties themselves.

The opening up of the Indian economy to the global market, initiated by Rajiv Gandhi and hastened by IMF conditionalities in 1991, unleashed a consumerism previously unknown in a country that combined an ethic of conserving wealth for the next generation with an underproduction of luxury goods. While the Tamil middle classes have been migrating to English-speaking countries for some time, it is the combination of the longstanding opposition to Hindi being taught in schools and colleges (English is preferred) and the DMK's more recent strategy of making Tamil Nadu a global IT centre that has attuned even working-class families to the possibility of well-paid work abroad.[3] This positive attitude towards the potentials of globalisation is slowly chipping away at the integrity of Tamil symbols by creating a desire for the consumerist and individualist gratifications of the western Other. Outside the main cities, where the facilities for and acceptance of western forms of consumerism are much more limited, this desire is most visible in the popularity of a new breed of Tamil language film. No longer do western clothes, a college education and platonic love automatically signify female immorality and superficiality in Tamil films, as they did a decade ago. Instead, these are the traits of non-transgressive heroes and heroines – non-transgressive because their parents, no longer the kind demanding submission to parental authority, are glad to accept what will make their children happy. These films do not consciously reconfigure Tamil identity, they demote it; where once Tamil identity was the leading protagonist, now the best it can hope for is a character role.

In the political arena, a similar shift can be seen in the narrowing of Tamil nationalism. This is being replaced by a creeping Hinduisation of state policies and political discourse. Initially based on racial as well as cultural difference, Tamil nationalism is now largely restricted to a pride in the distinctiveness of an ancient language and classical literature. Since the formation of Tamil Nadu as a Tamil-language state in the 1960s, the Dravidian parties have moved towards a national agenda and away from one that was initially separatist and later regionalist. In the late 1990s, the two main Dravidian parties' ambitions for influence in Delhi led them to ally locally and nationally with the North Indian party of Hindu nationalism, the Bharatiya Janata Party (BJP). In the early 1990s, the AIADMK leader, Jayalalitha, sought to revitalise Hinduism in the state through renovating temples and participating in Hindu festivals. The DMK's alliance with the national BJP compromised its ability to promote inclusive Tamil identities, based as they are on defining the North Indian as Other. This erosion of a clearly defined non-Tamil Other, has created the space for a revitalisation of caste identity, a multiplication of caste-based parties and increasing caste violence. These are in part a response to the Dravidian parties' elision of the specificities of Dalit oppression at the hands of non-Brahmin castes. In part they are a consequence of the Hindutva combine's strategies to break the non-Brahmin/Dravidian basis for Tamil identity by appealing to individual castes' perceptions of their own dominance (Geetha and Jayanthi, 1995). While this may have been an early strategy, the current one appears to be the normalisation of Hindu nationalism. Instead of attempting to break Tamil identity, the aim is to incorporate it under a dominant Hindu identity, hence Tamil BJP politicians are actively promoting the Tamil language in order to present local Hindutva ideology as 'Tamil-Hindu-Hindustan' as opposed to 'Hindi-Hindu-Hindustan' (Pandian, 2000). In doing so, the BJP's objective is not only to accommodate the middle classes who, by 1990, had already retreated from a political definition of Tamil to one focused on its linguistic and cultural heritage, but also to absorb within itself, and thereby dissolve, working-class and low-caste struggles by appropriating the rhetoric of the Dravidian Self-Respect movement – as they did by defining the issue of whether children in primary schools should be taught in Tamil as one of self-respect.

The Hindu Munnani's strategy is to normalise Hindutva ideology by taking advantage of, rather than confronting, the history of religious tolerance in the state. They have done so by downplaying their opposition to non-Hindus in favour of promoting a heightened consciousness of a collective Hindu identity. The means has been to capitalise on long-running broadcasts of Hindu mythological soap-operas (Rajagopal 2001) by Hinduising public space, largely by transforming private rituals into public ones and by revitalising public forms of worship. By the late 1990s, women's groups and organisations were making elaborate ceremonies of the originally domestic *Saradu Pooja*; now a collective expression of female marital fidelity (Geetha and Jayanthi 1995). The Hindutva combine have selected a pan-Indian god favoured by Tamils, Pillaiyar (also known as Vinayaka or Ganesha), to create a massive public spectacle that is now widespread throughout Tamil Nadu. Its success can be measured in its ability to draw participation from Hindus who do not regard themselves as subscribing to Hindutva ideology; in their view they are there to get *darshan* (be seen by the god), make a *puja* (prayer) and give the priest a donation just as they would do at any temple or shrine.[4] The interpellation of Hindu Tamils by Hindutva discourse is facilitated by the way Tamil identity has focused on female chastity, purity, motherhood and valour, values that are widespread in South Asia. While for Hindu men, the Rashtriya Swayamsewak Sangh (RSS) divides these values in the same way as the Dravidian movement – that is, attributing valour to men – the Rashtra Sevika Samiti (the female wing of the RSS) provides the added attraction for women that valour is now also attributed to them and religious piety is raised from a private individual practice to an essentialised and public attribute of the Hindu woman (Sarkar, 1995; Fuller, 2001). It is exactly the ability of the Hindutva combine to absorb Tamil values, in terms of gender and language, and to combine it with a heightened sense of religious devotion while playing down their communal intolerance that makes Hindutva ideology appear to be common sense, unmarked by a strident Hindu or North Indian framework.

Yet Tamil identity is a long way from displacement, *tay Tamil* is still spoken of with reverence, the DMK's demand for primary education to be conducted in Tamil remains a politically tenable stance (though strongly resisted by the middle-classes), the Dravidian parties remain dominant in the state and the old Tamil movies are still being watched on television.[5] However, by the year 2000 there were noticeable differences in Chennai and more significant ones in Coimbatur District where Hindu-Muslim rioting in the district's capital left many dead in the late 1990s. Coimbatur District is now a Hindutva stronghold, its elected representative is a BJP member, the RSS are conspicuously generating goodwill by providing labour and a vibrant atmosphere at key ceremonies in neighbourhood temples and, they are actively recruiting college students and Dalits alike. In 2000, I could not elicit any critique of the RSS from any caste or Dalit Hindu I spoke to on the subject in Coimbatur District, but more significantly nor could I elicit much in the way of an argument in favour of them other than that they are disciplined and that they do voluntary work. It is this apparent innocuousness of the RSS at the local level, combined with reports of Muslim bombings in Coimbatur and elsewhere in India, and the heightened pleasures, vibrancy and sociality of collective, public worship, that facilitates the inscription of what is, at its essence, a revitalised Hindu identity *over* an increasingly linguistic framing of Tamil identity. Now it is permissible in non-Muslim company for Tamil Hindus to unselfconsciously describe Muslims as 'a nuisance', to feign ignorance of Muslim religious practice, to ascribe unfettered fertility to them and to conflate Muslims with Pakistan and India with Hindus.[6] This is a significant departure from a decade earlier when North Indians and Brahmins were seen as the primary Other by Tamil non-Brahmin Hindus and Tamil Muslims alike.

Having argued that the residents of socially heterogeneous settlements can only draw on discourses generated in wider social contexts to forge a common neighbourhood identity and to establish a positive reputation for the neighbourhood, the remainder of the chapter develops this argument in relation to the contexts of a low-income squatter settlement in a large city and an urbanising and gentrifying settlement in a small administrative and industrial centre.

Low-income settlement, Chennai 1990–92

Defining the neighbourhood

Gandhi Nagar is a densely occupied, socially heterogeneous squatter settlement which, at the time of study, was about 30 years old. The majority of its residents were either born in Chennai or are long-term Tamil migrants to the city, many having moved to Gandhi Nagar from nearby neighbourhoods. In-depth research was initially focused on a stratified sample of 56 women selected on the basis of the informants' age, marital status and occupation, or lack of occupation, and then broadened to include their households and those of their neighbours and relatives resident in the locality. Seventeen per cent of informants belonged to Scheduled Castes or Tribes, twelve per cent were Tamil Muslims and the remainder belonged to the castes designated by the Government of Tamil Nadu as Backward Classes or Most Backward Classes. At the time, the overwhelming majority of people who worked did so in the informal sector. They engaged in petty retail, construction work, drove cycle-rickshaws and auto-rickshaws, or worked for middle-class families as drivers, night-watchmen and maids. The few men who worked in either the government, public or organised sectors did so as unskilled and semi-skilled labour. Barring two women employed as casual workers, no women worked in these three sectors. Thus, the residents of Gandhi Nagar were divided by caste, religion and occupation.

Despite what might appear to outsiders as clear boundaries (formed by a major road to the south, a river to the north and east and an area of middle-class housing to the west) the settlement's boundaries are not at all obvious. Initially, the land was uniformly squatted and this provided the material basis for both the common experience and external characterisation of the locality; subsequently distinct tenurial contours emerged which differentiated the economic potentials of the area for its residents. The land bordering the sewage-laden Coovum River is *porumbroke* land, defined by the government as 'objectionable', that is unsuitable for habitation, so its residents are never likely to secure land titles. This land was predominantly occupied by Muslims. The ownership of the central, and largest, area of Gandhi Nagar was disputed. Residents claimed they bought the land from the non-resident owner, a 'North Indian', through a 'party man', but had no proof. They had been told that the North Indian's sons denied a sale took place.[7] The southern section, which borders the road, is government land and here the residents were buying land titles. While each of the three tenurial contours demonstrated a degree of economic differentiation afforded by the possibility of slow investment in building improvements or subdividing property in order to rent, the long-term economic potential of the southern section of Gandhi Nagar is considerably greater than that of the *porumbroke* land. Reflecting their differing legal positions, each of the tenurial contours has its own name. In 1990 these names only bore significance in relation to public institutions; the name, most frequently used by residents and non-residents to describe the whole area in social terms, Gandhi Nagar, is that belonging to the largest tenurial contour, that is the squatted land that residents claimed they had bought from the 'North Indian'.

Not only did the tenurial contours differentiate the economic potential of the area for its residents but they also differentiated its political potential both for residents and for non-residents seeking political support in the area. In India, local leadership, and the drawing of people into wider political networks and institutions is dependent on being seen to help local people access national and state government schemes.[8] In Gandhi Nagar the Dravidian and Congress parties used this tactic, but it was the two Dravidian parties which had greater success in securing access to state government schemes. These schemes are of two kinds: ones which apply to individuals such as widow's pension and loans to buy equipment for self-employment, and others which are applied to localities, such as tiling roofs, provision of communal water taps or tanks, the right to buy land title and so on. The different tenurial contours qualify for different schemes, those on *porumbroke* land being covered by fewer schemes than the other two. Some schemes apply to all the contours or to only one or two of the three. In these circumstances, the boundaries of what was defined as the neighbourhood by residents, party organisations and institutions varied and were contested with the challenge 'why are you doing this for them and not us'. Further, these forms of garnering political support raised questions of belonging between residents who let property and their tenants: are government schemes directed only at 'house-owners' or are they supposed to benefit the locality as a whole, that is, can landlords justifiably raise rents? Thus, the locality's boundaries and the question of who belonged were not fixed, rather institutions, residents and non-residents alike were engaged in a ceaseless contestation over how boundaries and criteria of belonging were to be defined.

Rather than having a strong sense of neighbourhood with clear-cut boundaries, residents of Gandhi Nagar had a more diffuse sense of 'neighbours'. Neighbours range from the most inclusive category, 'people living around here' (*inge irrukirranga*), through 'known people' (*therinthavanga*) in the area, to 'next house people' (*pakkutuvittukaranga*) who live adjacently.

Neighbours are those people living beyond the household who know you, or know of you, to the extent that they can and do comment on you, your household and your relatives. Such people were not limited to immediate neighbours, although they were the ones most likely to be in a position to claim authoritative knowledge of one's family. Nor, indeed, were they limited to the networks of 'known people' that men and women engaged with to meet household needs. Rather, they included the 'people living around here' whose reputations became imbricated with one's own.

Neighbourhood as panopticon

At the time of fieldwork in Gandhi Nagar, Tamil identity was the dominant discourse operating in the settlement. It set the criteria for individual behaviour and family relations as well as the standards by which the neighbourhood assessed a family's honour, that is, its *maanam*. In this way the neighbourhood attempted to assert and maintain a reputation for respectability, a respectability that accorded well with values dominant in the wider society and to which the diverse castes and religious groups in the locality could readily subscribe. While neighbours could not formally impose these standards on each other, they could do so informally through numerous, and sometimes coordinated, acts of exclusion. In a context where neighbourhood networks are rooted in little more than the shallow ties of residential proximity, and where these networks are critical for the inputs necessary for one's daily and social reproduction (such as work, customers, tenants, credit, water, impartial arbitration, spouses for one's children and so on) individuals had little choice but to comply.[9] The problem for the individual residents of Gandhi Nagar was how to combine the Tamil values of purity, chastity and motherhood for women and valour for men with the realities of living on a low, irregular income. This required not only reconciling oneself and one's family to the tension between the ideal and the necessary, but also negotiating around the judgements that neighbours could and would make. The way round the problem was to persuade the 'neighbours' that the course of action being taken, while not strictly in line with the ideal, was as closely aligned to it as possible in the family's circumstances; that one's family was conforming with, not contesting, Tamil values.

In a very real sense, therefore, Gandhi Nagar combined a subaltern's version of Foucault's panopticon analogy (Foucault 1979) with Butler's concept of performance (Butler 1990). People in Gandhi Nagar were heavily surveyed by their neighbours, a situation facilitated by building materials (predominantly mud and thatch), housing form and subdivision and the congested nature of the settlement.[10] While housing was constructed to minimise the degree to which outsiders could see in, all properties were set around common space, a yard or alley-way, to which other families (related or otherwise) had access. Without resorting to whispering, aural privacy was negligible for most households. In this moral economy neighbours and relatives made it their business to know the circumstances of those in their networks lest they be seen as condoning immoral behaviour; it is this fear of condemnation by association which makes this system of surveillance so effective. Together these two factors, building form and the vested interest neighbours had in surveying each other, had three consequences. First, there was no arena of life which was not open to the neighbours' evaluation. Second, Tamil values were performative in the sense that they could not be attained once and for all but had to be continuously reinacted. Third, residents of Gandhi Nagar experienced and riled against their neighbourhood as an oppressive place full of jealous people who wilfully misconstrued their actions and delighted in spreading malicious gossip. Resentment against neighbourhood surveillance should not be read as a rejection of either the system of surveillance nor of the values being safeguarded; rather it was a manoeuvre in the claim to conformity on which inclusion in neighbourhood networks depends.

During this period of fieldwork, male valour amongst the working classes was demonstrated by men's ability both to provide financially for their families and to protect them by a strong and ready response to insults. The kinds of work men undertook and the social contexts in which it took place were seen as requiring mental and physical strength, courage, skill and knowledge. As long as men were able to provide for their families, their *maanam* and self-perception accorded well with Tamil concepts of masculinity. The problem faced by men working in the informal sector was that, because their incomes did not rise annually, they were unavoidably caught between what are ultimately incompatible measures of masculinity – the ability to sire children and the capacity to provide for them. As families expanded and demands on fathers increased to cover children's consumption (including the costs of schooling, marriage, etc.), men had to rely on women's financial support, thereby not only exposing both their masculinity and their family's *maanam* to potentially negative evaluations, but also destablising self-perceptions rooted, as they unavoidably are, in inter-subjectivity. Men's response to this situation varied considerably: most tried to conform to Tamil conceptions of masculinity by arguing that their wife's or daughter's need to work was due to factors outside their control such as ill-health or bad luck, or by defining women's contribution to household income as negligible or, more controversially, as unnecessary. Some claimed that the problem lay with women's tendencies either to be profligate with family income or, more seriously, to give the man's earnings to her natal family. Many men retreated into alcohol abuse and domestic violence in a complex and ultimately unsuccessful effort to underpin their masculine identity by taking on the hyper-masculinity of the Tamil cinematic villain. Some, although less commonly, either started a second family, which by definition would be unaffordable, necessitating female incomes, or deserted their wives and children altogether. The problem with these responses is that while trying to shore up their masculinity in terms of their ability to provide, they undermined their masculinity in terms of their ability to protect, a key component of Tamil valour, by compromising their wife's reputation for chastity.[11]

As stated before, Tamil identity is predicated on female chastity and a veneration of motherhood which locates women within the domestic sphere. While people accept that women are not always able to remain at home, and wives and daughters of drunkards, who are by definition deemed to be non-providers, are thought to be incontrovertibly forced to work, women who are deemed either to be working unnecessarily or unnecessarily exposing themselves to the possibility of sexual encounters are defined as unchaste. Hence, women were obliged to present themselves as working solely because of their filial or protective and self-sacrificing mother roles. This was not mere packaging, these women *did* see themselves as dutiful daughters and sacrificing mothers because they were brought up expecting to be dependent on valorous men. For them, working, despite its prevalence, was seen as an exception and, bearing in mind the harsh conditions and poor earnings of petty trading and factory work, as well as the difficulties of domestic work for which working mothers remained responsible, it was experienced as a misfortune.

The need to be seen to be conforming as closely as possible to Tamil values not only determined whether women and girls in Gandhi Nagar worked, it also constrained how women and girls entered work and the incomes they earned (Vera-Sanso 1995). They were forced to select the context, site and hours of work according to how they thought neighbours would judge their family's need. Those with working sons and husbands/ fathers were generally considered to have no need to work, although a few women did evoke the ideal of motherhood to justify working from home. These women positioned their work as a considerable sacrifice aimed solely at educating their children. Those with a large number of dependants, aged, sick or drunken husbands / fathers and those whose husbands / fathers had a second family were considered to have more grounds for working. Need had also to be balanced with what was seen as the differential likelihood that women and girls have of engaging in sexual activities, whether by force or otherwise. Consequently, there was a broad but clear structuring to women's participation in the labour market (Vera-Sanso 1995). The younger a woman and the less her need to work, the more her work had to be either heavily supervised, sex-segregated or located within the home. The older the woman or the greater the need for her income, the freer a woman was to work at a distance from home in unsupervised, mixed-sex contexts. Thus, unmarried girls worked either at home, with a parent or in heavily supervised, sex-segregated factories and young married women worked from their home, within their immediate area or with their husbands. From approximately age 30, women with limited economic need worked from home while those with greater need worked unsupervised in Gandhi Nagar, the adjacent middle-class area or in local markets. In the latter case women operated a system of mutual chaperonage. The only constraints on late middle-aged and old women's work were their capacities, their position within the labour market (largely as petty traders), access to credit and the degree to which their family wished to be seen to be providing for the elderly; at this age female chastity was not deemed to be at risk. Barring the young, unmarried women working in factories, it was these older women who generated the greatest incomes because they were free to travel as far afield as they wanted seeking cheaper inputs and better prices for their trading. Constrained mobility forced the remaining petty traders to buy dear, at local retail rates, and to sell cheap to their neighbours, who were not only known to them (and are therefore able to enforce neighbourhood norms through boycotts) but were themselves living on very low incomes.

By ensuring their neighbours' behaviour conformed as closely as it could to Tamil values, the residents of Gandhi Nagar were attempting to create and maintain a positive reputation for their neighbourhood. Inevitably there were people who did not conform. These people become spatially and socially isolated within the settlement; the networks to which they had access were narrower and had less social and economic potential. Heavy drinkers and women defined as 'cheap' or uncontained (having had more than one relationship or a love marriage) could only find tenants, rooms to rent and spouses for their children amongst people with similar reputations, and their sources of credit and work were much more limited. One case, though extreme, reveals the processes by which families were isolated or, in this case, forced out of the neighbourhood. During her husband's terminal sickness, Rani, a young mother of two children, returned with her family to her father's house where she remained after her husband died. As her father was too ill to work she and her non-resident brother were the only ones supporting her father, step-mother and her unmarried half-sisters. Conflict between Rani and her step-mother over how much of her income Rani should be spending on her own children's education (as opposed to her half-sisters' dowries) resulted in Rani renting a room elsewhere in the settlement. Unable to accept the situation Rani's step-mother would shout abuse at Rani from the street, accusing her of seeking sex. Having already placed their *maanam* at some risk by letting their property to a woman without an adult male in the household, Rani's landlords were unwilling to further risk their *maanam* and asked her to move out despite considering the accusations baseless. This fear of condemnation by association prevented Rani finding alternative accommodation within the settlement.

Up to the early 1990s the dominant discourse operating in Gandhi Nagar was that appropriated by the Dravidian movement and propagated by Tamil cinema. While this discourse was consciously utilised to shape neighbourhood reputations in order to enhance residents' social and, hence, economic position, it also provided the grounds for inclusive definitions of 'people living around here', frequently countering social and economic differences based on caste, religion and tenurial status as well as overcoming the characteristic divisions of those working in the informal sector.

Gentrifying neighbourhood, Coimbatur District, 2000

Defining the neighbourhood

Kasturibai Nagar is an urbanising and gentrifying neighbourhood on the outskirts of a small industrial and administrative town in Coimbatur District. Once a coconut farm, in 1979 the land was subdivided into 158 house sites of which 40 per cent still remained undeveloped when fieldwork was undertaken in 2000. The remainder comprised a mix of modern family homes and a small number of thatched and mud dwellings. The area houses a wide social mix; from wealthy entrepreneurs and landowners, retired farmers, senior government and state sector staff, professionals and semi-skilled mill workers to poorer auto-drivers, impoverished craftsmen and open prostitutes. The overwhelming majority of people came to Kasturibai Nagar from elsewhere in the town or from nearby villages. Additionally, the area is visited, on a daily basis, by herds-persons bringing buffalo, goats, sheep and cows to graze on the empty house sites. There is a mix of castes; one-third are from the Tamil land-owning Gownder caste, a fifth are from the Tamil merchant Chettiar caste; and a further third are Naickers. The latter originally came from what is now Andrah Pradesh and although their first language is a form of Telegu, they identify themselves as Tamil and express a high regard for *tay Tamil*. The remaining people are Brahmins, Muslims and Christians. The area is predominantly BJP-supporting.

Despite its age, Kasturibai Nagar is still in the process of becoming a place. It is physically undeveloped and its social integration remains weak; very few people have relatives in the neighbourhood and there are no common facilities within Kasturibai Nagar. Instead, schools, shops and places of work, public worship and entertainment are all located outside the neighbourhood. The lack of facilities both reflects and encourages residents' outward orientation, away from the neighbourhood, in their engagement with the institutions and people most significant to their lives. While residents do not depend on neighbourhood networks to find work, credit, spouses for their children and so on, as residents of Gandhi Nagar do, the locality's reputation does have significance for their social status and for their sense of who they are and who they want to be.

The *raison d'être* and ethos of Kasturibai Nagar are a function of the town's economic expansion, national consumer-led growth policies of the late 1980s and 1990s, and creeping Hinduisation. Indeed, the dominant discourses that the residents of Kasturibai Nagar repeatedly encounter through their most regular forms of entertainment, that is temple visiting, film, television and the print media, promote and combine modern and Hindu forms of consumption (Rajagopal, 2001; Fernandes, 2000). While in the 1980s houses were chiefly seen as investments, by the 1990s they had became expressions of their owners' modernity, aesthetic values, creative powers and spirituality as well as their economic success. New homes, and extensions to older ones, are now built in a larger, more costly, modern style.[12] In Hindu households, which are the overwhelming majority in the locality, the house has also become the focus of a more public Hindu identity; domestic rituals relating to the house and the family's gods are now elaborate functions to which the extended family, neighbours, friends and colleagues are invited. These occasions are bigger, more frequent, more public and have more of a party atmosphere than they did ten years ago; demonstrating the success of the RSS, whose strong presence in this area of Tamil Nadu has done much to invigorate people's self-perceptions as Hindus by expanding the scale, number and frequency of Hindu festivals and by heightening their vibrancy and entertainment value.[13]

The physical appearance of the neighbourhood and the way residents see it are at variance. The large tracts of land covered in scrub and on which herders graze their animals are, for the residents, clearly bounded house sites bordering well-defined streets. Developing the area as a 'respectable' neighbourhood is the main basis for bringing the residents together as a whole. An informal neighbourhood organisation exists, based on voluntary and *ad hoc* arrangements as residents perceive the need for action both in relation to the settlement's boundaries and the settlement itself. For several years, the neighbourhood organisation has unsuccessfully petitioned the local government to lay metalled roads. It organises the clearing of bushes on the empty house sites in order to reduce the number of snakes in the area. To do so the organisation traces non-resident landowners, asserts they belong and presses them into shouldering a portion of the expense. If necessary the organisation facilitates important social duties – for example, hiring a bus to take mourners to a resident's funeral if it is held outside the town. The issue which exercises the neighbourhood organisation the most is an illegal bar operating on the road just beyond the main entrance to the settlement. The drinkers' comments and stares are thought to make the route unsafe for women and their propensity for being found sleeping under bushes or propped up against compound walls gives the neighbourhood a bad name. In dealing with common problems, the neighbourhood organisation serves as the locality's main integrative force; it attempts to promote a common identity based on dominant values, sets criteria of belonging and police the neighbourhood's boundaries.

The organisation works with what it sees as an unmarked, 'commo sense' view of what represents respectability. While this framing, in terms of 'common sense' rather than a Tamil identity, reflects the Hindu majority's perception that they and what they think constitutes the norm, there is widespread agreement amongst Hindus, Christians and Muslims that female chastity is *the* foundational moral value on which family and neighbourhood reputation depends. Consequently, the issue which exercises the neighbourhood most, and which they can do little about, is the presence of a self-declared prostitute and households in which married women are reputed to have more than one sexual partner. The latter women are defined as 'cheap', as indulging their uncontained desires. As far as the neighbourhood is concerned these women 'do not belong'. Unable to drive them out, because they have land titles, the neighbourhood excludes these women and their households from the domestic celebrations and rituals which form the main means of defining the neighbourhood's social boundaries; for to do otherwise, that is to treat immoral women in a decent manner, would be to mark oneself as immoral. Yet even the determination to exclude these women and their families is context-dependent. When the women's water supplies were temporarily disconnected the neighbourhood had the opportunity to force them out of the area for a period. Despite having declared their intentions to do otherwise, in the end no 'respectable' households refused them water – it felt too callous to do so.

Inevitably, these women's isolation from the rest of the neighbourhood throws them together socially while remaining spatially dispersed within the locality. As these women live in thatch or mud buildings it might be supposed that it is their comparative poverty which predisposes them to such treatment. This would be a mistake because other impoverished families are not just tolerated but actively, although very irregularly, helped with the provision of water, work, credit and second-hand clothes by individual households within the settlement. Nor is there any tension regarding the herders who graze their animals in the area as long as the animals are kept outside compound walls. Rather, it is only those women deemed as unchaste who, along with their families, are defined and treated as the neighbourhood's Other.

Throughout the period I have worked in Tamil Nadu, concerns about female sexuality have always been at the forefront of discussions about individual behaviour, social interaction and how society should be organised (Vera-Sanso 2000b). In 2000, these concerns were not framed in the context of Tamil identity, as previously, but in a general common sense, 'this is the way it is', manner. The prostitute and 'cheap' women were unacceptable in Kasturibai Nagar because female chastity is a key criterion of respectability, irrespective of religion, class and caste, not because they are identified as transgressing uniquely Tamil values. Most women in Kasturibai Nagar behave in such a way as to ensure their reputation for respectability. This means that even those women who used to work in the cotton mills, effectively become 'gated' in their homes if they have to stop working because of ill-health due to working in enclosed environments with high levels of airborne cotton filaments. The main difference between Kasturibai Nagar and Gandhi Nagar is that the privacy afforded by large, well-spaced houses reduces the immediacy of social surveillance; but it cannot obviate it altogether because neighbourhood reputations are managed and sustained through the surveillance of neighbour by neighbour.

Conclusion

Rather than being merely a methodological problem, defining the neighbourhood, setting its boundaries, determining who is included and on what terms is the crux of local politics. People and institutions address and define neighbourhoods selectively; selecting those boundaries and criteria of belonging which advance their interests and objectives. Hence, neighbourhood boundaries and criteria of belonging are not fixed but contested. As identity and locality are founded on exclusion and Othering, this contestation of definition is a feature common to all neighbourhoods; the question is whether different socio-spatial forms impact on the framing of neighbourhood identity.

The comparison of a densely settled, low-income squatter settlement and an urbanising and gentrifying neighbourhood highlights two issues in neighbourhood identity formation. The first is people's concern to control the way outsiders perceive their neighbourhood. The second is the way people in socially heterogeneous neighbourhoods are forced to resort to discourses circulating in the wider society in order to find criteria of belonging which the majority, if not all, residents will accept. During the two periods studied, the need to be deemed to be living in a 'respectable neighbourhood', defined in terms of controlled female sexuality, not only shaped gendered subjectivities but also provided strong discursive weaponry for determining who belonged and who did not belong to the neighbourhood. The framing for this discourse, either within a Tamil identity, or a more general, unmarked 'common sense' is tied to larger economic and political processes. The shift to an unmarked framing, rather than an explicitly Hindu framing, reflects the extent to which Tamil identity is being fractured and displaced by economic and political processes; now Tamil identity takes second place to an identity which, while not explicitly labelled by Tamil Hindus as being 'Hindu', is founded on the view that the Indian norm is a Hindu one.

The comparison between a densely populated squatter settlement and an urbanising and gentrifying neighbourhood also reveals that structural features, in terms of settlement patterns, building materials and differentials in tenurial status, expose poorer families to greater levels of scrutiny from people living within their neighbourhoods than better-off families. Further, because poorer families' economic and social survival is more dependent on the neighbourhood networks that a reputation for respectability lubricates, they experience their neighbourhoods as more oppressive, and have a greater need to conform, than do better-off families. It is precisely because the latter's networks are orientated beyond the neighbourhood that they are less vulnerable to the sanctions neighbours can impose.

In settlements which are undifferentiated in terms of tenurial contours, as Kasturibai Nagar is, attempts to define the character and social boundaries of the neighbourhood can only be realised through social isolation. Whereas in settlements which have them, such as Gandhi Nagar, tenurial contours can provide further grounds for redrawing neighbourhood boundaries. Whether they are used, and whether the strategy is successful, depends both on what is at stake and what is discursively defensible. If an inclusive Tamil identity suffers further fracturing, the Muslims squatting *porumbroke* land in Gandhi Nagar, whose only source of water and access to the road is through the other Hindu dominated tenurial contours, may find the boundaries of the wider neighbourhood begin to exclude them.

Acknowledgements

I would like to thank Lionel Caplan, Swapna Sundar, Gordon Talbot and the participants in the South Asia Anthropologist Group workshop on urban neighbourhoods, especially Henrike Donner, Geert De Neve and Chris Fuller for their comments on earlier drafts.

Notes

1 Derne (2000) makes similar points in relation to Hindi films.
2 A feature common to boundary marking in other contexts; regarding caste boundaries see Unnithan-Kumar (1997), for communal boundaries see Jeffery and Basu (1998) and Caplan (2000), for national boundaries see Chatterjee (1993).
3 By 2000 the state government was laying down cable throughout the state and even small villages could boast private IT training.
4 See Fuller (2001) for a full account of the Vinayaka Chaturthi.
5 Younger people's readings of old Tamil movies are less stridently Tamil than they were a decade ago; they are read in terms of commentaries about action, emotion, intention, and gender and class relations rather than as presentations of a specifically 'Tamil' identity.
6 This equation of Muslims with Pakistan can be seen almost daily in local newspapers.
7 It is likely that the sale was an elaborate deception on the part of the 'party man'. As there is no agreement in Gandhi Nagar as to which party the man belonged, he may have been merely posing as a representative of a political party. The labelling of the landowner as a 'North Indian' may have been part of the deception; in their recounting of the story residents emphasised the landowning family's non-Tamil identity, for them this adequately explained why the sale had been denied.

8 This is done by most organisations seeking support from amongst the poor, including fan clubs (Dickey, 1993) and the Hindutva combine (Rajagopal, 2001).
9 Water supply, for example, is extremely irregular: the municipality only releases drinking water during the middle of the night, compelling women to find female chaperones to the communal water pumps. Similarly, residents' poverty and illegal residence inhibited their access to formal means of adjudication, forcing them to rely on neighbours to arbitrate in local disputes.
10 Gandhi Nagar is, according to the Madras Metropolitan Development Authority's definition, a slum, that is at least seventy-five per cent of the housing is made of mud or thatch.
11 For a more detailed discussion see Vera-Sanso (2000a).
12 This desire for the modern is probably best seen in the building of *en suite* bathrooms with electric water heaters. These remain unused in favour of showers and toilets located in outhouses where domestic waste and dead coconut branches are burnt to heat water.
13 See Kaur (2003) on the use of spectacle and religion for political mobilisation in Western Indian.

References

Butler, J. (1990) *Gender Trouble: Feminism and the Subversion of Identity*, New York: Routledge
Caplan, L. (2000) 'Iconographies of Anglo-Indian women: gender constructs and contrasts in a changing society', 34, *Modern Asian Studies*
Chandavarkar, R. (1994) *The Origins of Industrial Capitalism in India: Business Strategies and the Working Classes in Bombay, 1900–1940*, Cambridge: Cambridge University Press
Chatterjee, P. (1993) *The Nation and its Fragments: Colonial and Postcolonial Histories*, Princeton, NJ: Princeton University Press
Derne, S. (2000) *Movies, Masculinity and Modernity: An Ethnography of Men's Filmgoing in India*, Westport, CT: Greenwood Press
Dickey, S. (1993) *Cinema and the Urban Poor in South India*, Cambridge: Cambridge University Press
Engels, D. (1999) *Beyond Purdah? Women in Bengal 1890–1939*, Delhi: Oxford University Press
Fernandes, L (2000) 'Nationalising "the global": media images, cultural politics and the middle class in India', 22, *Media, Culture and Society*, 611–28
Foucault, M. (1979) *The History of Sexuality* 1, London: Allen Lane
Fuller (2001) 'The "Vinayaka Chaturthi" festival and Hindutva in Tamil Nadu' *Economic and Political Weekly*, May 12
Geetha, V., and Jayanthi, T. V. (1995) 'Women, Hindutva and the politics of caste in Tamil Nadu', in Sarkar T. and U. Butalia (eds), *Women and the Hindu Right*, New Delhi: Kali for Women
Gupta, A. and Ferguson, J. (1997) 'Culture, power, place: ethnography at the end of an era' in Gupta, A. and Ferguson, J. (eds), *Culture, Power, Place: Explorations in Critical Anthropology*, Durham, NC: Duke University Press
Gupta, D.C. (1991) *The Painted Face: Studies in India's Popular Cinema*, New Delhi: Roli Books
Jeffery, P. and Basu, A. (eds) (1998) *Appropriating Gender: Women's Activism and Politicized Religion in South Asia*, New York: Routledge
Kaur, K. (2003) *Performative Politics and the Cultures of Hinduism: Public Uses of Religion in Western India*, Delhi: Permanent Black

Lakshmi, C.S. (1990) 'Mother, mother-community and mother-politics in Tamil Nadu', *Economic & Political Weekly*, Vol. October 20

Pandian, J. (1987) *Caste, Nationalism and Ethnicity: An Interpretation of Tamil Cultural History and Social Order*, Bombay: Popular Prakasham

Pandian, M.S.S. (1992) *The Image Trap: MG Ramachandran in Film and Politics,* New Delhi: Sage

—— (2000) 'Tamil-friendly Hindutva', *Economic and Political Weekly*, May 27

Rajagopal, A. (2001) *Politics after Television: Hindu Nationalism and the Reshaping of the Public in India*, Cambridge: Cambridge University Press

Rowe, W. (1973) 'Caste, kinship and association in urban India', in Southall, A. (ed.), *Urban Anthropology: Cross-cultural Studies in Urbanisation,* New York: Oxford University Press

Sarkar, T. (1995) 'Heroic women, mother goddesses: family and organisation in Hindutva politics', in Sarkar, T. and Butalia, U. (eds), *Women and the Hindu Right,* New Delhi: Kali for Women

Unnithan-Kumar, M. (1997) *Identity, Gender and Poverty: New Perspectives on Caste and Tribe in Rajasthan,* Oxford: Berghahn

Vera-Sanso, P. (1995) 'Community, seclusion and female labour force participation in Madras, India', 17(2), *Third World Planning Review*

—— (2000a) 'Masculinity, male domestic authority and female labour participation in South India', 12(2), *European Journal of Development Research*

—— (2000b) 'Risk talk: the politics of risk and its representation', in Caplan, P., (ed.) *Risk Revisited*, London: Pluto

10

THE RITUALS OF REHABILITATION

Rebuilding an urban neighbourhood after the Gujarat earthquake of 2001

Edward Simpson

On any weekday and most Saturdays, Vipul, an administrator for a private trust, would leave his home in the west of Bhuj at 8.30am by motor scooter. Sometimes, if it was a pleasant morning, he would take the road to the south of the lake in the centre of Bhuj and appreciate the fine views onto the palaces of the former royal families. If he was in a hurry, or if the weather was inclement, he would take the narrow and congested route that ran to the north of the lake. Either way, he would arrive at his brother's house at around 8.40am, park his scooter and walk the few yards to the *aksara* (caste temple) for worship. Ten minutes later, he would be sitting under a neem tree with his brother and a couple of friends enjoying a cigarette and tea, and examining the pages of the local newspaper. Typically, he sat there for half an hour exchanging views on the news and on the latest developments in the locality. He had been born within a stone's throw of the tree but had recently moved away from the area when his employers provided him and his immediate family with a house. On most mornings, just as Vipul was returning to his scooter to head for work, he would greet Rajesh, a government clerk, as he weaved his own way towards his office. Sometimes, Rajesh stopped to say hello; on other occasions, if a minute or two early, he paused to share tea under the tree. Rajesh's scooter was small and the engine not very powerful, and it struggled on the slight incline sending a plume of delicate purple smoke into the air above the narrow street. His slow progress allowed him to say a leisurely hello to Sohag who would be sitting on the steps of his hotel reading the newspaper. Rajesh would turn the corner into the main bazaar, smiling at the owner of the sweet shop as he did so, before passing out of the town's gate and towards his workplace. At lunchtime, both Rajesh and Vipul returned to their respective houses passing a similar set of familiar faces. In the early evening, after work, Rajesh would visit a Swaminarayan temple and idle away half an hour or so in conversation with the Swamis who resided there. Afterwards, he would leave his scooter, walk up to the railings

206

overlooking the lake and watch the birdlife, turtles and the passing traffic before returning to his mother and brother's family for his evening meal. At about the same time, Vipul would return to his seat under the tree to while away another half an hour or so before going home to his wife and daughters. In the evening, Sohag and his brother could also be seen under the tree; before dusk, they would wander back up the slope to their separate apartments above the hotel.

The tree and the benches under it were in the heart of Soniwad, a neighbourhood in the north of the old town of Bhuj. For these residents, Soniwad was an intimate place; time was marked as much by the regular comings and goings of acquaintances as it was by the ritual cycles of religious festivals celebrated in its temples and mosques. The neighbourhood constructed their routines as much as their routines constructed the social life of the neighbourhood. Both had developed over decades. These men, with their different places of work, different devotional practices, families and homes, were brought together under the tree or at the tea stall. They favoured these areas of the town over all others; they also felt comfortable and at home in the streets and the alleys they knew so well. And they passed in and out of the area several times during the course of the average day. Although Sohag frequently left town on business trips, he, like the other men, returned whenever he could to the familiar tree in the shadow of the walls of the former royal palaces.

All this was to come to an end in January 2001, when an earthquake destroyed the neighbourhood (see Figure 10.1).

Figure 10.1 Soniwad cleared of rubble after the earthquake

Space and neighbourhood

The dominant style of ethnographic monograph that emerged from the discipline of social anthropology has typically located its subjects on a regional map, sometimes a sub-regional map and, in most cases, a specific map of the village showing its main human and physical features. At best, the presentation of this spatial trope spoke in shorthand of the village in a wider context; at worst, it implied an isolated village community. However, labour migration, transhumance, wars, changing patterns of governance, sea and land trade routes, natural disasters and so on necessitate movements of people that fragment the monographic presentation of a bounded village nestling in the bosom of its region. Space has become more theoretically and empirically complicated. But it is not just physical movements of people that call for a more careful reckoning of the landscapes of social relations, because 'space' can also be ordered socially and morally in relation to broader cosmological notions of time and its qualities. Representative of the turn to deconstruct our understanding of 'space' and its implications, Lewis and Wigen (1997) have suggested that the division and naming of continents, culture areas, civilisations, world regions and so on is arbitrary and discursive rather than scientific. Tracing the origins of spatial classification, they show how imperialism and hegemony have underpinned the tendency to map cultural centrality directly onto economic centrality. They further suggest that to properly understand spatial relationships then ideas, human practices, and social institutions should be considered rather than political and ecological boundaries.

Recent work in urban studies has also attempted to deconstruct essentialist notions of 'neighbourhood' and the associated concepts of 'identity' and 'community'. Eade (1997), for example, has shown that neighbourhoods can be composed of sets of people who have very little interaction with one another and who can have radically different images of the same residential area. Similarly, Massey (1993, 1994) has shown how places are articulations of social relations, established over time through periods of decay and renewal, and that competition between such articulations goes a long way to determine the character of a place.

While these common-sense suggestions are laudable, it is also important to note that dominant social boundaries can also coincide with political and economic ones. The arbitrary boundaries drawn by the Radcliffe Boundary Commission at the time of Partition, or the planning lines translating into social division drawn in Chandigarh by Le Corbusier in the 1950s, clearly have had dramatic effects on social practices and the ways in which people think about themselves and others. National or administrative boundaries are at times articulations of certain kinds of identity that sometimes coincide or are transcended by other loyalties expressed through the deployment of spatial tropes. Furthermore, there is a considerable literature on South

Asia, especially in relation to kingship (see Dirks 1987), which shows precisely how political and economic boundaries lie at the very heart of the ways in which social order is understood and maintained. The approach taken by Lewis and Wigen (1997) and others appears to ignore the significant fact that political and ecological boundaries are also ideas, often supported by social institutions, which have a great deal of influence on other kinds of ideas and social practices, and indeed on the way that the academy comes to understand them. The rhetoric of Hindu nationalism, for example, is premised on the fact that ideally national and cultural boundaries coincide and are supported by an array of congealing social institutions (van der Veer 1994: 28; Hansen 1999), a vision in which a religious community is naturally fitting to the country, the region, its towns and its neighbourhoods.

However, while there is a striking congruence in the form that these various levels of spatial construction take in Western India, different reactions to the destruction of Soniwad illustrate that there is nothing primordial about an attachment to a locality. Faced with the tasks of finding a place to live and restoring a sense of normality, some residents, such as Vipul, have invested considerable effort in reconstructing the symbolic and physical boundaries of their neighbourhood, while some, such as Rajesh, have begrudgingly left forever to settle in other parts of the town. Others, such as Sohag, have remained aloof from the committees established to oversee the future of the area and have preferred instead to concentrate on the preservation of their private property over and above anything else. For all three of these men, Soniwad retains an importance as a neighbourhood, but what it means for each of them differs – largely depending on how they inhabited the locality, experienced its destruction and partook in the ensuing discussions about its reconstruction. Therefore, the material in this chapter suggests that, instead of dismissing ritual, structural, national or neighbourhood boundaries as arbitrary or even artificial in favour of the analysis of human practices, boundaries themselves should be viewed as part of human practice and their wider implications should be given due consideration.

Today, Bhuj town, with a population of around 160,000, is a municipality covering an area of nearly 20 square kilometres. The town consists of an ancient walled area known administratively as the *gamtal* which is surrounded by a newer sprawling development, the *simtal*. The municipality has 12 wards, 8 of which are in the old city. In the months after the earthquake, the Government of Gujarat implemented legislation contained in The Gujarat Town Planning and Urban Development Act 1976 (as amended on 9 March 1999). Contained in this legislation are guidelines for the establishment of Area Development Authorities and details of their powers. In essence, the Act gives the government greater powers to claim and redistribute land, and, for the most part, the Area Development Authority has powers that exceed those of the local municipality. Thus, in 2001, the Bhuj

Area Development Authority (BHADA) came into existence to administer and regulate the reconstruction of the town.

The old town, the commercial centre, was densely packed with a population of nearly 40,000. The guild and caste buildings that sprung up as the town developed were mostly to be found within the city walls, as were the majority of the historic temples and mosques. The *simtal* area had expanded rapidly in the last few decades fuelled by investment from Non-Resident Indians (NRIs) and local property speculators. Like many towns in Western India, the expansion had been marked both by the growth of new housing societies and the development of apartment blocks. Inside the walled town, however, where property prices were very high, there was little room for legal expansion and as a consequence many illegal additions had been made to existing buildings. The twisting lanes, narrow bazaars and dead ends were ordered loosely around caste and commercial interests. Hindu, Muslim and Jain neighbourhoods were each clustered together, each ending in a cul-de-sac or a series of cul-de-sacs (for parallels, see Dossal 1996). Each neighbourhood (*falia, mohalla*) or street (*seri, marg*) was associated with particular religious and occupational groups, or named after particular *chowks* (squares) or temples. The majority of them, however, were known for the caste that either founded them or predominated in them in the past. In recent decades, such neighbourhoods had become decidedly more mixed as wealthier families had left the area leaving their property rented in order to settle in the new residential colonies to the south of the town.

The wall and gates surrounding the city were more-or-less intact before the earthquake. They had been first constructed during the reign of Rao Godji in the early eighteenth century and strengthened considerably after an earthquake in 1819. As a consequence of this earlier earthquake, some 7,000 houses were destroyed and more than a thousand people perished in the ruins (Gazetteer of the Bombay Presidency 1880: 16; MacMurdo 1820). Despite this disaster, and up until the 2001 earthquake, the town had many buildings of architectural and historical value. The present walled city has five main entrances – the Mahadev, Vaniawad, Bhid, Sarpat and Patwadi gates – as well as a smaller but no less celebrated entrance known as 'Chattibari'. In the past, the walls were heavily fortified against the predations of aggressors and the gates were locked at sunset. Each gate was also associated with various protective deities to ward off evil and bring prosperity to the town. Each gate also carried with it particular social connotations – for example, Vaniawad Gate with Jainism and affluence and Sarpat Gate which, in years gone by, was associated with prostitution and illegality. The town and each neighbourhood within it was a collection of areas, streets and buildings, each of which was known for particular social and moral groups of people and activities. The earthquake did not just destroy life and property: it also destroyed the pathways and routines that those in the town had developed.

Rajesh was out of town on the day of the earthquake but returned home as soon as he heard the news. He arrived at Sarpat gate, the northern entrance to the walled city, and was shocked by what he saw. He recalls seeing the dead and injured lying in or on the rubble; some were without limbs and others were of 'unconscious mind' and crying for help. It took him, he estimates, around an hour to climb over the debris to where his house had been; normally, it would have been a five-minute walk. Familiar landmarks had disappeared and roads and streets were indistinguishable from the rubble of the houses that had fronted them. Like many people who experienced the earthquake, he found he could identify his house by the tree that eerily still stood at its entrance. He could not find his family but there were four people lying injured who recognised him and told him that his family were safe and that they had left for the open space of the park some hours earlier. A few hours later, he was reunited with them; it was then he discovered that two tenants, who had been renting a part of his house, had been killed by falling masonry. Their bodies were concealed in the rubble on which he had stood talking to the injured. Buffalos and cows, tethered in the alley leading to his house, had also been crushed. Rajesh, his family and many others of Soniwad allegedly lost many of their personal possessions in the following few weeks as properties were looted and scavengers moved in to work alongside the rescue workers. For a while, Rajesh considered leaving Kachchh District for a big city, but decided that they did not have enough money to relocate; he also looked for accommodation in villages outside Bhuj but the rents were too high given the shortage of accommodation after the earthquake. For three or four months, his family stayed together in a tent in the compound of a temple before they were allotted temporary accommodation in 'tin city'. The small corrugated tin hut was to be their home for the following two years. It proved to be mercilessly hot in the summer, leaky in the monsoon and freezing cold during the winter nights. Despite the discomforts, health problems and lack of privacy in 'tin city', Rajesh and his family decided they would not return to Soniwad. They said they had seen too much suffering there and would always be haunted by the memories of the earthquake and the spectres of death that haunted the neighbourhood. Their family had been in Soniwad for many generations; they were well known in the neighbourhood and were very troubled by the difficult decision to leave. They surrendered their land to BHADA to be redistributed in the town planning schemes. Rajesh took me to the site of his old house a few times during 2002 and 2003. They were always very sad visits; he would look at the ground on which his house had once stood with a mixture of disbelief and sorrow; on all these occasions, he imagined where each ground-floor room had once been, tracing a rough outline in the dirt with his feet. The first time we went after the site had been cleared, the water and sewerage pipes that had served the bathroom still protruded awkwardly from the razed earth. When we visited again some weeks later, the pipes were gone and white marks on the ground suggested that the property had been divided and shared between adjacent plots. As his house, the alleys that led to it and other familiar landmarks were slowly erased from the landscape, Rajesh and six other members of his family continued to live in the tin shed. They did so in the hope that they would be allotted a new plot in a suburban area far away from the old town.

Vipul was waiting for his daughter to return with his breakfast when the earthquake struck. He had sent her to buy deep-fried corn flour to eat with his morning tea. After the shockwaves had subsided, he ran out into what remained of his street, desperately searching for his daughter. Her leg was injured, but she was alive when he eventually found her. In the following days, Vipul placed many of his family's belongings in a storehouse owned by his employers and went to stay with relatives on the outskirts of the town. There he and his family remained for many months before they returned to their partially damaged home in the west of the town. In the following months, he was to play an active role in the committee formed to reconstruct Soniwad – the area of the town in which he had been born.

Three months or so before the earthquake, Sohag had completed an eight-storey residential high-rise block on the southern borders of Soniwad. On its lower floors, he had opened a hotel which he hoped would generate income for him and his family. He had borrowed a significant sum for the structure, which miraculously survived the earthquake with little damage. Before the earthquake, the legality of the structure was questionable and had brought him into conflict with other local residents who were concerned that the building was unsuitable and intrusive. The top floors of the structure afforded fine views over Bhuj and into the private courtyards of the erstwhile ruling family. Now he was determined that his building was not going to be demolished by either the town planners or the new safety laws that demanded retrofitting and placed restrictions on the height of structures in the town. Consequently, Sohag was also to play an active role in pressure groups and public consultation meetings – not primarily for the benefit of the area, but in order to safeguard the structure in which he had invested his savings.

Some years after the disaster, these men are nostalgic for the intimacies of life before the earthquake; and in different ways they also desire to recreate some of the familiar places that were lost. Their wanderings in the town were not random; they were embedded in ritual and social practices and ideas that had long histories. To some extent, the disaster has made them appreciate what they had, but it has also forced them to consider who they are, what they know and what they want as well as the more pragmatic question of what is it possible for them to gain from the disaster. Haresh, a bank manager in Bhuj, claims that, although the earthquake took thousands of lives, the aftermath has slowly killed many more. He suggests that the tension of life after the earthquake ate away at peoples' brains and steered them quietly towards premature deaths. 'Tension', a commonly used term in Gujarat, is life threatening, more than mere stress; in its more dangerous forms, it is caused by the separation of the body from its familiar habitus – in the sense of environment, routine and consumption habits. Financial and physical insecurity, the uncertainty of the government's plans, the predations of the *saat bagari* (the seven crows: contractors, engineers, demolition crews and the like) and the uncertain future have preoccupied people, in Haresh's view, initially to the point of distraction and later to death. However, the most potent ingredient in this fatal malaise is the discontentment caused by the lack of routine. Each man in his own way has reassembled a compromised routine: Sohag sits on the steps of his hotel and worries about the paucity of customers, and Rajesh and Vipul journey to their offices to sit under-employed amid precarious columns of scaffolding.

How people have responded to the crisis and the loss of property, and what moral frameworks they have put in place to deal with the catastrophe, varies considerably. Personal, material and emotional circumstances account for many of these differences, as do the ways in which people experienced Soniwad as an urban neighbourhood prior to the earthquake. However, there is a dominant discourse on how the area should be reconstructed; formalised by myths and rituals, this discourse suggests that the ideal boundaries of the new neighbourhood should reflect the ways in which those of the kingdom were ideally constructed. This is a totalising discourse, familiar to all three men, which constructs the residential area as a microcosm of a larger ritual complex – a discrete entity amid the larger discrete entity that was the royal kingdom of Kachchh. This discourse and the ancient sources of authority it draws upon is not derived from a manual or a proscribed way of doing things but emerged at the complex interface of interaction between the government, the planners redesigning the city and the many of the residents themselves.

The following sections of this chapter explore the creation of this discourse as the first step in a long process of reclaiming the neighbourhood as a suitable location for residence and routine after the alienating excesses of natural disaster and the bureaucratic processes that emerged in its aftermath.

Ritual rehabilitation and the neighbourhood

On a warm day in February 2003, Rajesh, Vipul and Sohag were among a group of around 50 people who gathered under a *mandap* (tent-like structure) to inaugurate the reconstruction of Soniwad. The various rituals they performed and the claims made for the status and organisation of the area were to auspiciously demarcate its boundaries and to reassert the area's fundamental Hindu character. The meeting climaxed with the insertion of a metal stake into the earth (see Figure 10.2).

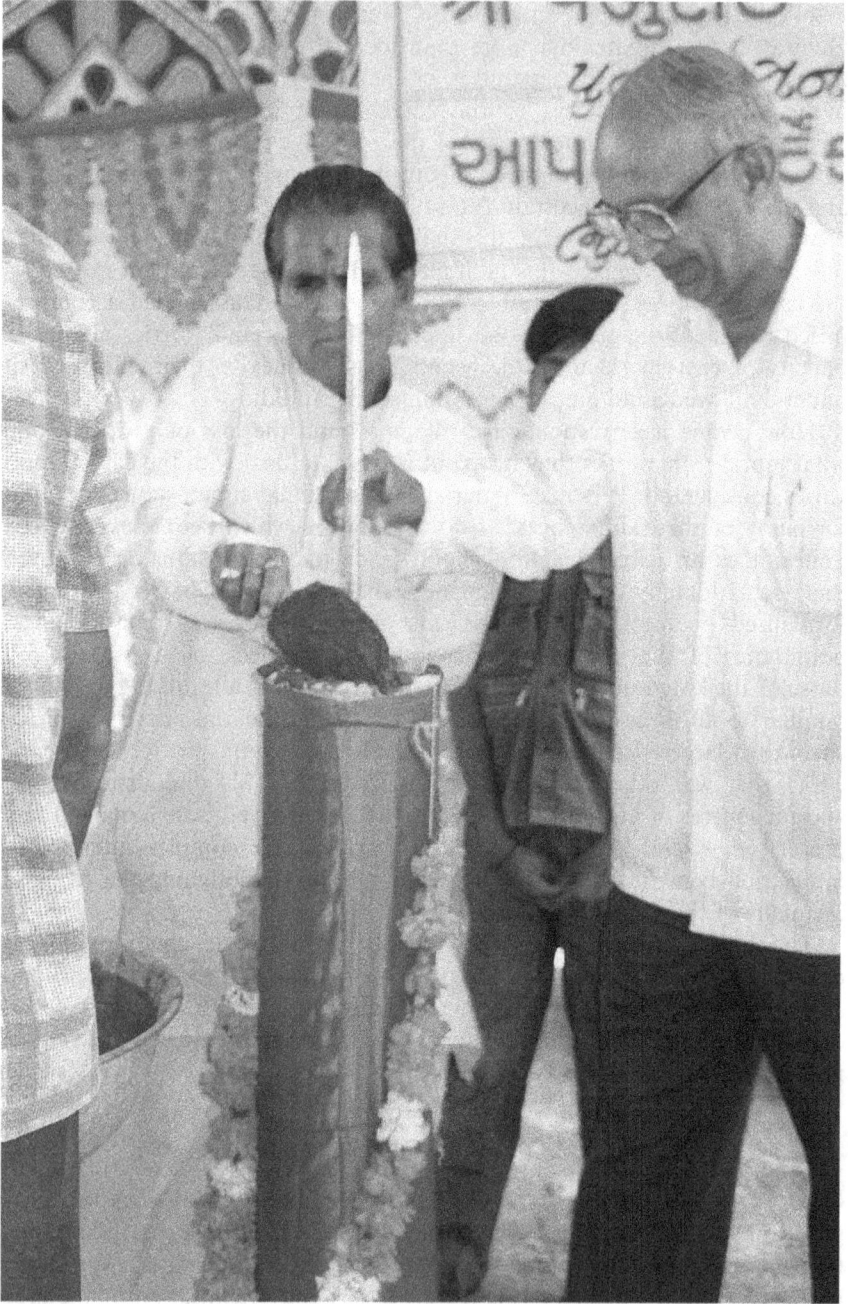

Figure 10.2   Kili Pujan

In this section, I explore some of the relationships between the reconstruction of Soniwad and broader ways of thinking about the town, region and country of which it is a part – in other words, what its boundaries might signify. Here, the rituals and myths of the land and its people used to re-consecrate Soniwad reveal how the ideal boundaries of this modern neighbourhood ideally coincide with those of the ritual complexes that sustained Kachchh as a Princely State and to some extent continue to define it in federal India. The analysis illustrates the changing relationship between ancient ritual boundaries and their modern political manifestations. It is suggested that in this case the construction of a neighbourhood mirrors that of a pre-Independence kingdom, and could perhaps best be thought of as a modern ritual reconstruction of that kingdom and, in turn, of modern nationalistic constructions of India.

These rituals took place more than two years after the earthquake struck. The disaster left around 14,000 people dead and tens of thousands injured. Swathes of the principal towns of Bhuj, Anjar, Bhachau and Rapar in Kachchh District were reduced to rubble. Hundreds of villages totally collapsed or suffered severe damage; temples, mosques, schools, marriage halls and other communal buildings also crumbled.

Prior to the earthquake, Soniwad was a highly densely populated area of Bhuj. The eighth of the eight municipal wards in the walled city, it had a pre-earthquake population of 6,500, around 360 of whom were living in each square hectare. This was a slightly lower population density than the other wards in the *gamtal* and reflects its relative prosperity. In ancient times, the area is said to have been a lake known as Babu Rai, but gradually, as the town expanded, it was settled predominantly by Sonis (goldsmiths), from where it takes its name. As with the neighbouring areas of Delo and Jethi Sheri, which Soniwad has incorporated today, it had also been home to other high-status castes in the service of the ruling families of Kachchh. Among them were the Jethis, a Brahmin caste, whose men were traditionally the royal bodyguards and wrestlers, and whose women acted as wet nurses for the ruling family. The area had been very prosperous during the heights of royal power but had slowly fallen into decline as people moved out and the large houses were subdivided to accommodate tenants. The area was severely affected by the earthquake and, along with other areas to the north of the town, suffered the highest casualty rates as buildings collapsed. Many of the survivors in Soniwad were either resettled in temporary camps or fled to stay with relatives in the suburbs or further afield. For the best part of two years, the neighbourhood was practically deserted, and, when the demolition of dangerous and ruined structures and the removal of debris gradually got under way, most of Soniwad and the areas surrounding it were razed to the ground.

The initial stages of planning were subcontracted to a private agency; their product was then to be implemented by BHADA. The private agency was keen to create a participatory planning process at both conceptual and developmental stages. While this desire is laudable and in many cases very genuinely pursued, it was also encouraged by the funding practices and monitoring protocols of the World Bank, the Asian Development Bank and some departments within the government of Gujarat. 'Participation', in this case, generally meant generating public feedback on the location of relocation sites, temporary markets, road networks and land-use zoning; but public 'participation' was not intended as an exercise in determining the mechanisms for decision making; rather, it was to aid decision making among planners.

Given the level of destruction, the remaining residents were asked to suggest ways in which to redesign and reconstruct the entire area. The planners rapidly found that most of the people were not experienced in making decisions on future urban forecasting. Consequently, they changed tack and started to present specific options to the 'stakeholders' they identified. They worked closely with non-governmental organisations (NGOs) in the town and attempted to foster close links with community leaders. They identified key figures, such as amateur historians, elected and administrative figures in local councils and in the government of Gujarat, representatives of the media, eminent citizens and notable figures in trade and industrial associations. They also attempted to nurture the growth of community-based organisations, which they felt were lacking in the town, in order to give direction and support to planning initiatives and as a method of understanding the 'needs' of local people in an urban space. In the first round of consultation, they surveyed the town and got a feel for the issues they would face in drafting a plan. In the second round, they 'took the plan to the people' in an attempt to solicit a response. Over 150 consultation meetings took place, the majority of which were with individuals. Eventually, the planners decided that they would use the boundaries of administrative wards as an approximate method of designating different planning schemes and as a way of organising consultations.

However, ward boundaries in the town were not coterminous with communities or even particular neighbourhoods. 'Ward 8', for example, encompassed Soniwad but also other areas known as Delo, Jethi Sheri, Ashapura Mandir and, to the north, Minyan ni Wadi, Pakhali Falia, Arab Falia and others. The areas to the north, as their names suggest, are predominantly Muslim settlements. But most of the opinion leaders nurtured by the planners, with one or two exceptions, were middle-class Hindus. Likewise, key social institutions identified by the planners were the Lions Club, the Rotary Club and the Chamber of Commerce, again the refuges of the elite Hindu and Jain populations. It is impossible to condemn the planners for this as these institutions have a strong public face in the town, they are the most accessible institutions and the most likely to speak of the issues involved in a language understood by the planners themselves. The result, however, is that there is a notable bias in representation towards vocal Hindus, many of whom have held public office, are accustomed to public speaking and presenting supported arguments, and have an interest in the future of the town. The activities of the planning agency are of course only half the story as some of the residents of Soniwad and other areas took a proactive role in putting themselves forward as decision makers and spokespersons. Initially, the private agency received a rough time in the local media and they were widely resented for coming from 'outside' (Ahmedabad) to make decisions on behalf of local people. However, despite this resentment there was also a great deal of curiosity about their activities, personas and personal habits. Some people in Soniwad quickly realised that through this agency they had an opportunity to voice their concerns and indeed to safeguard their own interests. Those who stepped forward were generally well received and their worries duly noted.

In Soniwad, as elsewhere in the town, one of the consequences of this confluence of interests was that Muslims were, by and large, excluded from the consultation planning procedures. Taking an active role in the first months after the disaster in public meetings, they were gradually sidelined by the more prominent Hindu residents. By nurturing the neighbourhood associations and by encouraging individuals to take a lead, positions of responsibility and power devolved to those best equipped for the challenge and to those able to converse with a range of public figures. Such positions invariably fell to individuals and organisations with a stake in local politics or business, which again were mostly local Hindu elites.

The residents of the southern parts of Soniwad were well equipped for the tasks of public participation, being relatively well educated, well represented on many of the town's boards and having the influential incumbents of the palaces and a wealthy hotelier as neighbours. They formed the *Soniwad Mohalla Samiti* (Soniwad Neighbourhood Committee) and the Soniwad Rehabilitation Committee in attempt to congeal local interests. The representatives of the two bodies coincided and sometimes it was impossible to separate the actions of one from another. Nevertheless, these organisations were slow to form and came about through the efforts of one or two particular individuals resident in Soniwad. Together, these interest groups developed close relationships with the planning consultancy. As previously mentioned, Soniwad lies within the boundaries of municipal 'Ward 8' and was classified under 'Town Planning Scheme 8' but the *Soniwad Mohalla Samiti* was not acting in the interests of the entire ward, but for the relatively prosperous Hindu sections to the south.

It is testimony to the agency of some residents of Ward 8, and to the favourable relationships they initially fostered with the planners that in the final Draft Development Plan submitted under Section 16 of the Gujarat Town Planning and Urban Development Act 1976, that they are the only community to be subject to a detailed case study.[1] While their case was put before the government as an example, it was the only community study conducted in this round of the planning process. However, at a meeting between planners and residents of the municipal wards in the old city in August 2001, some Soniwad residents disrupted proceedings and asked the assembled to disperse as they had not been consulted in the drafting of the redevelopment plan. Among the most vocal of these protestors was Sohag, who was under severe pressure to demolish his hotel. He had commissioned a private engineer to survey the structure who had issued a certificate attesting to its structural integrity. Many people doubted the professional integrity of the surveyors.

The *Soniwad Mohalla Samiti* and its Jethi members in particular have been far more proactive than others in speaking for or against the town-planning scheme through the particular channels fostered by the private consultancy. They were interested in promoting Soniwad as a model for other wards and took an active role in campaigning for some of the area's *chowks* (residential areas) to be left intact in the town plan.[2] Others, former residents of the area, have also been active and creative in warding off the predatory advances of the bulldozers. Both planners and NGOs working in the town have rightly encouraged a sense of nostalgia towards heritage sites and have attempted to be 'culturally sensitive' in rebuilding the town. And, for example, in August 2001, the resident of a house in Soniwad wrote to the planners expressing his concerns over the future of his property. It had been classified as a moderately damaged building but he was worried that it would be demolished to make way for new infrastructure. Promising to repair the house to a suitable standard once he received compensation money from the government, he wrote that: 'We say that our house land is sacred, – as Lord Swaminarayan's "footprint" [is] also existing in it. Everyday some pilgrim[s] and visitors are coming to pray at this place.'[3] The issue here is not whether the claim is genuine or not but the fact that the letter writer was able to appeal for the preservation of his house on such grounds is testament to the efforts of the planners and the levels of awareness they contributed towards generating among local people.

As the residents of Soniwad gathered in early 2003, the government of Gujarat had finally approved the Bhuj Development Plan.

Permission had been granted for reconstruction to commence in the area. A number of speakers at the event stressed how the earthquake had laid waste the holy places of Kachchh and how the people had suffered with loss and grief. They emphasised that there was a bright and hopeful future and that they would rebuild Soniwad with energy and enthusiasm so that in three years it would be unrecognisable. The speakers had to compete with the noise of the endless stream of tractors carrying rubble from other parts of the town, the overhead manoeuvring of military jets, and the warbling and tweeting of mobile phones that had been introduced into Kachchh immediately after the disaster. Others spoke of the pragmatic issues they faced in the coming months, their frustration with the local administration and of technical and planning procedures. The event was held to stage two public rituals for the neighbourhood: *bhumi puja* (purification of the land) and *kili puja* (worship of the stake).

Bhumi Puja

The attendant Brahmin announced the date, time and precise geographical location of Bhuj so that the deities could find their way safely to the site. He requested Hanuman and other gods to accompany them in Soniwad to purify the land. By these announcements, he was attempting to establish a precise channel with Sanskrit verses and familiar ritual items through which the divine forces could offer their blessings for the reconstruction of the neighbourhood. The rituals were informal and those congregated wandered through the small crowd greeting friends and acquaintances. According to Vipul, the informality was a key part of the ritual because the gods would see there was a community of friendly neighbours and would bless them accordingly. However, the main purpose of the *puja* was to placate those hundreds of people who had met premature and unnatural deaths in the neighbourhood. It was widely rumoured that restless ghosts travelled the area at night and, in particular, many people who found themselves unwittingly roaming the rubble after dark had seen a female doctor who died in the earthquake. Some years before the earthquake, Devendra Vyas, a local journalist and educationalist, had explained to me the purpose of *bhumi pujan*. He had said that:

> I can say this is my land because I have purchased it, but what was here before we do not know. We cannot say who the landlord was millions of years ago nor can we tell of those who passed unknown lives on this ground. Small creatures were born and died here and men may have met with natural or unnatural deaths on this land. It is because we do not know that we perform this *puja*. We pray that every life that passed away through this land may be silent for us and for our offspring.

In other words, the ritual brings comfort and prosperity to those inhabiting the land. I reminded him of this conversation in 2003 and he provided a further example of the importance of *bhumi puja*. He said, ' . . . sometimes my father says, "See that honey bee – why don't you remove it [from your house]?" But I say, 'How can we know that the land does not belong to the bee and that it is we who are the newcomers?"' In his view, the land is a silent witness and repository of past events that can influence the living.

Kili Puja

The events in Soniwad climaxed with the symbolic insertion of a metal stake (*kili*) into the earth. By this time, the audience had returned to their seats and had fallen silent. The location for *kili puja* had been determined some time in advance by community representatives and the Brahmin with a little help from a cartographer. Together, they had made a map showing the boundaries of Soniwad and key religious and social sites on its periphery. Key to plotting the parameters of the area were the locations of temples, including the temple for the tutelage deity of the royal family and other temples with a history of royal patronage. They had drawn lines from these peripheral locations to determine the exact centre of the neighbourhood. This system, the Brahmin said, was derived from *vastu shastra*, the ancient science of structure, widely believed to be a cause of prosperity of moral well-being. The Brahmin had isolated key sites in the urban landscape – some had collapsed but others remained intact – on or around the ward boundary and had triangulated the middle-most point. This spot, where the *kili* stood, the *brahmsthan kendra* (central place of creation), was to be marked by a ceremonial house (*puja kilinu smargh* or *kendrasthan*) for future community activity. In Gorringe's discussion (in this volume) of neighbour-hoods and Dalit identity politics, he suggests that flagpoles, markers of spatial identity, remain hollow banners until acted upon. In many ways, the point of the ritual activity in Soniwad was to establish a clearly defined terri-tory, embellished with royal and Brahminical traditions, which could be traced to a particular location and periodically brought to life as a symbol of the neighbourhood. In other words, *kili*, associated structures and other paraphernalia were to become the symbolic and ritualised centre of Soniwad, which as the following section demonstrates is an idea derived from ancient ideas about kingship and governance.

History and foundation myths

In Western India, ideas about kings and the cities in which they lived were never static. However, a number of canonical texts were written on the ideal relationships between a royal personage and the kind of space that should surround him, such as the *Mansara*, *Mayamata*, *Samrangana* and *Rajavallabha* (for discussion see Sachdev and Tillotson 2002). These writings are known as *vastu shastra* – treaties on city design, architecture and the division of space. The texts are in broad agreement that legends and deities associated with a site will influence the cities' fortunes and well-being. Before any construction can commence, offerings must be made to propitiate demons and deities during *bhumi puja*. The texts show a number of square diagrams (*mandala*) aligning deities, temples and castes with the cardinal points. Such diagrams range considerably in the complexity of their sub-division. However, at the centre of all these diagrams is the *brahmasthana* or, as in this case, the *brahmsthan kendra*, the seat of Lord Brahma – the creation deity. This principle applies whether the construction relates to a town, a neighbourhood or a single house. The literature is clear that the smaller units are ideally architectural microcosms of larger spatial units (Sachdev and Tillotson 2002), but does not spell out that such relationships are echoed in human relations and in relations between royalty and deities. However, as Smith (1989) has discussed for other contexts, the Vedic universe was composed of mutually resembling and interconnected, but also hierarchically distinguished and ranked, components. Such ideas are evident in contemporary ritual activity, and the events in Soniwad can be seen as a classificatory activity and as an attempt to reunite the neighbourhood with encompassing ruling and divine hierarchies.

Kachchh was one of around 565 semi-independent kingdoms in India. It was ruled by Jadeja Rajputs from the sixteenth century until 1948. Within the principal domain were smaller Jadeja fiefdoms, which were semi-autonomous tributaries. Within these domains there were villages and hamlets with lesser headmen, who together formed a political unit known as the Bhayad (younger brethren and political subordinates of the main Jadeja lineage). Political authority, although having a centre at the *darbar* (assembly) in Bhuj, was dispersed throughout the kingdom into provincial political centres, which formed ritual and political microcosms of the central Jadeja lineages. Here, the term *darbar* refers to rulers and their representatives, whose interests and activities ideally coincide at a *gadi* ('throne', central seat of power) in Bhuj. The *darbar* was thus a broad collection of people, buildings and institutions connected through ritual and ideological elaboration. At the head of the Darbar sat the king, a relationship succinctly described by Fuller:

> The king's first responsibility is to protect his kingdom and subjects, by guaranteeing their safety, prosperity, and well-being. But these depend on preserving the order of the kingdom in the widest sense, so that, for example, the king is responsible for maintaining the hierarchical caste system within his realm; he must protect the privileges of Brahmans and the rights of all the different castes, confirm their relative rank, and uphold the authority of caste courts. Order in the kingdom, moreover, is ultimately continuous with order in the universe; the kingdom is correspondingly conceptualized as a micro-cosm of the universe and ideally their boundaries coincide. To put it differently, the order of the kingdom is itself part of the sociocosmic order or *dharma*, and it is ultimately preserved by king and deity together rather than by king alone (1992: 106).

In this worldview, the Jadeja Rajput rulers and their principal deity, Ashapura Mata (Hope-Giving Mother), preserve the integrity of the kingdom. Ashapura Mata is a lineage goddess and, simultaneously, a tutelary goddess, a royal deity and a state deity. An integral part of ruling power, she is the source and representative of *shakti* (power) in the kingdom, and is

221

commonly linked to the earth as soil and territory. In this sense, she is identified specifically with the lands of Kachchh and with the rulers who are literally regarded as the sons of her soil. Vital in the relationship between deity and king is the royal lineage, which is also derived from and perpetuated by the *shakti* of the Mother Goddess. This relationship is complex and is informed by other symbols of royal power such as thrones, swords, turbans, horses, palaces, city walls and non-Brahman mediators (see Mayer 1985). The *darbar* is to the Bhayad what the Mataji is to the tutelage deities of fief lineages, and, thus, gradations of goddess and ruled territory are hierarchically ordered but encompassed by the apical goddess and king.

As with other kingdoms, the disintegration of Kachchh as a political entity, shortly after the Independence of India, only partially eroded the symbolic power of Ashapura Mata and the significance of kingship as a socio-religious institution. The worship and rituals of the goddess remained important, replicating traditions of the past in the absence of actual political authority in the post-Independence era, and more recently the traditions of the goddess have become a rallying cry for Hindu exclusivity. The traditions of the goddess, as they now appear, are undoubtedly selective in what they include and exclude of the past, just as the dominant myth of the foundation of Bhuj, discussed later, tends to obscure competing versions of the same story. Lesser known tales of the foundation of the town, for example, include those of foreigners who sacrificed their lives to the earth for the creation of a strong fortress, and of particular heroic individuals who are said to have led or lured the rulers to the land that was to become their kingdom. The point here, however, is not to suggest that one form of the tale contains more truth than others; rather, that the dominant version of the foundation mythology and the practices associated with the goddess have become so successful that the past is also interpreted through the parameters they provide.

Within this overarching structure, there are a series of lesser ritualised structures that give each town, village and neighbourhood a stake in the grander narrative. While many of these accounts were recorded in the Gazetteers of the British Colonial period and in the records of bards in the pay of the erstwhile rulers, they have also been firmly resurrected in the post-earthquake period. In July 2001, the current incumbents of the *darbar* in Bhuj wrote to the Chairman of BHADA. They were concerned that proposed post-earthquake town-planning schemes would encroach on the grounds of their palaces on the southern boundary of Soniwad. They wrote:

> . . . this part of the scheme militates against the very ethos of Bhuj town, demolishes its history dating back to 1549, affects its excellent architecture, and violates its cultural heritage. Bhuj being the capital town of the former princely State of Kutch, it has given lead to other towns and villages in Kutch in these respects and the

proposed destruction of the fort wall will adversely affect the whole of Kutch.[4]

In order to substantiate such a claim, the writers did not turn to UNESCO statutes for the protection of heritage sites nor to the support of the Archaeological Survey of India (which has again and again taken a critical stance towards such Hindu nationalist discourses); instead, in what might have been a ploy to gain popular support, they turned to the foundational myths of the kingdom. The dominant story tells us that Bhuj was founded in, or around, 1549 when the first ruler, Kengarji, drove a *kili* (peg, nail or stake) into the ground around which palaces, walls, the town and the kingdom developed concentrically. This stake, which is still existent, marks the centre of the kingdom and the moment of its foundation. There is more to this story, however, than the letter writers acknowledged. According to popular legends, as the future ruler was passing what was to become Bhuj, he saw a hare fighting with a dog. Impressed by the courage and strength of the hare, he concluded that the people of this place must also be abnormally able so he decided to build his capital on the site. As he hammered the stake into the ground, as part of the rituals to purify the land, it bounced back, its tip covered in blood. The attendant priest opined that the king had injured the celestial serpent known as *gujan* or *shersnaag* that is mentioned as 'Bhuj-bavan or the fifty-two yard snake' in the Gazetteer (Vol. V. 1880: 216). The term 'Bhuj-bavan' appears to refer to the structure within the walls of the *darbar* in which the original stake is housed. In other versions of this tale, the king is said to have been attempting to drive the stake into the head of the serpent to harness its power and to prevent its writhing from causing disruption to the kingdom. Unsure of whether he had found his target, he again removed the stake but, when blood issued forth from the land, he realised he had been successful and when he went to replace the stake the serpent had moved. This time, instead of pinning the hood of the serpent, Kengarji pierced its tail. From that day onwards, the snake has been writhing in its subterranean home causing the earth to quake. In order that the snake would remain quiet, it had to be regularly propitiated; accordingly, a temple was constructed on Bhujia Hill to the east of the town, and, from that time onwards, the annual procession that takes place from the former royal palaces to the temple has been the largest and most spectacular public festival held in the town.

What the writers of the letter were referring to was not so much that Bhuj was simply the town of principal importance in Kachchh, but that it stood at the very centre of the ritual complex that gave the lesser towns, neighbourhoods, villages and hamlets of the kingdom sustenance and power for governance.

The principles of *vastu shastra*, focusing on the central point of creation, the *kili*, contribute to the hierarchical resemblance between different social and spatial units, and are derived from ancient and obscure sources. However, in this case, as suggested in the following sections, such principles are actively used as vehicles for contemporary political concerns.

The boundaries of community

The Soniwad rituals, conducted in the shadow of the *darbar* walls, have clear parallels with the symbolism of the foundation rituals of the kingdom: the *kili* ideally stabilises the earth and the other rituals propitiate the dead and the deities in different ways. Within a month of the *pujas* taking place, there was a book launch in Bhuj. The volume detailed, among other things, the failures of the local administration after the earthquake. In a congratulatory speech, one prominent member of the ex-ruling family called for a Kachchh independent of the governance of Gujarat. His utterances were not unprecedented and represent the views of a small but resilient minority who resent the loss of local power and autonomy. Many of the ancestors of Soniwad's residents once (and this is as true for Muslims as for Hindus) held positions of responsibility and respect in the kingdom. Many of them were trusted by the *darbar* and had privileged access to its secrets and resources until Kachchh passed to rule from Delhi in 1948. In 1956, Kachchh, along with Saurashtra and Gujarat, became part of the bilingual Bombay state, which was subsequently divided into Gujarat and Maharashtra in the 1960s (Wood 1984). The inclusion of Kachchh in the linguistically defined state of Gujarat has always been the source of some resentment in Bhuj. Kachchhis feel they are underrepresented in the Gujarat Legislative Assembly and that the government neglects their interests and development. It may well be the case that the mainstream political life of Gujarat tends to sideline the border district, but Kachchhis have a number of genuine claims for their distinctive regional character such as language, customs, traditions and geographical affinities, which they also feel are unappreciated by the government ruling from Gandhinagar.

Furthermore, there is clearly resentment in Soniwad about their own loss of power to bureaucrats from outside the district and their relegation to a mere neighbourhood committee in decision-making processes. Vipul put it like this: 'Today there are no Maharajas only Collectors and Government. In the old times only some families of our area had access to the kings now anyone can come to the Collector'. The democratisation of governance in federal India did not only remove the rights of kings to rule but also stripped whole auxiliary communities of their privileges. While the immediate effects of Independence did not apparently radically alter hierarchical patterns of social relations in the town, as the decades have passed and the old guard have begun to die off, many of those claiming hereditary status because of positions their ancestors held in the kingdom have been sidelined, such as Rajesh whose ancestors were jewellery manufacturers. However, as

Harold Tambs-Lyche (1997) has also noted for Saurashtra, the rallying cry for the king and the traditions he represents has recently undergone something of resurgence.

So far it has been suggested that at the level of public representation and decision making the interests of ward and neighbourhood have become coterminous through the actions of planners and the Soniwad neighbourhood organisation. The coincidence of ward and neighbourhood is expedient for excluding Muslims from participating in local politics and neighbourhood-level decisions. It has also been suggested that the coinciding boundaries of ward and community have been constructed as a microcosm of Kachchh as a Princely State, drawing on its symbols of power and Vedic spatial concepts as sources of legitimacy. After a fashion, the way the construction of the kingdom is remembered has been imbued with nostalgic and nationalistic overtones. As such, and as discussed later, it mirrors political discourse on the construction of India as a mythic and fitting land for its Hindu population. However, and importantly for the proponents of the small but sustained campaign for independent rule, the foundational traditions of Kachchh are not a microcosm of the traditions of Gujarat. They see Gujarat as a relatively recent and unjust invention, its boundaries have little emotional or symbolic purchase and there is no plausible mythology around which to congeal a suitably powerful and Hindu past. The disintegration of Kachchh as an independent political entity only partially eroded significance of kingship as the premier social and religious institution. The traditions of kingship and the rituals of tutelary goddesses continued to have a great following and are being integrated into the older myths of Indian unity recently resurrected by Hindu nationalists.

Many Hindu residents of Soniwad identify strongly with the Hindu nationalist turn in Indian politics, participate in its meetings and sponsor its organisations. In this vision, the development of Hinduism and the emergence of the land, landmarks and history are intimately related; India is a whole, a unity that has been eroded by successive invasions first by Muslims and later by the British. It has clearly defined boundaries that are ideally inviolate; in this sense, the new cartography of Hindu nationalism and the mapping of new neighbourhood boundaries have more than a passing resemblance to one another. Hinduism has been described as a related assortment of many faiths, doctrines and sects, rather than an integrated religion (Miller 1991: 786). This is disputed by the leaders of the new forms of nationalism who present Hinduism as a unified religion that is naturally fitting to the country (van der Veer 1994: 28). In Gujarat, the BJP is largely thought of as a Hindu party; it is attempting to redraw the country's history within the divine landscape of the continent. India has become the Hindu motherland, progressively weakened by Muslim infiltration and torn asunder by the Partition. In their rhetoric, the historical presence of Muslims in India is variously ignored or demonised. At the state level, the

BJP and associated organisations are animating the landscape with new temples and symbolism invested with new meanings, and in the process they are recreating religious contest and dispute in order to reclaim the past and the land as their own.

Following the earthquake, this process took on a new vigour in the rural areas of Kachchh. In the urban centres, reconstruction is just getting under way and the inevitable communalisation of the landscape is yet to become apparent. However, in the past, tensions have periodically erupted between Hindus of Soniwad and Muslims of adjacent Sumara Deli. A number of the 'heroes' of these confrontations died in the earthquake and were informally remembered after the *pujas* were complete. Perhaps unsurprisingly, none of those present at *pujas* were Muslim and, as has happened elsewhere in Kachchh, Muslims and Hindus have largely gone about reconstruction after the earthquake independently. The creative interface between the people and the state has been predominantly Hindu in character and Muslims have not participated extensively in the public consultation process, although many of them went to some of the initial meetings. For the most part, they have rebuilt their mosques in the original locations and have generally shifted their residences further to the north of the town. The apparent illegality of many of these constructions has further enraged some Hindu residents. In their view, it confirmed what they already knew: Muslims are expansionist, aggressive, secretive and prone to illegality.

The nationalist and anti-Muslim turn in the politics of Gujarat has been accompanied by religious violence, systematic and organised attacks on minority communities, disruption of civil life in the cities, and high-profile attacks by Muslims on trains as in Godhra and temples as in Akshardham. These events have determined the political atmosphere in which much of the reconstruction work has taken place, and, to some extent, it is impossible to separate patterns of polarisation and community creation in Soniwad from the macro-polity of Gujarat. In the state, Hindu speechmakers and political pundits are increasingly turning to electioneer on the basis of religion rather than caste. The rise of the BJP has largely been facilitated by the eradication of those in its ranks who have manipulated caste divisions among Hindus in order to gain votes. Similarly, residents of Soniwad are attempting to unite – across caste divisions – around a series of common rituals that combine the traditions of kingship, with Brahminical and nationalistic Hinduism. While these elements are often ideologically contradictory, they are being combined as a way of cementing the idea of a neighbourhood that is exclusive and bounded.

Many of the Soniwad residents who came to the foundational rituals had not previously considered where the boundaries of their community lay. Even before the earthquake, the neighbourhood was defined primarily as a space between royal power and predatory and aggressive Muslims. The foundational rituals have given the area a more clearly defined and articulated presence, with boundaries formed by invisible but potent lines. In Soniwad, the traditions of kingship have incorporated political nationalism into their foundational rituals and thus perhaps into the future mythologies of the neighbourhood.

The dominant Hindu universe, as imagined in Western India, is composed of mutually resembling and interconnected, but also hierarchically distinguished and ranked, components, ranging from the house and neighbourhood to kingdom and nation. The rituals of rehabilitation described in this chapter are classificatory activities that reunited the neighbourhood with this hierarchy. The rites for purification and prosperity held in Soniwad have created a mythological and theological infrastructure for the minutiae of reconstruction and routine to take place. Many of those who came to the *pujas* moved away from the area before the earthquake or are planning to construct houses further to the south once they receive official permission. Why did these people attend the rituals of reconstruction? I started this chapter with a brief description of the overlapping daily routines of three former residents of Soniwad; it is to the issue of routine, urban boundaries and forms of identification that I wish to return by way of conclusion. Notwithstanding the fact that Rajesh or Vipul no longer live within the boundaries of Soniwad, they still return there regularly and increasingly so as reconstruction gains pace. They both strongly identify with the neighbourhood, its heritage and sociality – Vipul more so than many of those still living there. In Bhuj, neighbourhoods leave their imprint on people. Residents' bodies and practices reflect, in part at least, a portion of the daily struggles, disputes, hierarchies and relationships that characterise life in the area of town where they live. Each neighbourhood has a literal character of its own formed by the aggregates of population it houses and the kinds of relationships they entertain with one another. The neighbourhood into which individuals were born and the kinds of relationships they develop there with others play a significant role throughout later life. Straddling caste and sectarian relationships, neighbourhood connections provide men with access to employment, opportunities and resources: both Rajesh and Vipul trace salaried appointments back to the assistance of older residents in Soniwad; and Dilip left the neighbourhood over 20 years ago but continues to have a steady stream of visitors from the area to his suburban door. Those born in the neighbourhood continue to be firmly identified with it even after they have moved out. Thus, the idea of neighbourhood is not only that of a physical space with clearly defined ritual boundaries but it also a marker of character defined by particular kinds of social relationships interwoven with routines. The networks of residents and former residents form a super-locality that does not simply correspond to geographical space. Those forming such networks are connected as the progeny of a bounded geographical area and this form of relatedness sits alongside those of caste, religion and sect. Thus, as the atypical circumstances of post-disaster reconstruction reveal, the neighbourhood in which you reside is not necessarily the one in which you live.

Conclusion

In this chapter, I have discussed the imposition of parameters on an urban neighbourhood and its imagined position within wider designs of the city and the nation. However, despite the strength and prominence of this design in public discourse, I have shown how this design emerged from social fragmentation, physical destruction and from the interaction of competing visions of what the neighbourhood is and was to become. At different times and in different ways over the last few years, the neighbourhood has been variously dressed in moral, convivial, caste, administrative, religious and nostalgic clothes. While neighbourhoods exist as political, ideal and intellectual tools to both outside observers and those who live within them, neighbourhoods are also constructed by any number of invisible lines signifying trust, co-operation, affinity and their opposites.

There has been considerable public reflection in Bhuj over the last three years as to what the town is, what it means to live there and how people should live in it in the future. A great many people have contributed their ideas, suggestions and complaints. The implementation of the new town plans has been met with mass demonstrations, organised letter-writing campaigns, litigation and hunger strikes. The majority of these agitations have been about the preservation of private and community property, especially those buildings and open spaces to which the population is sentimentally attached. In the initial months after the earthquake, the government of the time was in favour of abandoning the old core of the town and building a new settlement afresh. This idea was rapidly abandoned in the face of critical opposition from the public. It was felt that there was too much of value inherent to the chaotic structures of the old city for it simply to be deserted. The religious places, community halls, historic sites and trees under which men sat together to drink tea gave the city its identity. Indeed, the word 'identity' took on a life of its own because, overnight, faced with their loss, the gates, chowks and ancient buildings of the old town came to mean much more than they had before.

Eventually, an uneasy compromise was reached in which three vast areas beyond the existing suburbs were to be prepared for the resettlement of some of the population. These 'relocation sites' were for those who had lost their houses, for those who surrendered their old property to the government and for those displaced by town planning schemes. Hundreds of hectares of land were gradually possessed, cleared and laid with infrastructure for the new 'housing societies' or 'colonies'. While the process of 'suburbanisation' in Bhuj may have been accelerated because of post-earthquake planning, migration from the densely populated old city to the societies had started some decades ago. The first housing societies were built outside the fort walls in the 1960s and their growth has continued steadily ever since. Increasing pressure on the land also forced new developers to build upwards. Thus, housing societies, consisting of rows of detached or semi-detached houses each with separate compound walls and apartment 'culture', had already secured a place in the urban landscape. The new planning regulations may have put pay to the development of further medium-rise blocks of flats in Bhuj but the relocation sites have been chalked out in the shape of mass housing societies.

Before the earthquake, both housing societies and apartments were associated with the wealthy, modern and upwardly mobile. The spectre of a town made up primarily of housing societies has alarmed some elements. Ideally, although it was rarely the case in reality, the old town was comprised of a series of *falias* (semi-gated cul-de-sacs) within which there was a communal courtyard in which people would share news, views, chores and celebrations. Such *falias* formed smaller communities within a larger neighbourhood. While they were often architecturally and historically rich places, they were difficult to service with adequate modern infrastructure because of the density of the buildings and the irregularity of the streets. As a consequence, they also tended to be dirty, airless and congested. Those most vocal about preserving this heritage and rebuilding sections of the town in the *falia* style have been those who live in detached and gated society houses. While they are rightly concerned about the town's heritage and its identity, they are also concerned, in a rather conservative manner, as to how people who lived in the *falias* will adjust to life in a housing society. The principal idea behind this concern seems to be that life in the old town involved sharing, mutual co-operation and interdependence because individual houses were open to the courtyard. Conversely, life in the housing society is regarded as alienating and tantamount to privatising family interests and affairs. Was life in the *falia* really so great? Would life in the housing societies really be so bad? Why had many people who could afford to do so already left the old town for the relative tranquillity, cleanliness, spaciousness and privacy of the housing societies?

The truth behind the choice is probably not as clear-cut as I have implied. There is no reason why *falia*-style housing with modern amenities could not be constructed, and, as the burgeoning new housing societies on the outskirts of Bhuj are beginning to show, there is no reason why suburban life should be particularly alienating. Although the either / or choice is stark in the Bhuj case, people making the decision to leave the older areas are changing the face of towns throughout Western India. Urban areas are expanding rapidly and, as a result, so are the ways people live in towns and cities, and think about neighbourhood and locality; it is also forcing people to travel much further to enjoy a cup of tea under their favourite tree.

Acknowledgements

Stuart Corbridge, Henrike Donner, Christopher Fuller, Isabella Lepri, Geert De Neve and Jonathan Parry kindly commented on previous drafts of this paper and the ideas contained within it. I am also grateful to B.R. Balachandran, Pramod Jethi, Azhar Tyabji and Dilip Vaidya. The time for research and writing this chapter was generously supported by a Nuffield Foundation New Career Development Fellowship (NCF / 00103 / G).

Notes

1 *Draft Development Plan* prepared by Environmental Planning Collaborative; Babtie Consultants (India) Pvt. Ltd; JPS Associates and Theotech Engineers.
2 *Bhuj Town Planning Schemes. Report on Public Consultations.* 1 January 2003. Environmental Planning Collaborative.
3 Letter from the Additional Assistant Engineer to the Incharge Officer, EPC; also published in *Draft Development Plan for Bhuj, 2011AD. Part 3: Support Documents*. Bhuj Area Development Authority.
4 Letter from The Darbar Gadh to The Chairman of Bhuj Urban Development Authority dated 7 July 2001; also published in *Draft Development Plan for Bhuj, 2011AD. Part 3: Support Documents*. Bhuj Area Development Authority.

References

Dirks, N.B. (1987) *The Hollow Crown: Ethnohistory of an Indian Kingdom*, Cambridge: Cambridge University Press

Dossal, M. (1996) [1991] *Imperial Designs and Indian Realities: The Planning of Bombay City 1845–1875*, Delhi: Oxford University Press

Eade, J. (ed.) (1997) *Living the Global City*, London: Routledge

Fuller, C.J. (1992) *The Camphor Flame: Popular Hinduism and Society in India*, Princeton, NJ: Princeton University Press

Gazetteer of the Bombay Presidency,Vol. V (1880) *Cutch, Palanpur, and Mahi Kantha*, Bombay: Government Central Press

Hansen, T.B. (1999) *The Saffron Wave: Democracy and Hindu Nationalism in Modern India*, Princeton, NJ: Princeton University Press

Lewis, M.W. and Wigen, K.E. (1997) *The Myth of Continents: A Critical Metageography*, Berkeley, CA: University of California Press

MacMurdo, J. (1820) 'Papers relating to the earthquake which occurred in India in 1819', in Hurst, R., Brown, O. and Murray, J. (eds), *Transactions of the Literary Society of Bombay* 3, London: Longman

Massey, D. (1993) 'Power geometry in a progressive sense of place', in Bird, J., Curtis, B., Putnam, T., Robertson, G. and Tickler, L. (eds), *Mapping the Futures: Local Cultures, Global Change*, London: Routledge

——(1994) *Space, Place and Gender*, Minneapolis: University of Minnesota Press

Mayer, A.C. (1985) 'The king's two thrones' 20(2) *Man* (N.S.) 205–21

Miller, B.S. (1991) 'Presidential address: contending narratives – the political life of the Indian epics' 50(4) *Journal of Asian Studies* 783–92

Sachdev, V. and Tillotson, G. (2002) *Building Jaipur: The Making of an Indian City*, New Delhi: Oxford University Press

Smith, B. (1989) *Reflections on Resemblance, Ritual and Religion*, New York: Oxford University Press

Tambs-Lyche, H. (1997) *Power, Profit and Poetry: Traditional Society in Kathiwar, Western India*, New Delhi: Manohar

van der Veer, P. (1994) *Religious Nationalism: Hindus and Muslims in India*, Berkeley and Los Angeles, CA: University of California Press

Wood, J.R. (1984) 'British versus princely legacies and the political integration of Gujarat' 44(1) *Journal of Asian Studies* 65–99

INDEX

Abu-Lughod, Janet 17
Acharis 94–96, 97
adoption 108
alcohol abuse 197
All-India Anna Dravida Munnetra
    Kazhagam (AIADMK) 187, 191
Ambedkar People's Movement 55, 57
anthropology: holistic approach 3;
    terminology 141; traditional organi-
    sation 7
Appadurai, Arjun 10, 55, 169
Archaeological Survey of India 223
Area Development Authorities 209–10
'argument' 89
aristocrats 98–99
Arundhadiar 65n.14
Ashapura Mata 221–22
Ashraf, A. 87n.13
automobiles 106–7
Awas Vikas colony 121

bad/dirty people 162–63, 178
Bairagimadam temple 101
Balija Naidus 93–94, 97, 101
Banaras Hindu University 125
Beeri Chettiars: overview 14; businesses
    111; charity vegetable garden 108;
    headmen role 100; Komati rivalry 89–
    90; riots 93–94; temples 96–97
beggars 162–63
behavioural codes 99–100
benefactors 108–9
Bengali culture 148, 155
Bengali Hindus 143
Bensman, J. 48, 56
Berreman, Gerald 160

Bharatiya Janata Party (BJP): Dravidian
    politics and 191; education 126, 132,
    138; as Hindu party 225–26
Bhavani 13, 23–31, 34–40
Bhuj: overview 17; descriptions of 209–10;
    earthquake 211; history 220–23; subur-
    banisation 227–28; see also Soniwad
Bhuj Area Development Authority
    (BHADA) 215–17, 219–21, 222–23
'Bhuj-bavan' 223
bhumi pujan 219
big people 163–64
Bijnor: overview 15; difference and
    educational spaces 123–27; educa-
    tional institutions 117–22; relational
    webs 122–23
BJP: see Bharatiya Janata Party (BJP)
Black Town 14, 91, 93
Blaustein, Jessica B. 145
Bloch, Maurice 164
Bombay (film) 160
Bombay state 224
Bose, Nirmal Kumar 68
boundaries: of community 224–28;
    economic centrality 208–9; graffiti
    56; movement markers 56–59;
    neighbourhoods 38–40; political
    spaces 60–63; ritual rehabilitation
    213–19; rituals 25–26, 219–20;
    Untouchable settlements 46;
    women's bodies 145
Bourdieu, Pierre 59, 170
Brahmans 97–98, 101, 187, 114n.2
Brockett, C.D. 87n.10
business houses, decline in 110–11
Butler, Judith 195

Calavala family 108, 109–10
Calcutta: overview 13–14; community
  activities 150–53; community of
  neighbours 153–54; mapping the
  neighbourhood 144–48; mobility
  148–50; neighbourhood organisations
  79–85; as premature metropolis 68–
  70; religious mix 142–44; representation and the everyday 154–57;
  residential patterns 72–74; slums 70–
  79; socio-economic differences 75–79
Castells, Manuel 122
castes: overview 13, 14; class and 151–
  52, 170–71; classifying 160; exclu-
  sions 47–48; identity and 191;
  leadership 99–100, 112; opposition to
  187; right-hand/left-hand 90, 92–93;
  stereotyping 66n.18
Chakrabarti, Indranil 11, 13–14, 51
Chakrabarty, Dipesh 171–72
Chandavarkar, Raj 70, 184
Chandigar 6
charity 113, 120, 125–26, 136–37;
  opulence and 104–10
Charity Garden 101, 102–4
chastity 188–89, 197, 201
Chatterjee, Partha 155
Chennai: overview 11, 14; films 185–87;
  governance 90–91; low-income settlement 193–95; riots 93–94; see also
  George Town
cheris: see Untouchable settlements
'Chetpet' 108
Chettiyar manufacturers 34–35
childlessness 108, 109
Christian College 99
citizenship 48–49
class: overview 16; antagonism between
  24–28; caste and 151–52, 170–71;
  idioms of 162–64, 180n.4; interactions between 153–54; lower caste
  representation 42n.7; markers of
  164–71, 178–79; socio-economic
  mobility 22–24, 37–38; see also
  middle-class neighbourhoods
cloth merchants 106
Coimbatur District 192, 199–202
Collah Ravanappa 98–99, 101–3, 104,
  113
collective action 68–70, 86
colleges 120
colonialism 5–6

colonies 60–61, 117
Communist Party of India (Marxist)
  (CPI [M]) 14, 81–83, 86, 87n.7
communities, boundaries of 224–28
complexions 164–66
conformity 184
Congress Bastion 14
Congress Party 83–84, 86, 150, 187,
  87n.16
consumerism 190
controlled space 61–63
corporal punishment 132–33
courts, access to 99–100, 112
Cybriwsky, R. 55–56, 57–58

'Dalit' 64n.1
Dalit Panther Movement: overview 13;
  foundations of 47–48; identity 45–46;
  movement markers 56–59; political
  spaces 60–63; slogans 65n.15
dance 139n.18
Daniel, Valentine 30
darbar 221–22
de Certeau, Michel 9–10
De Neve, Geert 13, 21–43
debt relations 32–33
decentralisation 69
defended neighbourhoods 56–57
Deliège, Robert 61
department stores 111
Dickey, Sara 153, 160, 186
diet 168
Dirlik, Arif 2, 5
dirty people 162–63, 178
diseases 168
distancing 172–78
domestic violence 53, 151, 197
Donner, Henrike 11, 15, 141–58
Dover Terrace 70–79
Dravida Munnetra Kazhagam (DMK)
  185, 187–88, 190–92
dress 53, 166–67
Driver, Edwin D. 160
dubashes 90
Dumont, Louis 47
Durga puja 149, 152, 175–76
dyeing industry 31, 34–36, 38–40,
  42n.4

Eade, John 208
earthquake myths 223
East Bengali refugees 145–46

East Delhi 15
economics, centrality of 208–9
education 116–38; charity and 109, 120, 125–26, 136–37; contesting meanings 135–37; difference and educational spaces 123–27; disciplined bodies, docile behaviour 132–33; employment and 76; environments 15, 116; fees 124–25; functions 127–30, 132, 135–37; importance of 37; institutions 117–22; motherhood 149; Nehruvian secular project 131–32; as political resource 133–34; relational webs 122–23; women 156
Ekambareswarar temple 101
emblems 56–57
emigration 190
employment: caste work 61–62; class and 48–49; dirty work 50; experience of 31–32; government jobs 50; isolated social groups 68–69; male youth 76; women 39, 197–98, 65n.9; workplace/home boundaries 38–40
enclosure 16, 171–78, 179
Engineering College: overview 120–21; buildings and grounds 125; functions 127–30, 132, 135; Nehruvian secular project 131
English East India Company: headmen 99–100, 112–13; purpose 90; right-hand/left-hand 93–94; trading castes 89–90
English-medium public school 120–21, 124–25
Escobar, Arturo 2, 49
ethnicity: overview 16; religion 74–75, 78–79, 87n.6; social life 74–75, 79; socio-economic differences 75–79
ethnography 4, 5
exclusion 47–48, 62, 183–85
export trade 104–5

falias 228
family businesses 104–7, 110–12
fashion 166–67
Feld, Steven 169
female seclusion 155
Ferguson, James 4, 21, 64, 183
Fernandes, Leela 9, 22, 156, 66n.18
fidelity 191
films 185–87, 188, 190–91
Foucault, Michel 4, 62, 153, 195

foundation myths 220–23, 224
Founder's Day 130
Fox, Richard 3
Frøystad, Kathinka 16
Fuller, C.J. 221

Gandhi Nagar 193–99
Gandhi, Rajiv 190
Gandhian nationalism 6
Gans, Herbert 8
Garcha: see Dover Terrace
Geetha, V. 191
gender: overview 15–16; male-female relations 185; neighbourhoods 142–48; social restrictions 65n.9; subjectivity 189
gentrifying neighbourhoods 199–202
geography, spatial concepts in 3–4
George Town: overview 14; phase 1 93–99; phase 2 99–104; phase 3 104–10; phase 4 110–12; temples 91
Gidwani, Vinay 22
globalisation debates 21
globalisation, potential of 190
Goffman, Erving 159
good people 163, 170, 178
Gorringe, Hugo 13, 22, 220
gossip 153
government jobs 50
government schemes 194–95
graamam 30
graffiti 56
Gujarat 17, 224–25
Gujarat Town Planning and Urban Development Act 1976 209–10, 217
gunny trade 104
Gupta, Akhil 4, 21, 64, 183, 188

Hansen, Thomas Blom 5
headmen, power and 99–100, 112
heritage sites 222–23
heterogeneous settlements: see socially heterogeneous settlements
Hindu Mahasabha 125
Hindu Munnani 191–92
Hinduisation 200
Hinduism 191, 225
Hindus: banal Hinduism 132, 139n.13; education 117, 124, 132, 137–38; nationalism 126, 209
Hindutva politics 190, 191–92
history of urban environments 5–6

Hobsbawn, Eric 69–70
home/workplace boundaries 38–40
home/world 53–54
homogenous neighbourhoods 184
hospitality 152
housing: apartment buildings 111; for
  castes 46, 60–61; extended families
  147–48; foundation myths 220–23;
  mobility and 37; privacy 195–96;
  public/private areas 53–54, 152;
  rituals 25–26; status symbols 200
housing societies 228

identity: overview 16–17; caste and 191;
  exclusion 183–85; fracturing of 185,
  190–93; locally constructed 60; politics and 45–46; socially
  heterogeneous settlements 182–85
ideologies 16–17
Ilaiah, Kancha 168
illiterates 163
IMF conditionalities 190
immorality 201
import trade 105
income disparities 77–78
India as mythic land 225
industrialisation 6, 34–38
information technologies 3, 190
inside/outside 49, 53, 171–72
Inter-College 120–21, 124, 130, 131–32,
  135
Islamic city 17

Jadeja Rajputs 221
'Jansi Rani Complex' 57, 62
Jayanthi, T.V. 191
Jeffery, Patricia 15
Jeffery, Roger 15
Jeffrey, Craig 15

Kachaleswarar temple 96
Kachchh 221–22, 224–25
Kaikkoolars 94–96, 97
Kalahasteswarar temple 96
Kaligambal temple 97
Kandasami temple 96, 97, 100
Kanpur 161–62
Kanyakaparameswari 102
karmayoga 14, 90, 109
Kasba: see Swinhoe Lane
Kasturibai Nagar 199–202
Kaviraj, Sudipta 12, 53

kidney sales 32–34
kili puja 214, 219–20, 223–24
kingdoms 220–22, 225
Kodankipatti 47–48, 61
Komati Chettiars: overview 14; Beeri
  Chettiars rivalry 89–90; charity and
  opulence 104–10; charity vegetable
  garden 101, 102–3; decline 110–12,
  113; headmen role 100; influence of
  97; riots 93–94
Komatla Tottam 101, 103
Kotwal Chavadi 101, 103
Krishnaswami temple 101
Kumar, Krishna 123, 132
Kumar, Palani 44–45
Kumarapalayam 32, 33, 34–35

landlord/tenant 72–73, 76–77, 87n.3,
  87n.4
landowners 106
languages 169, 190
Lawrence-Zúñiga, Denise 4
Lefebvre, Henri 24, 29, 34, 40–41, 55
Left Front 81, 87n.7
left-hand castes 91, 94–97, 114n.2
legal system 99–100
Lewis, M.W. 208, 209
Ley, D. 55–56, 57–58
local/cosmopolitan 122–23
local governance: see Calcutta
locality: construction of 60–63; terminology 10, 141
love marriages 149, 154
low-income settlement: as panopticon
  195–99; as socially heterogeneous
  settlement 193–95
Low, Setha M. 4, 9

McDowell, Linda 11
Madras City: see Chennai
Madras South Maratha Railways (MSM
  Railways) 105
Madurai 45–46, 62, 153
Maharashtra 224
Mahila Samiti 150–51
Malaviya, Madan Mohan 125–26
male-female relations 185
manual work 31–32
marriage 29–30, 149–50, 154
masculinity 196–97
Massey, Doreen 3–5, 60, 63, 208
master/servant 161

material space 24
Meerut 148, 150
Melavassel: overview 13; locality 49–50; location of 65n.5; Melavassel Riot 44–45, 51; movement markers 56–59; occupants 50–52; political spaces 60–63; public/private 53–55
memory 10
merchant castes: *see* Beeri Chettiars; Komati Chettiars
middle-class neighbourhoods: community activities 150–53; community of neighbours 153–54; history 142–44; mapping 144–48; mobility 148–50; representation and the everyday 154–57
migration 8, 208
Mines, Mattison 6, 11, 14
Mitchell, D. 63, 64
mobile enclosures 173–75, 178
mobility 22–24, 37–38, 148–50; *see also* Vanniyars
mohallas 116–17, 118
Mohangani 161–62
money lending 104
Moore, Henrietta 141
moral communities 29–34
motherhood 149, 189, 157n.4
movement markers 56–59
Mudaliyar manufacturers 34–35
Muduvarpatti 65n.17
Muslims: bombings 192; dance 139n.18; education 124, 132, 138, 139n.8; infiltration by 225–26; Pakistan and 193; service elite 118; status 25–26
myths 220–23

Nagorik Samiti 81
Narayana Guruviah Chetty's Charities 108
nationalism: overview 16–17; boundaries 209; Tamil nationalism 187–90; visions of 6
Nehru Sports Stadium 120
Nehruvian nationalism 6
Nehruvian secular project 131–32
neighbourhoods: overview 9–12; boundaries 38–40; community of neighbours 153–54; defended 56; gender 142–44; as industrial localities 34–38; as moral communities 29–34;

organisations 79–85; as panopticon 195–99; representation and the everyday 154–57; ritual rehabilitation 213–19; space and 208–12; terminology 7, 10, 141; traditional/modern 145–46, 148; *see also* socially heterogeneous settlements
nuclear families 147–48

Old Boys function 128
opulence, charity and 104–10
Orsini, Francesca 117
Osella, Filippo and Caroline 160
Other Backward Classes (OBC) 124
outcastes 100

Pakistan 193
Panchalars 94–96
panopticon, neighbourhood as 195–99
Parry, Jonathan 8
participation 69, 216–17
Partition 208
Pattali Makkal Katchi (PMK) 26, 28, 29
performance 195–96
permanent enclosures 175, 178
pilgrimage processions 91–92
Pillaiyar 191–92
place, globalisation debates 1–3
political association markers 56–59
'political opportunity structure' 83, 87n.10
politics: education and 133–34; neighbourhood organisations 79–85; political spaces 60–63; religion and 226; women's involvement 150–51
population density 51
post-colonialism 117–22
poverty: *see* slums
power: loss of 224–25; spatial concepts 3–4, 64; topography of 60
powerloom industry 34–38
Prakash, Gyan 9
privacy 53–54, 195–96
processions 90, 91–92
property rights 100
prostitutes 201
public health 80–81, 87n.12
public/private 53–55, 150, 153–54, 155–56
public spaces: access to 159–60; community activities 150–53; enclosure 171–78; movements in space 55–56; negotiation of 64; slums 74–75

pujas 25–26, 151–52
Pure Tamil movement 188–89

qasba 118

Radcliffe Boundary Commission 208
Raghavan, V. 97–98, 99
Ramachandran, M.G. 188
Ramlila celebrations 176–77
Rao Bahadur Calavala Cunnan Chetty's
   Charities 109–10
rape 189
Rashtra Sevika Samiti 192
Rashtriya Swayamsewak Sangh (RSS)
   192
Ratnam, Mani 160
Ray, Manas 146
Ray, R. 68–69
refugees 145–46
rehabilitation 213–19
relational webs 122–23
religion: charity and 109; ethnicity 74–
   75, 78–79, 87n.6; festivals 151–52,
   175–76; tolerance 25–26
remarriage 189
rented rooms 72–73, 76–77, 87n.3
representational spaces 24, 29, 41, 55
representations of space 24, 28, 41, 55,
   60
respectability 185, 195, 200–201
right-hand castes 97–98
right-hand/left-hand 90, 92–94, 114n.2
ritual: boundary marking 219–20; foundation myths 220–23; past events 219;
   processions 91–92; rehabilitation
   213–19; space/place 55
Rosch, Eleanor 164
rural cosmopolitans 22

safety 146
Salmon, Thomas 91
Salway, S. 69
Saradu Pooja 192
Sarva-Deva-Vilasa 98–99
Sassen, Saskia 3
satellite towns, rise of 8
Scheduled Castes 55, 60, 124, 138,
   139n.9
school buildings 116
school uniforms 124, 157n.4
schools, outside tuition 136
Sebring, James 160

secondary schools 120
secular project 131–32
segregation: political spaces 60–63;
   urban environments 48–49; villages
   47–48; *see also* Calcutta
Self-Respect movement 187, 189
Sengadu Thottam: overview 13, 23; as
   industrial locality 34–38; as moral
   community 29–34; Vanniyar legacy
   24–28
serpent myth 223–24
servants 153–54
shopping exhibitions 177–78
shops, enclosure and 175
Siddique, Mohammed K.A. 7
Simpson, Edward 6, 10, 17
Sivaramakrishnan, K. 22
slums: charity and 109–10; citizenship
   and 48–49; comparison of 70–79;
   definition 204n.10; neighbourhood
   organisations 79–85; residential
   patterns 72–74; social action 69;
   social life 74–75; socio-economic
   differences 75–79; worship 74–75; *see
   also* Dalit Panther Movement
small people 170, 178, 180n.4
Smith, B. 221
SMP colony 57, 62
social life, ethnicity and 74–75, 79
social reform programmes 46
social sciences 6–8
social space, dimensions of 24
socially heterogeneous settlements:
   gentrifying neighbourhoods 199–202;
   identity 182–85; low-income settlement 193–95; as panopticon 195–99;
   wider discourse 185–87
Soja, E. 55
solidarity 32–33, 41, 52, 70
Soniwad: aftermath of earthquake 211–
   13; boundaries of community 224–
   28; descriptions of 206–7, 214; foundation myths 220–23; planning
   reconstruction 215–18, 222–23, 227–
   28; public participation 216–17;
   reconstructing boundaries 209; ritual
   rehabilitation 213–19; rituals 219–20
Soniwad Mohalla Samiti 218
space: caste and 55–56; globalisation
   debates 1–3; neighbourhoods and
   208–12
spatial imagination, urban place and 3–5

spatial practices 24, 34, 41
Sports Day 127–28, 132, 135
squatter settlement 193–95
Sri Kanyakaparameswari Devasthanam
    (SKPD) 101–4, 111, 114n.3
Srinivas, Smriti 10
Srinivasa Ramanujan 106
stationery businesses 105
Stepputat, Finn 5
strangers, classification of 160–61
sweet speech 169
Swinhoe Lane 70–79
symbols 56–57

Tambi Chetti's pagoda 96
Tambs-Lyche, Harold 225
Tamil-Hindu-Hindustan 191
Tamil Nadu: overview 13, 16–17, 22–24;
    citizenship 48–49; identity 185, 190–
    93; nationalism 187–90; slums see
    Dalit Panther Movement; values 188;
    wider discourse 185–87
Tarlo, Emma 15
Taticonda Namberumal Chetty 105
tea shops 39
television 39, 186
temples: construction of 96–97; as polit-
    ical institutions 91, 100–101;
    processions 91–92
temporary enclosures 175–78
tenural contours 194, 203
Thevar Peravai 48–49
Tolen, Rachel 161
Town Pagoda 101
trade liberalisation, impact of 40
trade specialisations 104
transport 167, 173–75
tuition outside school 136

Untouchable settlements: see Dalit
    Panther Movement
ur 29–30, 41
urban environments: negative perspec-
    tives 7–8; research on 5–9;
    segregation 48–49; spatial imagina-
    tion and 3–5
Urban Land [Ceiling and Regulation]
    Act 1976 111

urban/rural 122–23
'urban village' 8
Uttar Pradesh 117, 118t, 120, 134

Vadianpatti 47–48
Vajpayee, Atal Behari 169
valour 192, 196–97
Vanniya Sangam 27, 29
Vanniyars: overview 13; as industrial
    locality 34–38; moral communities
    29–34; as moral community 29–34;
    socio-economic mobility 22–24;
    Vanniyar legacy 24–28
Vasavamba 102
Vatuk, Sylvia 148, 150
Veblen, Thorstein 167
Vedic universe 221
vehicles 167
Vellaalas 97–98, 101
Vera-Sanso, Penny 16, 46, 62
Vidich, A. 48, 56
village, concepts of 8
VIPs 163–64, 180n.3
Vupputur House 108, 111

walking 167–68
water 204n.9
Wigen, K.E. 208, 209
Wirth, Louis 7
withdrawal from public places 172–78
women: cheap women 201; community
    activities 150–53; community of
    neighbours 153–54; female exclusion
    155; male-female relations 185;
    middle-class neighbourhoods 142–48;
    mobility 148–50; public/private 150,
    153–54, 155–56; purity and chastity
    188–89; representation and the
    everyday 154–57; sexuality 201–2;
    social restrictions 65n.9; work 39,
    197–98, 65n.9
Women's Degree College 120–21, 125
Wood, G.D. 69, 85
work: see employment

Yelu Ur Vanniyars 29–30

For Product Safety Concerns and Information please contact our EU
representative GPSR@taylorandfrancis.com
Taylor & Francis Verlag GmbH, Kaufingerstraße 24, 80331 München, Germany